SLOW BOAT THROUGH ENGLAND

Frederic Doerflinger was born in the USA but has lived in England with his family since completing his World War II service with the US Army Air Force in Europe. Throughout his various careers as foreign correspondent and editor, marketing and merchandising consultant and author he has revelled in exploring the heritage of the inland waterways of Britain and Western Europe. An Inland Waterways Association member since 1947, serving as a member of council, national vice-chairman and chairman of its Inland Shipping Group, Doerflinger was awarded the coveted Cyril Styring Trophy as well as honorary life membership. He was founder member of the National Waterways Transport Association and maintains his links with the Permanent Association of Navigation Congresses.

Slow Boat Through England was first published in 1970. It has now been reissued with a new Postscript by the author.

Also by Frederic Doerflinger
and available in Comet:

SLOW BOAT THROUGH PENNINE WATERS

SLOW BOAT THROUGH ENGLAND

Frederic Doerflinger

With a new Postscript

A COMET BOOK

A Comet Book
Published in 1986
by the Paperback Division of
W.H. Allen & Co. Plc
44 Hill Street, London W1X 8LB

First published in Great Britain
by Allan Wingate (Publishers) Ltd, 1970

Printed and bound in Great Britain
by Anchor Brendon Ltd, Tiptree, Essex

ISBN 0 86379 119 0

To the First Mate
who neither jibs nor jibes

Publisher's note: In order to keep the cost of this new
edition of *Slow Boat Through England* as low as possible, we
have not been able to re-originate the text first
published in 1970. Readers are therefore advised to consult the author's 1986 Postscript for a note on present-
day boat hire prices.

CONTENTS

	Foreword	7
1	Our Inland Waterways	11
2	How to Choose a Suitable Holiday Craft	25
3	On Handling Boats	47
4	Getting Ready	67
5	Our Waterways Story	79
6	The Fetching Fens	90
7	The 'Little Med'	107
8	The Nowither Nene	118
9	On to the 'Grand Circle'	140
10	London's Waterways	159
11	Looping the Midlands Loop	169
12	Sensations and Spectaculars	187
13	Into Shakespeare's Country	207
14	Back Through Birmingham	221
15	Adventures to Come	235
	Postscript, 1986	240

FOREWORD

IN A WAY I was responsible for this book. Not that I suggested it, for it was the publishers who did that, and they chose the man who could best write it. No, my responsibility goes back fifteen years, to a June day when Fred Doerflinger and his wife Lisa chugged down the Upper Thames on my boat from above St John's Lock to the Rose Revived. As a result of that one day on the water Fred Doerflinger began to develop a strange malaise.

The symptoms of his growing addiction followed the usual pattern. If he was driving and came to a humped bridge he had a compulsive urge to stop and get out of the car to see if there were any boats in sight. At home, his study floor began to be covered with canal maps and his desk littered with pieces of paper on which were sums in peculiar units which he would explain to be 'lock miles'. A year or two later you might find him sitting on a bollard in darkest Camden Town or furthest Fenland, pensive as the ancient mariner about to hook a wedding guest and tell him about his latest voyage.

Fred Doerflinger's addiction to water sometimes showed itself under the most surprising circumstances. Once a very very important person from behind the Iron Curtain came to London and held a press conference at which he outlined his scheme for uniting Europe, or dismembering it—I forget precisely which. At the end of his prepared statement the very very important person indicated that if any of the world's press wished to ask a very very important question he might answer it. There was an awed silence, then Fred spoke up. What was the depth of water in the canal that led from Berlin across Poland to Moscow?

That Fred Doerflinger is a canal fanatic nobody could deny. But he does not want to keep the waterways for himself. The canals and rivers, he writes 'are in fact a key to a way of life almost unchanged since the eighteenth century, and they are all yours to explore and enjoy'. As I read that, I remembered how on an April evening Fred had rowed us dreamily along part of the Regent's Canal. Overhead the buds were breaking on the elms, the rooks were cheerfully sorting themselves into pairs. My wife and I sat in the stern of the dinghy, she trailing her fingers in the water and I myself looking up dreamily at the silhouette of the trees against the evening sky, amazed that such peace and beauty could exist right there in London. Only 30 ft above us the traffic was jammed motionless on Blow-up Bridge, but it seemed to belong to another world, incredibly remote. And so it did.

On the bend towards Maida Vale Fred eased off to lean out and pick up a used motor-tyre. It was a fine one, white-walled and expensive. No doubt it had once belonged to just such a smart executive saloon as those which were edging irritably along the road beyond the trees. Fred thought it would serve us as a fender, as it did through eight countries in the following years. Every time I hung it against a quayside it brought back to me a whiff of those canals which we had cruised with him, the Llangollen or the Oxford, the Grand Union and the River Weaver, and the nostalgic dereliction of Ellesmere Port. And often I wished Fred Doerflinger would write about those voyages so that others could explore for themselves the same world and the same way of life.

This he has now done, and what particularly delights me is not just his encounter with the mole-catcher, the story of Ben who spent a lifetime legging in Braunston Tunnel, or the rescue of Worcester the ginger cat, but that he has set out to provide all the information a newcomer to the waterways can possibly need. And he has done so in exactly the right way. So many of those who have written about the waterways have adopted an intolerance quite foreign to such a pleasant way of exploring the Britain which still survives, as genuine and unspoiled as ever, between the strands of a web of hurrying motorways. In this book, where his purpose is partly to tell people *how* to voyage into adventure, he is the gentlest of advisers, never hinting that if you don't think as he does about some aspect of boating or waterways you must be deranged.

Fred Doerflinger loves the canals and rivers, and he has travelled them more widely than anyone else I have met. There are not many English locks which he has not wound, and as lock-wheelers his family have padded scores of miles of towpath. I hope that many others will cruise the same canals and rivers, and find as he does that whatever waterways they may happen to have chosen they will have entered a new world.

ROGER PILKINGTON

CHAPTER I

OUR INLAND WATERWAYS

IT WAS all due to our golden Labrador, Brandonwood Bracken of Denewood, more affectionately known as 'Wiggers' because of the continual happy movement of his tail, that we became a family of inland waterway addicts. We enjoy holidaying as a family and our three children were adamant about including the dog in any travel plans. This, of course, ruled out holidays abroad and set us searching for holiday venues in Britain that would genuinely welcome children and dogs and cater for everyone's idea of fun and relaxation.

Such criteria are difficult enough to agree, let alone satisfy, but Britain's inland waterways proved to be the ideal passport to pleasure for every single member of the family, 'Wiggers' included, and although we have already cruised literally thousands of miles up and down the rivers and canals of this country they continue to offer new, different and more exciting adventures each year. I must warn you at the outset, until you have experienced boating on inland waterways you cannot imagine or appreciate how the habit surreptitiously creeps up and envelops you. Your first cruise will almost certainly be the forerunner of many more and if you are not careful you will quickly become an enthusiast.

The water roads of Britain, for that is what the inland waterways essentially are, constitute another world. The peace and quiet they offer are in striking contrast to our congested, noisy, smelly and dangerous roads and to our pounding and often unsightly railways where speed is undisputed king. Who goes for a drive for pleasure or relaxation these days? Who travels by train to see the countryside? Roads and railways are no more today than methods of transport, a means of getting from A to B and usually in the fastest possible time.

But the shallow, narrow ribbons of canal waters, defying the barriers of the watersheds with their tunnels, locks and aqueducts to form links with deeper and wider rivers and then the sea, almost magically convey us like explorers into a way of life touched only on the periphery by the so-called advances of the last two centuries. On a boat on the inland waterways the pressure is off and you are as free as the open air. The waterways greet you as a friend and companion and act as a catalyst to initiative.

Today, thanks to the vigorous campaign led for over two decades by an almost fanatically devoted Inland Waterways Association, and the recent belated but welcome recognition by the British Government of the tremendous amenities for recreation and leisure provided by the nation's inland waterways, more and more people are beginning to discover the countless attractions and peace of the 3,000-mile network of navigable rivers and canals that the vast majority of an increasingly tension-ridden public have strangely failed to notice for generations.

Once you cruise the inland waterways you will begin to delve deeply into many aspects of their fascinating story. For each of your holidays afloat will introduce you to many strange, unusual and unexpected phenomena, sights and people, as the accounts of some of my own boating holidays in later chapters reveal in some detail. A lot of places we come across look magical at first glance, but the waterways go on being constantly surprising.

Their courses silently penetrate a very different Britain

from that we are accustomed to in the course of our busy and hectic lives. Unspoiled and uncrowded even if pleasure-craft traffic were suddenly to double or treble overnight (and it has already done so on the River Thames and the Norfolk Broads) the inland waterways of Britain are uniquely remote yet easily accessible to anyone with the slightest tinge of inquisitiveness in their make-up.

For the most part our rivers and canals today are lost trade routes with little prospect of ever again contributing an important chapter to the economic and social history of the country. But in this crowded island where there are so few opportunities to escape from the burdensome effects of modern civilisation, the inland waterways are a unique heritage which, if you care to claim it, can add a new dimension to your leisure. Our canals and rivers remain part of another age when the pattern of trade and transport was quite different. This pattern has been long forgotten or ignored by modern business and indeed by the masses of the public. So the canals and rivers are in fact a key to a way of life almost unchanged since the eighteenth century, and they are all yours to explore and enjoy.

Although the inland waterways still flow through or near a number of cities and towns and villages across the land they do not enmesh you and your craft in the snarls of traffic on flyovers, roundabouts and shopping centres, nor grind you to a halt in noisy, teeming railway termini after a tour of back-door slum districts. You will be agreeably surprised at the way waterways tend to avoid congested conurbations, ribbon developments, power plants, industrial estates and other conglomerations of this technological age. Well over nine-tenths of the canals and rivers wander peacefully through a remote countryside on winding courses bordered by meadows and fields, pretty flowers and bird-laden rushes, isolated cottages and picturesque inns.

You will, as my family and I have, become smitten with certain waterways and even particular spots on particular waterways, but there isn't any waterway anywhere that doesn't possess a host of attractions and cater for a myriad interests. I find that each river and canal has a distinctive charm and character of its own and conjures up different memories from varied personal experiences. One thing, you will never be bored, for even though a holiday cruise sometimes brings you back over the same or much of the same outward route you will discover that they really do look entirely different when travelling in the reverse direction.

A glance at the map of the inland waterways will show you that the threads of water are rather like a massive spider's web, somewhat tattered admittedly, but nevertheless sprawling over much of the country, with odd bits of cobweb seemingly blown by the winds from the centre to some outlying areas. Boating holidays open up vast areas of the countryside which you might otherwise never really see or explore.

Whatever waterways you choose for most of your holiday you will be away from it all—free to potter or press on; free to bypass this town or that village unless you want to shop or sightsee; free to visit that stately home or country church or pleasure ground; free to picnic in that pleasant glade; free to dine in that handy waterside inn; free to take the children to that bird sanctuary or zoo or craftsman's cottage; free to swim or paddle or fish; free to saunter along that towpath with your dog, and like him, thoroughly enjoy nature's sights and sounds and smells.

You will pass over rivers and streams from time to time on aqueducts, some rather small and quaint and others breathtakingly noble and massive. You will slip under countless road bridges, most of them sited in the middle of nowhere and devoid of traffic except for a mooing cow or a farmer with a load of hay. There will be railway bridges too, most of them deserted and many 'Beeching'd', but should you by chance spot a train rumbling across, a hoot on your boat horn will often spark the response of a whistle or a wave of the driver's arm.

Suddenly, you will begin to appreciate the functional and aesthetic beauty of the different kinds of locks, from the ordinary to the staircase and guillotine types; the different designs of bridges dating back even to medieval times and including those delightful swing and split bridges; the period lock cottages, many with colourful gardens; the old wharves and warehouses; the stables now perhaps converted to a pub storeroom; and scores of other relics of yesterday when architecture and craftsmanship were based on ingenuity, good taste and durability.

You will also notice little things like worn bollards and battered balance-beam caps, cast-iron name plates, bridge numbers and curious signs that from another era warn you that this or that bridge 'is insufficient to carry a traction engine or any other extraordinary weight'. The youngsters may collect lock names or pub names or spot mileposts as you cruise along. It isn't just that your leisurely pace gives you time to take things in properly, but that from a boat you have a different perspective. It's only when you get on the water that you begin to take notice of so many things that are usually taken for granted.

While the inland waterways map in one sense only hints at the lost world we can so easily recapture it does usefully chart the many routes to pleasure across so much of this island. Whether in the North, South, East, West or Midlands there are waterways that will carry you into a fresh and refreshing appreciation of your own country.

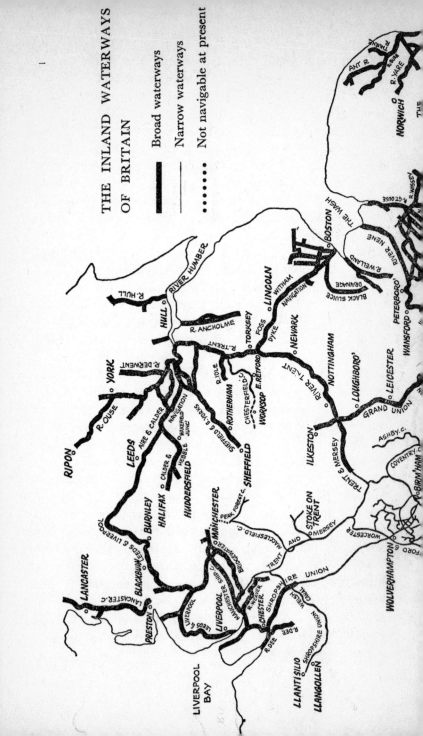

THE INLAND WATERWAYS
OF BRITAIN

——— Broad waterways
———— Narrow waterways
······· Not navigable at present

In the South, London's river, the Thames, is the major river navigation, navigable for over 200 miles from the tiny Gloucestershire village of Lechlade to the tidal locks at Teddington in London, and thence through the heart of the capital to the sea. The Thames is without doubt one of the most popular waterways for pleasure boating in the country, boasting an almost endless series of beautiful reaches and broad locks to take craft from kayaks and canoes to really substantial cruisers. Thousands of boat owners moor their craft on the Thames, and fleets of hire cruisers based on the river have grown to quite a size. This won't spoil your fun, however, for there's something exciting about passing through a lock with a number of other boats, with meeting other boaters at a mooring beside a cheerful pub, and certain advantages in having your every whim catered for. We have cruised the reaches above Oxford at weekends in the height of the summer and have encountered as few as half a dozen boats on the move.

There are smaller more remote rivers to cruise in solitude in the South, like the National Trust's pretty little River Wey, which from Weybridge to Godalming contributes more than its fair share of beauty to the periphery of London. The Medway too, from the tidal lock at Allington to Tonbridge, is sheer rural delight with its ancient bridges, wild garlic, hopfields and the odd 'folly' to make you ponder on the foibles of humanity. And there's the Lee & Stort Navigation which carries you from London's dockland into the depths of Hertfordshire along pleasant winding courses to Hertford or Bishop's Stortford, with views of old mills, stocks and lock-ups, water gardens and water-lilies galore.

However well you may know London you'll be amazed at the city you will discover when you explore it via the Regent's Canal. There's much more to it than a few miles of waterway with a baker's dozen of locks. It takes you into dockland, the East End and the curious hinterland running from the City of London to Camden Town and beyond. There are a couple of short tunnels, Regent's Park with 'Blow-up Bridge' and the zoo, attractive Little Venice, and more. From it you can enter the Lee Navigation, the tidal Thames or cruise along the Paddington Arm into the Grand Union Canal proper.

The Grand Union—our youngsters on their first trip along it dubbed it the 'Grand Onion'—is the major water link between the South and the Midlands. With its broad locks, the longest tunnel still open to boats in Britain, a smattering of commercial narrow-boat traffic, the fascinating Waterways Museum at Stoke Bruerne, charming canal villages and the changing panoramas of its pounds, this canal, whether you follow it from the Thames to Birmingham or to the Trent, will give you a little bit of everything that canal holidays have to offer.

Another route to the Midlands from the Thames is the Oxford Canal, without doubt one of the most beautiful canals in England, winding along the contours of the hills through unspoiled countryside with only rare contact with towns or villages. This is a shallow canal with narrow locks and delightful lifting bridges and with an intimate association with nature.

The canals of the Midlands are centred on Birmingham whose network of local navigations reflects the industrial England of a century or so ago. It's a rather sorry page of history to explore but with its own fascination, and many surprisingly pleasant and interesting stretches. From Birmingham the canals probe outwards in all directions with a choice of many different routes for years of holiday pleasure. To the south lies the recently restored Stratford-on-Avon Canal, several dozen miles of heavily locked waters, including a flight of nineteen locks in $1\frac{1}{2}$ miles, plunging through lovely Shakespeare country. Then there's the thirty-odd miles of the Worcester & Birmingham Canal running through hilly country to the River Severn. Although all the fifty-eight locks on this canal are concentrated in sixteen miles they are easy to work, and the famous Tardebigge Flight, the longest in the country and consisting of thirty locks with a total fall of over 200 ft, is an experience you'll always remember. Progress here will be slow but the magnificent scenery is in any case worth dawdling over.

The River Severn is also connected to the Midlands and indeed the River Trent by the Staffordshire & Worcestershire Canal, which averages less than a lock per mile in its forty-six-odd miles through really beautiful country, the haunt of many wild birds. On this canal you'll find such things as a 'canal lake', locks with picturesque names like 'Bumble Hole' and 'Stewponey', unusual split bridges which allowed the towline on horse-drawn craft to be passed through without unhooking, in addition to scenic splendour, good inns and attractive castles and manor houses.

The River Severn has few locks and few places to moor but it is a rather grand concourse connecting, via Tewkesbury, with the River Avon, which we find so idyllic and enjoyable that we return to it again and again. The word 'lovely' is too weak to describe the Avon along its twenty-eight miles between Tewkesbury and Evesham. The wooded countryside, the charming old mills, the pretty towns and villages, the unusual locks, the ideal moorings, the enchanting walks—and the local 'scrumpy' —are among the attractions that bring us back to the Avon so often.

From the Birmingham area the Shropshire Union Canal will take you over sixty-six miles through recurring deep cuttings with rocky and heavily wooded slopes, under towering bridges and over ingenious aqueducts to Chester, and beyond to Ellesmere Port and the Manchester Ship Canal. It is one of the most exciting and thoroughly pleasant canals we have ever cruised, every mile offering new prospects for admiration. The forty-six additional miles of the Welsh Section or the Llangollen Canal, from Hurleston Junction on the main line to Llantisilio in Wales, is, in the view of my family, the most beautiful canal in the country. It has simply everything from fine scenery including the Vale of Langollen and the 'Little Lake District' through narrow locks and lift bridges and tunnels and even an inland port to the thrilling Chirk and Pontcysyllte aqueducts, the latter over 1,000 ft long and carrying the canal breathtakingly over 120 ft above the rushing River Dee.

Not so spectacular but interesting in their own ways are the canals to the east of Birmingham, the Birmingham & Fazeley, the pretty Northern Arm of the Oxford Canal, the decaying Coventry Canal, all of which, while perhaps not selected as holiday venues in themselves, make possible circular tours which enable the exploration of a number of waterways on a single holiday. All have particular attractions worth seeking out as you get to know the waterways a little better.

Also part of the Midlands waterways is the Leicester Line of the Grand Union Canal incorporating the delightful River Soar Navigation, stretching over seventy-five miles from Norton Junction on the Grand Union main line to Birmingham to the Trent & Mersey Canal and the River Trent. It is a canal of great contrasts, varying from narrow to broad gauge locks, from canal to river navigation, from wild untidy country to pastoral landscape. It runs through fascinating villages and interesting towns and cities, features haunted tunnels, intriguing staircase locks and is one of the highest canals in the country, the summit level being 412 ft above sea level, with glorious views.

The River Trent and the Trent & Mersey Canal, you will note from the waterways map, form a vast semi-circle connecting the Mersey in the north-west to the Humber and ports of the north-east. The Trent & Mersey Canal is nearly a hundred miles long from Preston Brook on the Bridgewater Canal to Derwent Mouth on the River Trent, and from it you can also explore such scenic gems as the Macclesfield and Peak Forest Canals. The Trent & Mersey is another of those canals that combine broad and narrow locks, and a narrow-beamed craft with under 6 ft headroom is in any case essential because of the safe but sagging Harecastle Tunnel, which has a height gauge at each end which your boat must clear to be admitted. This 2,919-yard tunnel is only one of the exciting adventures on the Trent & Mersey as it wends its way through the Potteries and some of the most enchanting reaches anywhere in the country. Where the Trent & Mersey joins the broad sweep of the River Weaver in Cheshire you'll find the only boat lift in Britain. The Anderton Lift raises boats in massive caissons from the level of the Weaver some 50 ft to the canal level above, and passing up or down in your own boat is an exhilarating experience, to say the least.

The River Trent is tidal for fifty-two miles from the Humber to Cromwell Lock some five miles below Newark and, frankly glorious as these tidal reaches are, you must accumulate some boating experience before venturing along them as we have done into the Humber & Yorkshire Ouse and beyond to the city of York. A little experience will contribute to a greater enjoyment of the many canals of the North including the Sheffield & Yorkshire, Stainforth & Keadby, Calder & Hebble and the bustling Aire & Calder, famous for its trains of coal-carrying 'Tom Pudding' compartment boats which can still be seen daily. The finest cruising canal in the North, well suited to amateurs and rated the most pleasing in the country by many enthusiasts, is the 127-mile-long Leeds & Liverpool which takes you through the rugged moorlands of Yorkshire and Lancashire, and the farm lands of the Pennines. A broad canal with ninety-one locks and two tunnels, it mingles rustic scenery with grand navigation works like the unique sets of locks, grouped in sets of two, three and five, and the Burnley embankment which carries the canal literally over the centre of the town. The summit level of the Leeds & Liverpool canal is some 497 ft above sea level, and although the canal does run through some industrial areas many of the buildings are mellowed with age and quite interesting, while the open countryside is nothing less than magnificent.

The northernmost navigable canal in England is the Lancaster, separated from the main canal system and more like a river than a canal in appearance. There are no locks except on the short Glasson Arm leading to the sea, and the canal is beautiful with splendid sea views over Morecambe Bay.

And then there are the waterways of East Anglia. The ancient Fossdyke and Witham Navigations, a heritage from the Romans, penetrate rural Lincolnshire in almost the same straight line as a Roman road and are in a class of their own. They are mainly of academic interest to the enthusiast rather than of much interest to holiday-makers. We cruised them solely as a contrasting side-trip from a voyage on the Trent, but bird-watchers and anglers will find the Witham Navigable Drains at the Boston end most interesting.

It is the Fenland waterways of East Anglia that are unique, totally different in character from the other waterways of the country. They have qualities which can only be described as partly primitive, partly medieval. What we call the 'Nowhither Nene' is connected to the canal system by the heavily-locked and narrow Northampton Arm, and a cruise along this lovely winding river is not only scenically enchanting but a kind of historic pilgrimage. Our first love, however, is that conglomerate of rivers composed of the Ouse and its tributaries, the Cam, the Lark, the Wissey and the Little Ouse. Here there are hundreds of miles of the most unsophisticated cruising grounds in the country where you will move from one delight to another. These are perfect waters for the beginner and are guaranteed to convert amateur into enthusiast.

Of course, East Anglia also contains the Norfolk and Suffolk Broads, the most popular holiday centre in the country for boaters. The Broads have changed out of all recognition from what they were even a few decades ago. Today they are a commercialised holiday centre where three major rivers and their tributaries, broadening from time to time into inland seas, have been intensively developed to cater for those who want every facility and other holidaymakers about them. The Broads offer yet another kind of boating holiday which appeals particularly to young families who in pretty surroundings enjoy making new friends.

You'll find, once you board a boat for a holiday cruise, that whatever waterway you happen to have chosen, you have entered a new world where you are completely absorbed and there is never a dull moment. Each waterway, even after decades of boating holidays, offers new adventures and opens up new interests. Messing about in boats on our inland waterways becomes an engrossing hobby that opens the door to the wonders of nature and the achievements of humanity through the ages. On them you will find the closest thing to perfect peace in the world.

CHAPTER 2

HOW TO CHOOSE A
SUITABLE HOLIDAY CRAFT

A BOAT is the most important element in a boating holiday, but before broaching to family and friends the idea of getting on to the water for a holiday you will want an assurance that novices can easily cope with boats and boating. As you will all literally be living aboard a boat for a week or more, everyone will want to know if boats are safe and comfortable, if they can be handled easily by the inexperienced, what kind of boat should be selected for your particular holiday and how to go about obtaining a holiday craft.

When you set off on your first boating holiday on our inland waterways you won't exactly be ranked in history with Brendan the Navigator, Leif Ericsson, Christopher Columbus, Ferdinand Magellan or even Sir Alec Rose or Robin Knox-Johnston. Quite a few people living on or near the water have long been messing about in boats and they all began as amateurs. Although annual boating holidays by non boat-owners are a relatively recent development they are becoming increasingly popular.

At the start of this century it would have been fair to say that the inland waterways network was almost virgin territory. It wasn't until L. T. C. Rolt produced his classic *Narrow Boat* in 1944, triggering off the founding of the Inland Waterways Association, that public interest in our inland waterways network as a venue for holidays began to be aroused. Before the Second World War our waterways network carried very few people indeed on pleasure cruises. When the I.W.A. was formed in 1946, apart from the Broads and the Thames, only two firms offering hire craft were in existence.

With a small but growing band of enthusiasts creating a demand for more and more hire craft and spreading the word about the fun of exploring the waterways, a whole new industry catering to boating holidays gradually developed and spread to virtually every navigable waterway.

Types of hire craft

Today there are scores upon scores of hire craft operators based strategically over the length and breadth of the waterways system. They make it possible for the novice to enjoy a convenient and economical holiday on any particular stretches of navigable water that may take his fancy. Many types of craft are available for hire on our inland waterways. For those who want to see what a boating holiday is like without the responsibility of commanding a boat, cabins are available on hotel boats which cruise on a number of the waterways. These are usually pairs of converted traditional narrow boats, one with a motor and the other on tow. There are also bigger hotel-barges which operate on broad rivers. Both types have a professional crew who will let passengers steer or work locks if they wish, but the elderly or inactive passenger need not lift a finger if he doesn't want to.

Even cheaper holidays are available on hostel-boats, converted canal boats pulled by a horse. Accommodation on these is of dormitory type and passengers are expected to assist the professional crew.

Traditional camping skiffs and punts may be hired on some rivers like the Thames. These are flat-bottomed craft, usually paddled or poled, sleeping two to four. They are fitted with awnings which stretch over metal frames to form a tent, and cooking utensils and equipment can also be hired. The camping pontoon or barge, housing four to six, and motor-powered, has recently become available on a number of waterways. These inexpensive camping-cum-boating type holidays appeal particularly to groups of youngsters.

Sailing craft for hire on inland waterways are available on the Norfolk and Suffolk Broads and on rivers like the Warwickshire Avon. Most are equipped with an auxiliary engine and sleep from two to six people. Some skill is required to handle sailing yachts, however, and operators' brochures will spell out what degree of skill is necessary.

By far the most popular type of craft for inland waterway holidays are motor cruisers. Various types of modern craft are available with from two to ten berths and fully fitted with all modern conveniences and equipped with everything needed for a family holiday on the water. There is a choice of diesel or petrol engine and some of the smaller craft are powered by outboard motor. On rivers these craft are usually broader beamed and fitted with wheel steering, while on the canals the cruisers are mostly narrow-beamed, of shallower draught, and many are equipped with tiller steering. On some canals too it is possible to hire converted traditional narrow boats 70 ft long and 6 ft 10 ins in beam, and while they are somewhat more difficult to manoeuvre than the shorter cruisers the novice need have no fears about handling them.

I can readily recommend the self-drive river or canal cruisers as being ideal for family holidays. They give you the independence you want without having to rough it. They are safe and comfortable, easy to handle and are available right across our vast network of inland waterways so that your choice of holiday venue is unlimited.

Advantages of hiring

Hiring a river or canal cruiser for a holiday is the simple way to enjoy the pleasures of boating. For when you hire there is someone else to do the worrying and to cope with the countless details that are part and parcel of owning and running your own craft, from licensing and insurance to maintenance and servicing. For the first-timer, in fact, it would be folly to invest in a motor cruiser. Without any experience of boats and waterways you will not, quite apart from the financial investment required, know precisely what you want from your boat and what you want to do with it. Bringing a boat into a family should never be undertaken until you have spent some time on the waterways in boats owned by others and are not only enthusiastically fired by the idea of owning a boat but have an 'ideal' craft in mind.

Hiring gives you the opportunity to skipper different types of craft, including bigger and more lavishly equipped boats than you can probably afford to buy. Hiring not only provides you with a means of learning about boats but of acquiring sufficient waterways know-how to enable you to invest intelligently in the right type of boat for family use for years to come.

Early booking essential

Despite the rapid growth in the number of hire firms and the size of hire fleets the demand for hire cruisers is greater than the supply. To find a craft to suit your family on a particular waterway at a particular time it is essential to get your holiday dates settled and select the waterway on which you wish to cruise well in advance. Most hire firms get the bulk of their bookings for the season, which usually extends from late March to late October, very early in the New Year. This does not mean, however, that those who cannot, because of circumstances, make a firm hire cruiser booking before March will have to abandon hope of a holiday on the water. You may be lucky or fall heir to a cancellation and there are always other waterways— all of which are fun. But the earlier you book and the more flexible your holiday dates, the wider is your choice of both boats and waterways. Hire cruiser charges, which are scaled according to the number of berths per craft, are also scaled according to season, and are cheaper in spring and autumn than in the peak months of July and August.

Hire firm lists

Once you know when you can get away on holiday and have selected your holiday venue—the bulk of this book is devoted to detailed first-hand reports on the many waterways open to you, to help you and your family make an appropriate choice—you will need a list of hire firms. There is an extensive list of hire firms in the Appendix but no book can keep pace with the mushroom growth of this industry. Annually updated lists of hire firms can be obtained from a number of sources.

The Inland Waterways Association, 114 Regent's Park Road, London, N.W.1, publishes for 12½np post free, an annual *Waterways Holiday Guide* containing a list of hire firms offering all types of craft on all waterways. The British Waterways Board, Melbury House, Melbury Terrace, London, N.W.1, will provide information on the craft they have for hire at various bases on the nationalised waterways. The Association of Pleasure Craft Operators, The Wharf, Norbury Junction, Stafford, will, on receipt of a stamped self-addressed envelope, send you a copy of the Association's brochure listing names and addresses of their fifty-odd member firms describing the holidays they offer on the canals and some rivers. The Thames Hire

Cruiser Association, W. Bates & Son, Bridge Wharf, Chertsey, Surrey, will provide a list of member firms who between them offer over 200 hire craft on the River Thames. The Great Ouse Boatbuilders and Operators Association, Riverside Boatyard, Ely, Cambridgeshire, has a list available of member firms with hire craft at seven bases on East Anglia's Fenland Waterways. On the Norfolk and Suffolk Broads there are over a hundred hire firms offering well over 2,000 craft, most of them motor cruisers, and most of them can be reached through three associations that have been formed, each with central booking facilities. Craft belonging to the Norfolk and Suffolk Broads Yacht Owners Association can be booked through Blakes (Norfolk Broads Holidays), Wroxham, Norwich, NOR 41Z, who will provide a free colour booklet. The Broadland Owners Association publish a big colour catalogue obtainable from Hoseasons, 60 Oulton Broad, Lowestoft, Suffolk, and the Red Whale Boat Owners Association also produce a free colour brochure available from Bradbeer Ltd, Lowestoft, Suffolk.

Making enquiries

You need only enquire about craft in the first instance from those hire firms or trade associations which are based on the waterways or combination of waterways of your choice. If you state the number in your party and the dates or probable dates of your holiday it helps the hire firms to advise you about availability of suitable craft. And you should, before booking, always advise the hire firm of where you propose to take your hire cruiser, to ensure that the craft you book is suitable to your route. Of course, hire cruisers will always be suited to the waterways on which they are based and many firms offer hire craft that can range far afield, on broad and narrow canals and rivers as well. But problems can arise. For example, some hire craft on the River Thames may have superstructures too tall to pass under the low bridges of the upper Thames waterway between Oxford and Lechlade. If you intend to combine cruising on the Thames with a jaunt along the Oxford Canal you will require a narrow (6 ft 10 ins in beam) cruiser which can pass through the 7 ft wide locks of the narrow Oxford Canal. Should you plan to move from the broad Grand Union Canal to the broad River Nene a narrow canal cruiser is essential because the Northampton Arm, which links the two waterways, has locks only 7 ft wide. Another reason to advise the hire firm of your planned itinerary is that often canal cruisers are licensed for the nationalised waterways and not the Thames or Nene, and conversely Thames craft may not be licensed for the canals, and so on.

Preliminary spadework

It isn't necessary to plan your boating holiday in detail before you hire a cruiser, but if you have a particular itinerary in mind some preliminary spadework is advisable. It is relatively simple to figure out roughly just where and how far you can cruise in a given period with the aid of Stanford's Inland Cruising Map obtainable from Stanford's Ltd, 12 Long Acre, London, W.C.2, or the Inland Waterways Association, price 50p including postage. This useful map gives mileages, shows which waterways are broad and which are narrow, and gives the number and location of locks. We happen to enjoy locks, and have been known to average over a hundred a week on a three-week boating holiday, but the first-timer will not be so keen and will probably prefer a waterway or a route with relatively few locks.

There is usually a speed limit of four miles an hour on canals and six to eight miles per hour on rivers, depending upon whether you are cruising upstream or downstream. Speed limits should be strictly adhered to, to avoid damage to banks and harm to moored craft from excessive wash and indeed trouble with your own cruiser. It is rarely possible, in any case, to go much faster than the speed limit on canals because they are almost invariably shallow. Without going into technicalities attempts at excessive speed on canals will only result in your own wash overtaking you and slowing you down and can even cause your own cruiser to go aground.

Your speed is, of course, affected by locks. While experts can pass through locks in a few minutes when the gates are open and the lock ready and beginners will take only a few minutes more, the time taken to pass through locks is extremely variable. Timing can depend not only upon the proficiency of your crew but whether paddles or guillotine gates are stiff or easy to operate, upon the size of the lock and how long it takes to empty or fill, upon whether a lock is with you or against you, upon whether you have to wait for other craft using the lock or waiting to pass through, upon whether a lock-keeper holds you up until other boats in sight can join you in passing through, and upon whether locks are far apart or in flights where crew members can move ahead and get locks ready in advance, a process called 'lock-wheeling'.

The 'Lock Mile'

I have kept an accurate and detailed log of all my holiday cruises and experience shows that cruising time can be surprisingly accurately estimated by equating a mile of waterway with a lock. By adding locks to miles on any cruising route you get a total figure which can be quoted in 'lock miles'. Thus 60 miles of waterway and 60 locks would equal 120 lock miles, as would 90 miles of waterway and 30 locks. While it actually takes less time on average to pass through a lock than to navigate a mile of waterway, allowing equal time in your calculations will cover the variables in passing through locks mentioned earlier as well as others, including infrequent but nevertheless possible instances of rubble or rubbish obstructions preventing the complete closure of a lock gate. At times too you may pick up weeds on your propeller shaft, or a plastic bag or inner tube round your propeller, which will take time to clear.

My experience over the years shows without exception that it is safe to estimate that you can travel 4 lock miles per hour on canals and 6 lock miles per hour on rivers. River locks are generally bigger, deeper and take longer to empty and fill so that time gained on the open waterways is lost at the locks.

This calculation takes into consideration time lost on canal pounds or river reaches by the odd going aground, by slowing down for moored craft and fishermen, by easing off for blind corners and oddly angled bridge holes and the like. A combination cruise of rivers and canals can be estimated in the same way, i.e. a cruise involving roughly equal lock mileage on river and on canal will result in an average speed of 5 lock miles per hour.

Knowing in advance your cruising speed is helpful in planning an itinerary for your boating holiday, but there remains the question of how many lock miles you can comfortably cover in a day with ample time for seeing the local sights, shopping, visiting the local pub, chatting with interesting acquaintances, fishing, swimming, picnicing, bird-watching, sunbathing or just idling about.

A day's cruising is different for different people and different craft. Professional boaters with a pair of narrow boats will travel at a steady 60 to 70 lock miles a day. Experienced enthusiasts can manage up to 100 lock miles in a day in a canal cruiser, but these lock mileages are chalked up by being on the move for 12 hours or more, eating meals while under way, shopping only while in locks, consistent lock-wheeling at every opportunity, and what's more keeping on the move even in torrential rain. This is not for the holiday maker, whether a first-timer or a veteran of the waterways.

The beginner in a river or canal cruiser should not plan on covering more than two dozen lock miles per day on average. On canals this means 6 hours cruising, on rivers 4 hours, and on a combination of rivers and canals just under 5 hours cruising per day on average. As you gain experience this can be stepped up to 30 lock miles per day, which is what we have averaged over the years, but no more. This may seem a very short distance but I am talking about averages. Each day's cruising will be different. Some canal pounds and river reaches offer more in the way of sightseeing and other amenities than others. By planning on a 24 lock-mile-per-day average you will have ample time to 'sleep in', see the most interesting sights, complete your shopping, swim or fish or just laze about. And should it pour with rain all morning you can still do your 24 lock miles in the afternoon. An itinerary based on 24 lock miles a day will not exhaust you, however many locks are involved in the total cruise, and provides leeway not only for bad weather but for the odd battery failure or breakdown which can happen. It allows for lingering from time to time in particularly appealing places and ensures against straining the strength and patience of your crew.

So a week's boating holiday will mean 7 days at 24 lock miles a day, or 168 lock miles. For two weeks the total is simply doubled to 336 lock miles and for three weeks trebled to 504 lock miles. If you, as a beginner, plan your cruising itinerary on this maximum lock mileage basis, you will not be over-reaching yourself or be asking too much of your family or crew of friends. Your cruise will be halved, of course, if you return to the same starting point on a similar outward and return route. But in many areas of the country you can plan round trips on a combination of waterways so as not to retrace any of your outward journey or only a part of it. Then, too, quite a number of boat hirers operate from a number of bases and will make arrangements for your cruiser to be left at some other place, thus facilitating a holiday in which every day can be spent exploring new country.

I have provided these calculations as a guide only, a maximum which the beginner will not find it difficult in any way to achieve. It enables you to plan an itinerary with confidence and approach boat hire firms with sufficient information to enable them in turn to advise you that the craft you have in mind is suitable, or to advise you on what craft they have available for your planned cruise. If your planned itinerary is impracticable or will involve additional charges for licence fees on waterways for which the hirer's craft are not automatically licensed you will know the score in advance. The hirer is in a position too to suggest an alteration in your itinerary if necessary.

Writing for brochures

So with your holiday dates established and a feasible itinerary calculated you are ready to write for brochures to hire firms based along your chosen waterways route. One word of warning here. It is unwise to borrow a cruiser from a friend who may own one. Like borrowing money from a friend, it can lead to a broken friendship and on more practical grounds can lead to a spoiled holiday, for your friend's craft may not be properly serviced and you can hardly call him out should you break down with his boat. Nor should you hire a boat from the little man who can let you have it cheap, for it is unlikely to be in tip-top condition, and perhaps not even licensed for the waterways or insured. And the little man is rarely on tap to effect repairs in the event of a breakdown.

The professional hire firms belong to associations which require certain standards regarding the condition of craft let for hire, telephone repair services and fair conditions of hire.

Hire firm brochures vary enormously. Some are quite small and basic, while others are massive and packed with cruising hints and other helpful data. Do not be put off, therefore, if some boat hirers make a small charge for their brochure. Generally you will find it worth the token charge made to cover printing costs. All brochures will contain a bit of information on local waterways and usually a map of the waterways on which the firm's boats are permitted to cruise. There will be either a map or directions for reaching the boatyard by road and/or rail. There will be photographs, layouts, specifications and descriptions of the firm's hire craft, specimen inventories of equipment on board according to size of craft, hire terms (scale of charges for each craft according to season), notes regarding cancellation and baggage insurance, a booking form, conditions of hire and general information, often including advice on clothing to take, recommended holiday routes and even a list of booklets or guides you may wish to purchase. Some firms will send an up-to-date availability list of craft, while others will ask you to make alternative choices of craft in the event of your first choice being already hired.

It is a wise precaution to read carefully the all important conditions of hire so that you know exactly where you stand before you book, what deposit is required, what extras may be involved and what responsibilities you have to assume.

Criterion for hire craft

Is it possible to make a wise choice of craft from brochures? What should one look for in a hire craft? The vast majority of brochures are accurate and truthful and you have the protection of the Trade Descriptions Act. Our first hiring was such a success with the craft more than living up to its photograph and description that we booked from another firm on another waterway for the following year on the strength of the firm's brochure. When we arrived at the boatyard to start our cruise we found, to our dismay, that the firm's hire craft were very old and that maintenance was not all that it should have been. Our craft, while big and comfortable, not only leaked badly when it rained but the bilge needed pumping completely twice a day. Even though the firm slipped the craft to repair the leaks in the hull, losing us half a day, the repairs were not adequate. On the last day but one of our holiday, on a run of six hours after emptying the bilge, we moored at the boatyard with water lapping our floorboards. We found that other hirers had had similar experiences, one family abandoning their hire craft in mid-holiday and demanding their money back. That particular firm went out of business a few years later, which didn't surprise us in the least. As a result of that unhappy experience we have ever since visited the boatyard to check our hire craft before actually booking it. It has in every case proved unnecessary but we have come to enjoy these outings and hire firms have always welcomed our personal visit.

The first criterion in choosing a hire craft is its suitability for your planned itinerary. This will not arise, of course, if you decide just to potter along on the waterway on which the craft is based, or if you are booking a craft for a cruise on isolated waterways, such as the Broads, the

South Level of the Fenland Waterways, the Medway, the Lancaster Canal, etc. But if you are planning a cruise covering both broad and narrow waterways or a combination of river and canal, you will have to ensure that your craft will go where you want it to.

As a simple guide you can cruise virtually anywhere on the navigable waterways—except through the Harecastle Tunnel on the Trent & Mersey Canal where headroom is restricted to 5 ft 9 ins—with a craft with maximum dimensions of 45 ft in length, 6 ft 10 ins in beam, headroom 6 ft 6 ins and a draught of up to 2 ft or a bit more. Many canals and rivers will take craft up to 70 ft or more in length but you may not be able to enter some connecting waterways because the locks will not be big enough to cope with a boat this size. If the beam of the craft is over 6 ft 10 ins you will automatically be excluded from the narrow canals and limited to rivers and broad canals. All broad waterways will accommodate craft up to 10 ft 6 ins in beam and some will take boats up to 12 ft 6 ins or 13 ft wide. But once the beam reaches 14 ft most canals will be out of your reach and you will only have the larger rivers left as cruising grounds. If the draught is over 2 ft 6 ins canal cruising also becomes rather limited.

As long as you inform a hire firm where you want to go on your holiday you will have no worries. They will advise you of craft suitability including the aspect of size and whether the craft is licensed for the waterways on your itinerary or involves you in supplementary fees for travelling on non-nationalised waterways. There is one other important point. Many canal and river cruisers are equipped with flush toilets but there are waterways, like the Thames for example, which insist on chemical closets and do not even permit washing-up water to be drained into the river. Therefore, if your itinerary includes the Thames and you are hiring a craft from a boatyard on the Grand Union or Oxford or other canals within reach of the Thames, you will have to acquire one with a chemical closet and ensure you have a washing-up bowl aboard.

As important as the suitability of the craft for waterways is its suitability for your family or group of friends. Although the larger the boat the bigger the hire charge, it is unwise to hire a craft with insufficient room for a holiday cruise in comfort. The difference in handling boats of different size is minimal but you will certainly not enjoy being cramped for space. Most of our own boating holidays have been a combination of canal and river cruises and we usually hire a narrow cruiser. But on those occasions when we cruised exclusively on rivers or broad waterways we have invariably hired a broader-beamed motor cruiser.

Study the specifications and layouts of the craft in the brochures. Note how they are described in terms of berths upon which charges are based. Some brochures will give the exact number of berths, while others will quote adaptability, i.e. 2-3 berth, 2-4 berth, 4-6 berth, 6-8 berth, and so on.

Layouts will show you whether upper bunks are involved or if some of the crew will have to sleep under a boat canopy. Layouts of hire craft can vary tremendously and some layouts are much more spacious and comfortable than others, with better access, standards of privacy, deck space and sanitary and showering facilities. We inevitably select a craft for hire which is just a bit bigger than necessary.

It is impossible to describe in words the ideal layout in a hire craft, but you will find on page 40 good examples of a well designed narrow cruiser and a really comfortable river cruiser, both accommodating our basic five with guests from time to time. You will note that while the

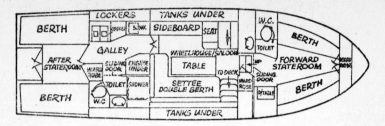

6 berth cabin cruiser

Length 34 ft. 6 in. Displacement 4.25 tons

Beam (maximum) 10 ft. 4 in. Draft 2 ft. 3 in.

Overall height 7 ft. 6 in. approx., normal waterline to top of windscreen

Headroom 6 ft. 0 in. minimum

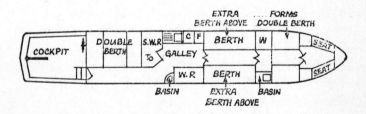

6/8 berth narrow cruiser (*Flying Mexican*)

Length 43 ft.

Beam 6 ft. 10 in. Draft 2 ft. 0 in.

Headroom 6 ft. 4 in.

river cruiser is broader beamed than the canal cruiser, the latter is usually longer than the former.

Many factors contribute to a comfortable layout. It is convenient if not essential to have a shower aboard. Even if you arrange baths for your crew in waterside hotels a shower provides extra storage room. Chapter 4 will cover what you should take with you on a boating holiday, but let me say at this stage that you will need at least one drawer per crew member and at least one hanging cupboard, apart from storage space for galley supplies.

A refrigerator or insulated cold box with renewable ice pack is a boon in hot weather and a worthwhile amenity at any time. We like ice in our drinks, the facility to have ice cream aboard, the convenience of frozen vegetables and meat at times, and butter that doesn't run.

Most craft, however large or small, have Calor gas stoves and even ovens, a sink and washbasins with running hot and cold water. While you will often dine ashore many meals will be prepared aboard and the scope of these as well as ease of preparation will depend upon the facilities. We find an oven a great advantage not only in providing more varied meals but in keeping food hot when delayed by locks or when running on a bit further to find a better mooring. Ovens can also be used for drying wet clothing and warming a craft on a cold or wet day.

You'll find that on boating holidays, you will be on your craft more of the time than inside her, so deck space should be available for every member of the crew, either in the steering well, in a bow well and/or on the superstructure. Crew members will want to see the sights as you cruise along or will want to sunbathe. I wouldn't hire a boat without a catwalk for ease in getting about the craft. It is a confounded nuisance to have to pass through a craft or climb over the top to get from stern to bow, particularly when dealing with warps or mooring lines.

Cruisers accommodating four crew or more should always have two points of access.

Water-flushed toilets are less trouble than chemical closets which have to be disposed of at least once a day, either at chemical disposal points or buried with the spade or shovel provided. But if you cruise on waterways which ban flush toilets you will have no choice in the matter and I would be prepared to bet that within the next decade more and more waterway authorities will insist on chemical closets, and introduce many more regulations against pollution.

Fuel and particularly water tank capacity on hire craft are important. Most craft carry enough fuel to take you through your entire holiday but many are fitted with inadequate water tanks. Watering points can at times be over a comfortable day's cruising apart. This can be inconvenient and I would say that every hire craft should carry at least fifteen to twenty gallons of water per person. You will be surprised how much water you will use on a boat and your crew will have to learn quickly not to let taps run.

Whether your engine is a diesel or petrol doesn't matter much although diesel engines are somewhat cheaper to run. On the other hand diesel engines are usually noisier than petrol engines. You will have to exercise special care with petrol engines because petrol is more inflammable than diesel fuel and although incidents are extremely rare, explosions and fires resulting from carelessness with Calor gas on petrol-driven craft are not unknown. I prefer a diesel engine every time and our entire crew has come to enjoy its distinctive throb.

Depending upon what waterways you choose for your holidays, you may have a choice of steering. River cruisers invariably have wheel steering, with the steering position either aft or in a centre cockpit. There is little to choose between them. Centre cockpit steering provides greater visibility as a rule but naturally affects deck space and general layout of the craft.

Canal cruisers usually have tiller steering, which is admittedly more direct, but which I personally find less comfortable. But many cruisers have wheel steering, some aft and some amidships, and I plump for wheel steering every time. This enables you to sit on a stool instead of standing. It is possible to sit while tiller steering but this can be awkward at times and controls can be inconveniently placed. I have found too that one gets much wetter at a tiller than at a wheel, for with wheel steering you have the benefit of bulkhead protection for most of your body. Many boating friends, however, prefer tiller steering. I don't honestly dislike it, indeed have found it fun, and would recommend beginners to compare it with wheel steering for themselves.

Both canal and river cruisers, particularly smaller craft, are sometimes designed to incorporate folding canopies. You will find that only on rare occasions can you cruise along with the canopy up, for there is usually a bridge hole too low on your course. Some hire firms insist that canopies can only be used when moored. My family and I enjoy an open cockpit even when it is raining, although not in torrential downpours. We have been on many cruises when we have never raised the canopy the entire time. On some craft, however, it is essential to erect a canopy when it rains, either because cockpit space under the canopy is required for sleeping space or because the combination of wind and rain makes it desirable. The important thing about folding canopies is to check that they are in good condition and all side curtains are aboard. Previous hirers may well have cruised with the canopy up and damaged it.

Take a good look at the layout of the craft you have in

mind from the standpoint of accommodation and privacy. Single bunks allow more space for each person than double bunks, for which reason my wife and I always sleep head to toe on the latter in sleeping bags. This makes the double bunk every bit as comfortable as the single. Age and sex of crew, whether family or friends, have to be taken into consideration when choosing a craft, so always work out which berths each member of the crew will occupy before a booking. If a friend or friends are joining the family a reallocation of berths may be necessary. Upper bunks are as comfortable as lower ones as a rule, and it is possible to tuck even a restless sleeper in one of these to obviate the danger of a fall. But those who sleep under an upper bunk will get less air, and this can matter to those people who like to sleep normally with bedroom windows wide open. You will want to be sure that cabins are separated by doors of one kind or another instead of being merely open gangways, for those times when privacy is desired. Doors should fasten back easily in an open position too because, particularly in hot weather, you will want them all open and a breeze flowing through the boat for sleeping comfort.

Cruiser equipment

Cruiser inventories listed in brochures do provide practically everything you will need afloat in the way of domestic equipment as claimed, and you will find it all supplied clean and ready for use. These inventories will vary somewhat from hire firm to hire firm and according to the size of the craft. Some hire firms provide items like soap, washing-up liquid, scouring powder and toilet rolls. In some cases all linen including pillow cases, tea towels, etc., are subject to a supplementary charge. And in all cases life-jackets for youngsters can be hired. The majority of hire cruisers today are fitted with radios and some firms even supply television sets for a supplementary charge.

Do not hesitate to be a bit fussy about the craft you select for the secret of an enjoyable holiday afloat lies basically in the craft rather than in your itinerary. You can, of course, obtain full information on all these points from brochures and correspondence with the hire firm, but for beginners a personal visit to the boatyard will give you and the family a much clearer idea of your mobile holiday home as well as an exciting preview of the fun to come.

As you become better acquainted with the waterways you may be as lucky as we were in finding an all-purpose craft which feels exactly right, which exerts a hold upon you and which comes up to the family concept of the ideal. You will sense this after your first few days of cruising aboard her and as you hire her again the following year, perhaps from a different base, you will come to feel that she almost belongs to you.

In our case, our favourite craft is a 'Toledo' class six to eight berth steel-hulled canal cruiser, 6 ft 10 ins in beam, 43 ft in length, 1 ft 9 ins in draught and with a superstructure clearance of just under 5 ft 9 ins without removing her spot-light or windscreens. She will go anywhere on the waterways network, apart from the isolated sections, and is the closest we have ever come to perfection in a cruiser, superbly laid out and equipped for comfort and efficiency.

You will find the diagrammatic layout of our favourite narrow cruiser, the *Flying Mexican,* at the bottom of page 40.

Hire charges

What do craft of this type cost to hire? The *Flying Mexican* can be hired at rates ranging from £46 per week early in the season, except for the Easter period, to a maximum of £80 per week at peak season (mid-July to the end of August), tailing off to £38 per week in late September and October. Four-berth canal cruisers with similar facilities range in price from £26 to £52 per week according to season. Two-berth craft can be obtained for a weekly charge of between £15 and £36 per week, according to season. Rates for river cruisers of equivalent size and standard are roughly the same. This means the cost per berth for hire craft varies roughly from about £6 to £22 per week, depending on the season and the type of craft. Some hire firms will let craft for shorter periods than a week and when hiring for three days or less the charge is usually half the weekly rate, while hiring for four days or more you will usually pay one-seventh of the weekly rate per day.

Some readers may at first consider these charges rather expensive but will realise that they provide good value for money when compared with hotel accommodation or caravan hire charges. After all, you are getting a comfortable fully equipped mobile home giving you an opportunity to explore and enjoy aspects of your country which can be achieved in no other way.

CHAPTER 3

ON HANDLING BOATS

Don't be put off by doubts about your ability to handle
a boat as all our craft are designed for easy handling.
A short trial run with one of our experienced staff is
all you need before you set out on your own.

Steering a cruiser is exceptionally straightforward,
but a trial run before finally leaving the boatyard is
always arranged to familiarise you with the simple
controls.

Generally if you drive a car you will certainly be
able to handle a boat; but non-drivers please take heart,
you will soon learn the basic requirements of boat handling. Controls are fewer than in a car and much
simpler : even the greenest of novices will be away on
their first voyage—waving goodbye to the boatyard—
within minutes of taking over after the trial run.

These three quotations, taken from the brochures of
three hire firms offering craft for hire on rivers, on canals
and on both rivers and canals, are representative of comments on boat handling expressed by all hire firm
operators. What's more they are perfectly true. I know
of no hire firm that will not let their craft to complete
novices or who will ask to see a car driving licence. To
do this, allowing amateurs with no experience whatsoever
to take charge of boats costing thousands of pounds, they
must be confident that hirers can cope.

Some hire firms offer advance tuition in boat handling for prospective hirers of nervous temperament but this course of special instruction is generally regarded as unnecessary and hire firms offering these facilities are few and far between.

Trial run

Every hire firm will supply you with a stencilled or printed list of instructions covering the most important points of boat handling and maintenance, or with a comprehensive booklet of cruising hints incorporating basic information on these points. So even if you should forget certain aspects of what you are shown on your trial run you will have a written reminder at hand.

Let us assume you and your crew are stowed away and on board your hire craft ready to cast off. One of the hire firm staff is with you and it will be he who starts up the engine, casts off bow and stern ropes, or 'straps' as they are sometimes called, pushes out the bows or entire craft, and gets you under way. You will find that he will let the engine run for some minutes before untying the boat, and will advise you always to give the engine a chance to warm up. You will also be told if you are aboard a sizeable cruiser that when you are not at a boatyard or designated moorings you should push out the stern first and reverse into mid-stream. This is because cruisers, and particularly long narrow canal cruisers, do not steer easily near the bank because they swing about on their own centres, i.e. the stern must swing into the bank for the bows to go out.

You will be shown that there are only one or two effective controls, a gear lever with forward, reverse and neutral positions, and a throttle. On some craft gear lever and throttle are combined. If there is a separate throttle it must always be closed down before going from forward to reverse and vice versa. If controls are combined you will be told to move the lever to neutral for a moment before changing from forward to reverse gear and vice versa.

Your mentor will show you the ignition switch, which in some cases will incorporate the starter, while in other craft there will be a separate starter button. He will locate the horn button, headlight switch and water pump switch and, in the case of a diesel engine, a control resembling a choke in a car or piece of wire with a loop at the end, which has to be pulled to stop the engine.

While you are cruising along he will show you where the gauges are which register oil pressure, engine temperature and battery charge, and advise you on normal readings. You will be told to check the oil in the sump regularly, just as you would in a car. You will be advised that when engine temperature rises unduly it will probably be due to debris wrapped round your propeller or shaft. You will be told how to clear this, and if your craft has a weed box for easy access from the 'engine room' to the propeller assembly your instructor will advise you always to ensure that bolts are firmly tightened after you replace it.

Even before you leave the boatyard you will have been shown where all of the equipment is stowed, and the positions of fuel and water tanks will have been made known to you too. Simple daily maintenance duties will be explained either before or during the trial run, i.e. checking oil, pumping bilges, turning grease points or pressing the lever of the shaft lubricant container, whichever is applicable, and topping up any header tank that may be aboard. Maintenance of both petrol and diesel engines is simplicity itself and literally takes only a few minutes a day. It's a good idea to take care of these easy but important chores first thing every morning as a matter of routine so that you don't forget them and cause unnecessary complications on your holiday.

Your mentor, in checking the inventory of the craft with you before the trial run, will give you some useful tips. You will be shown where the Calor gas is kept, and, if you are on a long cruise, how to change over the bottles and re-light any refrigerator aboard. If your craft is equipped with a cold box rather than a Calor gas fridge you will be advised to turn off the Calor gas at the bottle each night and turn it back on again in the morning. You will also be shown how to light the Calor gas heater pilot light and operate any levers that may enable you to obtain hot water heated by the engine rather than the gas heater.

More breakdowns are caused by flat batteries than any other single cause. In the great majority of cases where this happens it is simply because hirers don't run their engines every day. This does not mean that you must keep on the move, but it is mandatory to run your engine for at least half an hour every day, whether on the move or not, to maintain a good charge in your batteries.

There is much more equipment using electricity on a boat than in a car. Provided you run your engine daily there is no need to be parsimonious about using lights and electrical equipment aboard a boat.

One point that hire firms rarely if ever cover is use of water aboard a boat. Many hire craft have relatively small freshwater tanks and even on craft with water tanks of 100 gallons or more capacity, fresh water will vanish quickly, even if you do not use the shower or bath aboard. On a boat, you should establish a self-enforced ruling never to wash or wash up under a running tap. If you depart from this ruling you will almost certainly run out of fresh water frequently or have to make sure you reach a watering point every day for topping up. Showers are particularly wasteful of water and we invariably shower only when we are moored near or are approaching a watering point.

Steering

During your trial run you will quickly note that wheel steering on a boat is similar to wheel steering in a car, i.e. your craft turns in the direction that you turn the wheel. Response to the wheel of a boat is not as direct as that in a car, however. Your craft will not turn as quickly or as sharply as a car, and particularly if your boat is a sizeable one. With narrow cruisers in particular, as your mentor will demonstrate, when your bows swing left, your stern will come round to the right. Narrow cruisers steer rather like a pencil floats in a stream. Tiller steering is more direct, and although the craft reacts on the same principle, it reacts differently. To turn left with wheel steering, you turn the wheel to the left, but to turn left with tiller steering you push the tiller to the right. Whatever the type of steering on your craft you will grasp the technique easily during your trial run.

Boating on the inland waterways is quite different from motor-cruising or sailing at sea. Craft at sea can be left to run or drift for long distances, but on inland waterways the steerer must steer all the time that the craft is under way, or go hard ashore very quickly. Mooring and casting off and coming alongside, which happens once or twice a day at sea, is done a few times an hour on the inland waterways.

When steering on inland waterways of any kind you have to keep as alert as you do at the wheel of a car, even though there is comparatively little traffic. When you first take over the wheel or tiller of a boat, try lighting a cigarette, cigar or pipe and you will see what I mean. With practice you will learn to do this safely by hooking an arm over the wheel, or standing astride the tiller.

The usual 'rule of the road' on waterways is to keep to the right. This rule will frequently be broken for many good and bad reasons, but if in any circumstances you intend to veer left you should, if any other craft are about, give two blasts on your horn, or better still hold out your arm horizontally in the direction you intend to go. You can make your intention abundantly clear by a sharpish change of course in that direction. While there are no authentic hand signals on the waterways, you should do your best to indicate any change of course to moving craft around you. There are official sound signals, which you may find useful, but the trouble is that few hirers bother about or understand them. One blast of your horn indicates that you are altering your course to starboard (right); two blasts indicates alteration of course to port (left); three blasts that your engine is going astern, and four blasts followed by a pause and then two more means that you are turning round to port. Whatever methods you use to signal your intentions when other craft are about, always ease off.

Looking at a waterway, even a canal, it will appear to you to be wide enough to permit your craft to wander at will. But you will find on most canals and all rivers that the navigable channel runs down the centre of straight stretches, while the deep water is invariably on the outside of bends. The inside of a bend may be very shallow, even virtually dry, and you will note that long narrow boats usually have trouble on sharp corners. So keep clear of these craft on sharp corners and never moor at such locations.

Thus, although 'keep right' is the rule of the waterways, when no craft are in sight ahead or behind you, and provided you are not approaching a blind corner or angled bridge hole, it is wise practice to keep to the centre of canals and rivers on straight stretches and to the outside of bends. Of course, you must move over to the right for approaching craft or to permit a craft from behind to pass on your left. Normally, you too should pass to the left of craft, but do not overtake a working boat or pair of narrow boats until you are waved on by the steerer. Overtake on the side he indicates and have the courtesy to thank him as you pass. You will find that you will be unable to pass unless the working boat or pair is slowed down, in any case. This is due to the curious water-flow past the hull of a loaded boat.

Grounding

Attempts to cut corners, whether in passing other craft or not, will almost inevitably lead to going on the mud. It is no great tragedy if you run aground. In most cases, as you are moving forward you will only ground your craft at the bows. Your stern will probably be afloat. Immediately you touch bottom, you should put your engine into neutral. The deep water is back where you came from and your craft has almost certainly dug a trough in the mud as it went aground and is now lying in it. If your stern is afloat and your propeller has not churned up mud you may be able to reverse off the mud. If this does not work you should use your boathook or barge pole. There is no point in sending one of the crew to the bows to push off as his weight and thrust will only ground the bows more firmly and so make it more difficult to get off. The crew should push off from the stern and their weight alone will help lift the bows. Always push off backwards along the trough. If you still cannot get off, get a line ashore on the other side of the canal or river, and pull the boat out backwards from there.

Should you go aground at the stern, switch off your engine at once to prevent damage to rudder and propeller. Then lighten the stern by getting the crew forward to the bows. If the stern does not float free, then use your boat-hook to push off backwards and to the centre of the water-way. Never use your engine in any gear when your stern is grounded.

Should your entire craft be aground, and this can happen, for example, when the wash of a passing com-mercial craft pushes you to the shallow side of a waterway, cut your engine, move your crew to the bows and with your boathook try first to free the stern and then the bows and gradually edge your craft to the centre of the water-way. If your craft persists in sticking fast, try rolling it gently from side to side by shifting your crew from cat-walk to catwalk. In serious cases of grounding you may as a last resort have to lighten your craft by getting the crew over the side, or ask a passing craft to take a line from your stern and assist you.

Navigating bridge holes

Whatever canal or river you cruise you are bound to encounter bridge holes. Many are wide and easy to navi-gate but others will be both narrow and badly angled to the navigation channel. The easy way to navigate bridge holes is to line up your craft with the hole as you approach it so that you pass straight through. Never worry about the right side of your boat. Whether at wheel or tiller simple see that your left-hand catwalk will clear the left-hand side of the hole by a foot and you will invariably pass under the bridge without difficulty. Do not try to *just* clear the left-hand side of the hole, as a bend may follow and you will need the clearance on either side to allow your stern to swing when you steer round the bend. The height of your superstructure must always be taken into consideration. Your hire firm will advise you if there are any particularly low bridges or tunnels on your route. But do not take anything for granted. Ease off before bridge holes and tunnels to see if your craft will easily pass through. You will quickly be able to judge clearances, just as you become acquainted with the width of a new car. Rivers and canal pounds can be in flood, reducing normal clearance, and it is up to you to exercise due care.

It is bridge holes on blind corners or sharp bends on canals that sometimes cause concern to the inexperienced. Positioning a boat to go through a narrow opening on a bend is largely a question of practice. The most helpful advice I can give is to urge you to think of your craft as being steerable separately from both ends. There is little difficulty in aiming the bows so that the boat will enter the bridge hole. On a sharp turn this will mean steering for a point on the far side of the hole and then gradually bringing the bows round until they enter the gap. This done, you can turn your attention to the stern. If it is coming too close to either side of the bridge hole, you can move your rudder to bring the stern into line. Moving the stern over will have the effect of forcing the bows towards the side of the hole, but you will find that there is time enough to rectify this when the stern is past the danger point. You will find that most bridges on canal bends have bays cut in the outside bank on either side of them, and these are designed to allow for the stern swing of a 70 ft narrow boat. With a shorter craft you should have no difficulty in lining it up for the hole in plenty of time to see and avoid any craft that happens to be coming the other way.

Navigating tunnels

Tunnels are really no more forbidding than bridge holes although longer tunnels, which may stretch for over a mile, are dark. In many cases you will not be able to see the exit and this can be forbidding to the beginner, particularly as few long tunnels are absolutely straight. Ease off and proceed slowly until you are confident of your ability to steer through a tunnel. Use your headlight, of course, and pitch its beam so that it hits the centre of the curved roof of the tunnel about 20 ft ahead of your bows. You will find that this will illuminate both the top and sides of a tunnel. Also if you turn on all the cabin lights you will find that the brightly illuminated sides of the tunnel will make steering much easier. There are one-way tunnels which should be negotiated rather slowly as you may have only feet or inches clearance on each side. But canal tunnels which permit two-way traffic are wide enough for craft to pass each other, however narrow they may appear to you. If you feel a kind of astigmatism developing as you cruise through a long tunnel, reduce your speed. When passing oncoming craft, if you are worried, pull over to the right side and stop to let the approaching craft pass. After navigating a few long tunnels you will get the hang of it and enjoy your subsequent tunnels at normal speed.

Do not worry if you bump the side—your craft can take it. If you continue to veer against the sides, however, ease off for a more comfortable passage. Quite a number of tunnels are wet, even if they drip only at air vents. The helmsman should slip on a waterproof coat and if there is anything on deck that you do not want to get wet, store it below.

Stopping a boat

Boats, unlike cars, have no brakes. Steering in the almost frictionless element of water is only achieved by adding drag to one side of a boat, or applying extra drive to the other. Both forces make the boat turn in the same direction, but it will turn on an imaginary pivot slightly forward of amidships. The bows will therefore move sideways in one direction and the stern sideways in the other.

As the imaginary pivot round which a boat turns is

forward of its central point, its stern will obviously swing wider than its bows. There is therefore more likelihood of hitting something with the stern than with the bows. You will also find that when going full speed ahead a rudder will resist being turned and you will have to exert a good force on tiller or wheel to overcome this resistance, a breaking wake being formed as your craft comes round. But when you are idling along very slowly, rudder action will be light. If drifting with the engine off you will not be able to steer at all, for a boat must be under way to obtain steerage.

The only way of stopping is by going astern. A propeller is far less efficient for this than when going ahead. If you are moving forward, even at only four to six miles per hour, your craft will continue to move forward for some distance even if you put the engine in neutral. You will need considerably more engine to get any worthwhile stopping effect, and even then you will find it seems to take a long time before you lose way. To stop you should first put your engine in neutral and then into reverse— and don't hesitate to 'gun the engine'. Most bumps occur because boat handlers do not allow sufficient space or time to stop. Do practise stopping with your hire craft a few times so that you can see for yourself the distance required before the craft comes to a halt. Once you are aware of this, stopping will cause you no problem. You will find, once you have gone through a lock, that stopping in confined water is a much faster process than stopping in a wide reach of river or canal.

Reversing

While practising stopping it is a good idea also to try going in reverse. You will soon see that when going astern the propeller is the wrong side of the rudder and cannot deflect water off it. Unless you are going hard astern, which you usually do not want to do, the rudder will have virtually no effect. In fact, it is difficult, if not impossible to steer accurately when going astern. One way to change your heading, that is to come about, is to move to the right side of the navigational channel and then give your engine a brief burst ahead with the wheel hard over to the left. Put your engine in neutral, swing your rudder the opposite way, then go hard astern briefly. A few manoeuvres like this and you will be facing the opposite direction.

Of course, many waterways are wide enough to enable you to turn your craft simply by putting the rudder hard over. Canals have winding holes, i.e. turning points or deep indentations in one bank to permit a 70 ft narrow boat to turn. Navigational guides to waterways generally list winding points, and approaches to locks are often wider than the waterway itself, enabling all but the biggest craft to turn about.

Mooring

You will be mooring your craft several times a day. And mooring is really very little different from stopping in midstream. It is a simple matter to come to a halt beside a designated mooring—a quayside, platform or floating dock —because there is usually sufficient depth of water for your craft. You simply ease off and steer to bring your craft at a 10–15° angle to the mooring, first going into neutral and then using reverse gear and opposite rudder to come to a halt.

It is along the banks of rivers and canals, those rural, isolated or out-of-the-way spots that appeal to you, that mooring can require a little finesse. This is because many of the most scenic and desirable moorings have little depth of water. Whenever attempting to moor at undesignated moorings always bring your bows in first at about a 45°

angle with a member of your crew armed with a boathook to make soundings of the depth of the water. Even if you go aground, your stern will still be afloat in deeper water and you can reverse safely back into midstream. If your bows come in to the bank without grounding a member of the crew can leap ashore with the bow line and while he or she holds the bows in you can turn your rudder towards the bank and reverse your stern close enough in to enable other members of the crew to jump ashore with the stern line. This is also a useful technique to employ when mooring in a narrow gap between other craft.

It is possible to moor along shallow banks provided you keep your craft a foot or more off the bank and use a gangplank for leaving and boarding the boat. The main thing to remember about mooring is to do it slowly. On canals you can moor craft facing in any direction, but on rivers with a stream running always moor with your bows facing upstream. You will find that the stream will help you come to a halt and your craft will ride more comfortably when facing the stream.

Never moor on bends, in locks, on approaches to locks, in bridge holes or their entrances, or on sites with 'no mooring' signs. Don't run the risk of being rammed or clipped by other craft.

The most common method of mooring is to two points, at bow and stern, and this method is best for overnight mooring or for leaving the boat for any length of time. At recognised moorings you will find mooring rings or stakes to which you can tie your mooring lines. On occasions they may be too far apart for the length of your craft and it may be necessary to use one of your own mooring stakes and mallets or heavy hammers. For safe and comfortable mooring, drive these stakes into the ground at a 45° angle away from the bows and stern, siting the stakes about 6 ft ahead of your bows and 6 ft behind your stern. In a field positioning does not matter but obstructing a canal or river towpath with mooring lines can cause accidents—and it may be your crew who are the victims.

Mooring lines should never be taut with your craft pulled hard against the bank. Allow a little slack so that the boat can cope with the wash of passing craft and/or the natural flow of the stream. If your craft is equipped with fenders rather than rubbing strips do adjust the height of the fenders to take any bumps from quayside, posts, rails or the contour of the bank. The only time you will need knots is when you moor, and two half-hitches are what you should use. Ask your hire firm instructor to show you how to tie a half-hitch. This is simple to tie, is safe in that it cannot work loose and is easy to undo. In fact, if you simply pull the half-hitches down the stake after lifting it they will undo themselves.

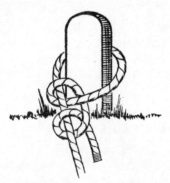

Another method of mooring, useful for short stops, for making tea, waiting a turn at a lock, or to let your dog ashore, is to use a 'breast rope'. This is simply a short line from midships to a stake, mooring ring or post in the ground abreast of the centre of the boat. It saves work and is amply secure in waters without tide or stream.

In the brief spell that your hire firm mentor is aboard he will not have sufficient opportunity to advise you on all these aspects of boat handling. As soon as he feels you are unlikely to wreck the boat, or drain pounds or reaches dry, he will wish you a pleasant voyage and leave you to get on with it. When cruising on inland waterways be assured that contacts with banks, lock-sides and even other boats are normal and inevitable. Inland waterway cruisers are designed to take bumps, though this does not mean you should be careless and ram or scrape everything in sight.

Locking

Locking is no doubt the most formidable aspect of inland waterways navigation to the amateur. When the boat-yard is near a lock, which is often the case, your mentor will take you to the lock and demonstrate exactly how it is worked. Even so, you may not take in all his advice and thoroughly understand the function of locks. A lock is simply a device to enable boats to go up or downhill.

Although rivers usually have a constant supply of running water the water would run too fast or be too shallow to float boats if it were not controlled by dams or weirs, and locks to raise or lower boats from one level to another without releasing all the water behind the dams. Canals are more heavily locked, for water in canals has no regular flow and each level is rather like a still lake. To get boats over a hill the next lake, usually called a 'pound', is constructed some feet higher up, and a lock permits the boat to be raised up to it. To make up for the water lost by working the locks, more water has to be fed into the canal on the highest or 'summit' pound. This means tapping reservoirs or other sources of water, is always most expensive, frequently very difficult and some-times virtually impossible. Therefore wasting water while working a lock is the most heinous offence you can commit on a canal.

A lock is really a simple device, first built by the Chinese over a thousand years ago, when rivers were split up into steps for the first time. There are various types and sizes of locks but basically a lock consists of a chamber or box of brick or stone or concrete or iron with gates at either end tough enough to withstand the huge water pressure. It is provided with primitive shutter-like valves called 'paddles' or 'sluices' at either end to allow water to enter or leave it. River locks can be huge, big enough to handle coastal steamers. On broad canals locks will be about 14 to 15 ft across and 72 or more ft long, with double gates at each end pointing towards the higher water level. Narrow canal locks are usually only 7 to 7 ft 6 ins wide and about 72 ft long. Usually they have double bottom gates but only one upper gate, opening in the direction of the higher pound. Many bigger river locks have gates opened by power but the smaller canal lock-gate is usually opened by pushing on a massive 'balance-beam' which projects from the gate over the lock side. The easiest way to manipulate these is by putting your seat against the balance-beam and pushing with your feet on the ground, rather than by pushing it with your hands.

Paddle gear may look very primitive to you but it is effective. A bar is attached to the top of a paddle, which in turn is attached to an iron rack with a double track. A pinion on a shaft with a square end engages this. The only equipment or tool needed to work a paddle is the lock key or 'windlass', an iron handle with one or more square sockets on its end, which fit the square end of the shaft. There are two basic sizes, $1\frac{1}{4}$ ins for gear on rivers and broad canals and 1 in for gear on narrow canals. Windlasses are supplied with hire craft, either double-socketed types or sets of both sizes when required, or simply the correct size windlass for the particular water-ways you are cruising. When fitted to the square end of the shaft and turned the windlass makes the pinion pull up the rack and paddle, and so open it. To prevent the paddle falling back again when the pressure from the windlass is removed, there is a ratchet and pawl on the pinion shaft. You should keep this in the 'on' position as you wind up the paddle so that, should your hand slip

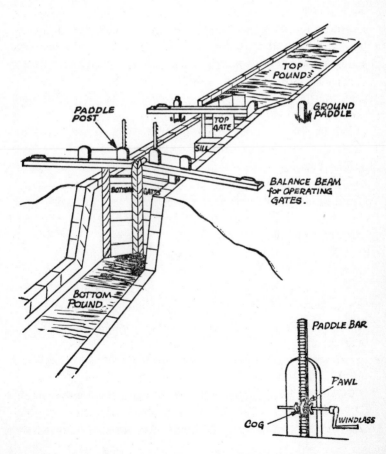

off the windlass for any reason, the weight of the paddle dropping will not cause the windlass to fly round. If no pawl is provided there is usually a wedge to place between the rack and pinion to hold up the paddle, either attached to a chain or fixed to a hinged stirrup.

When working paddles NEVER let go of the windlass while it is on the shaft and never leave it on the shaft while locking through. Always ensure the pawl or wedge is engaged and then remove the windlass once the paddle is raised. Careless handling of windlasses can cause serious accidents as they fly from the shaft with terrific speed.

When lowering a paddle either use a windlass to wind it down after disengaging the pawl or wedge or use your hand on the round part of the shaft as a brake. Don't let them run down on their own by taking the easy way out and simply knocking out the pawl or wedge as this can damage the paddle gear.

While it is certainly true that some locks are hard to work the vast majority are easy enough for women and children to handle. Despite the great weight of lock gates the heavy balance-beams make the gates easy to open. Guillotine-type or vertical gates are usually stiff and require some little effort to wind up but they are relatively rare on our inland waterways. The ease with which paddles can be raised will depend upon the weight of water on them, the condition of the gear and the state of lubrication. Some will be more difficult than others but in our experience we have found over 80 per cent are easy to operate, particularly those on locks on narrow canals.

I should mention here that locks often have several sets of paddles, some set in the ground of the lock-side and called 'ground-paddles' and others, set in the gates themselves, called 'gate-paddles'. Both are operated in the same way but when there are both types at a lock the ground-paddles should be raised first, quite slowly, as they do not cause such a rush of water as gate-paddles, and then the gate-paddles. It is unwise to open paddles too quickly when your boat is in the lock for the rush of water can throw the boat about.

Some locks, where water is scarce, have 'side-pounds'. These have special paddles of their own and should be used first in both emptying or filling a lock. By using these nearly half a lock-full of water is saved every time a boat comes up or down.

When passing through locks it is essential that the right procedure be used to avoid damage to craft or the locks. The best way for amateur crews to handle locks is to divide the various duties among the crew, so that each crew member knows exactly what he or she has to do.

All waterway guides have specific and detailed instructions on the operation of all types of locks on the waterways they cover and they need not be repeated here. When you come to a complicated lock or those ingenious 'staircase' locks you will find instructions posted and, most likely, a lock-keeper on duty. Proceed with care and you will meet no insurmountable problems.

One of the most pleasant pastimes on a cruise is 'lock-wheeling'. All of our crews, and particularly our dog, enjoy it. If you have sufficient crew members to cope with locking, one crew member can move ahead at flights of locks and consecutively prepare each lock in the flight. This will obviate mooring at each lock before entering it. Some holidaymakers take a bicycle along with them and the lock-wheeler can then cycle ahead along the towpath to prepare locks in advance and perhaps have time to shop or collect beer from a canal-side pub.

By watching others with experience you and your crew will develop a system for locking and you will soon be taking great pride in the speed and efficiency with which you can pass through. You will learn that fenders should be used in wide locks. You will quickly find the easiest way to land or take on crew members close to the lock head and tail, and that you will be able to control your boat on its engine in narrow locks without mooring lines, and in wide locks you will find that a crew member on both bow and stern lines, keeping them taut as your craft moves up or down, using bollards when available, will ensure smooth passage.

Handling boats on inland waterways is within the competence of any amateur who keeps alert, obeys the rules and practises common courtesy. Steering cruisers is great fun for all the family once the 'feel' of your hire craft is acquired and that glow of confidence arrives.

CHAPTER 4

GETTING READY

ONCE YOU have chosen and booked your hire cruiser your appetite for the waterways will have been well whetted and the real fun can begin. You will know your starting date and starting point and you will have a tentative itinerary roughly planned. You and your crew can now start preparing for your holiday in earnest.

Personally I find that much of the enjoyment of any holiday lies in anticipation and preparation and this is particularly true of boating holidays. Different crews can cover the same waterways journey and yet have quite different holidays. There is considerable scope in every cruise for individual choice—each waterway caters for a host of varied interests. You can set off without paying more than lip service to planning, other than reading your joining instructions from the hire firm, and thoroughly enjoy yourself. But the odds are that you will regret it when you run out of water miles from a watering point, when you go out to shop and find it is early closing day or when you discover from other boating holidaymakers that you missed that little antique shop, that marvellous restaurant, that charming pub, that outstanding exhibition or that wonderful view. What is more, you will have wasted a winter and spring of planning pleasure, which I regard as being almost as fascinating as the holiday itself.

Documentation

From the hire firm brochures you will note that most hire firms recommend or offer certain basic maps and booklets, including the Stanford's Inland Cruising map you have used to work out your tentative journey, or Imray, Laurie, Norie & Wilson's map of the Inland Waterways of England and Wales, which is equally well executed and informative.

Among the guides available will usually be a localised navigation booklet or cruising guide. These vary in content but all give an outline of facilities and amenities of waterways within the cruising range of the hire firm and are well worth the few new pence they cost.

Waterways outside the jurisdiction of the British Waterways Board are often covered by local charts and maps or even official guides such as *Gateway to the Avon,* published by The Lower Avon Navigation Trust. Also available for certain waterways like the River Medway and the Rivers Lee and Stort are handy inexpensive Inland Waterways Association illustrated handbooks.

For the nationalised waterways there is an entire series of sixteen invaluable Inland Cruising booklets, selling at between 25p and 30p, and they add enjoyment to your holiday out of all proportion to the cost. If not available from the hire firm they can be obtained from the British Waterways Board or the Inland Waterways Association. Each of these begins with a short but interesting history of the waterway or waterways covered. The courses are inevitably depicted as a perfectly straight blue ribbon running up and down the page. Locks, tunnels, bridges, basins and wharves are all indicated along with mileages and important characteristics of the vicinity. While these diagrammatic maps distort other topical features, they are easy to read and follow. Bridges are always numbered in sequence and as these numbers appear on most of the actual bridges they are constant guides to your exact whereabouts. Locks are also numbered and frequently named, and the booklets show which side of the waterway the towpath is sited. They also indicate the position of watering points, mooring points, winding points, post offices, pubs, public telephones, toilet facilities, garages, railway stations and other services. Along the side of each diagrammatic map is a running narrative describing some of the highlights of the waterway and the country through which it passes.

The one-inch Ordnance Survey Maps, from 32½p, showing in great detail just what lies either side of the waterways within striking distance are, I find, a great help in preparing for a boating holiday. And as the various booklets do not incorporate information like early closing days and market days, I have found an *ABC Railway Guide* most useful both for planning a cruise and for working out the most convenient method for picking up and disembarking guest crews.

Obviously you will need only those maps and guides relevant to your proposed journey and your hire firm will either stock these or will tell you what booklets are needed. It is possible that you will discover a certain amount of duplication in the hire firm's booklet and the B.W.B. Inland Cruising booklet. We have found from experience that no guide is fully comprehensive, and in addition to the documentation already mentioned we have added to our planning material by obtaining from the library official guides to certain cities and towns which we intend to visit as well as the so-called county books, such as the *King's England* series, the *County Books* series and the *Companion* series.

The advance log

Most boating holidaymakers tend to keep some sort of diary or log of the holiday but I believe that an 'advance log' is of great value. When planning my own boating holiday I buy a loose-leaf notebook in which to set down the collated net results of planning. This I keep by me throughout the holiday as a reminder of potential opportunities and for handy reference. Of course, I also take the relevant maps, charts, navigational booklets and guides but one can hardly keep spreading these out to find exactly what is available round the next bend, particularly when steering or when it happens to be windy or wet. This notebook can be kept open by the wheel or tiller and can be transferred quickly to the pocket in inclement weather. It will tell you your rate of progress and enable you to judge whether you can reach a certain place in time for lunch or whether it is feasible to get through a flight of locks before dark.

The preparation of this advance log will give you considerable advance knowledge of what lies along the route and will make for the most enjoyable of holidays.

Tentative schedules

Once I have completed my advance log I select a series of tentative mooring points for tying up overnight and even for lunch-time halts. In short, I work out how far I am likely to cruise each day, taking into consideration average cruising time on the basis of lock miles and facilities available along the route. Each day's cruising will vary in lock miles covered. One day I may plan to cruise only twenty lock miles because this enables us to moor overnight at a place with a host of facilities. Another day I may plan to cover thirty lock miles because there are long canal pounds with few locks and few apparent amenities along the waterway, while a particular water-side town would seem ideal for overnight mooring and shopping next morning.

We do not, of course, rigidly adhere to this tentative schedule. Heavy rain, fishing or excursions may upset a particular day's cruise. In making a tentative plan I take into consideration too that the crew may well have had enough in working a couple of long flights of locks in one day, and may want to moor early for the night. It is also necessary to allow for locking times. All river authorities specify the hours of locking. On the Thames where all locks are manned, lock-keepers are on duty from 9 a.m. to sunset, with an hour off for lunch. While there are no specified hours on canals, flights of locks can be padlocked at night, about 7 p.m., and it is not unusual to find yourself separated from the pub outside which you intended to moor overnight by several miles of padlocked locks. On the Oxford Canal there have been silly experiments in closing locks to craft over certain periods of certain days to allow fishermen to pursue their sport in absolute peace. The literature you receive from your hire craft firm should contain this information as well as information on stoppages. Except for emergencies the waterways authorities do not suddenly close locks for repair but plan these well in advance and publish a list of planned stop-pages for many months ahead. You will find that only rarely will a planned stoppage affect your holiday, for most repairs are carried out during the off-season periods.

If you prepare your advance log on the left-hand pages of your notebook, each right-hand page can then be used for an actual log of your holiday cruise. My own logs are very simple, noting time of departure from the overnight mooring each day, times taken through locks or flights of locks, times of passing underneath selected bridges and aqueducts, times of mooring for lunch, watering, shopping, sightseeing and times of mooring for the night. I make brief notes when warranted of the condition of locks or stretches of waterway; comments on moorings, waterside pubs and restaurants; observations of excursions, shopping facilities, scenic beauty spots, noteworthy items of waterways architecture or engineering; and I invariably add such items as unlisted watering points and meetings with working craft. Each evening after mooring I quickly calculate and note the actual cruising time for the day and the number of lock miles covered. Simple division then provides accurate statistics on average speed per lock mile.

You will find that keeping a simple log of this kind in conjunction with your advance log takes very little time, yet is most useful for the return trip along the same waterways and for planning other holiday cruises. After a few days you will be in a position to estimate accurately whether your planned itinerary is practical; whether you can indeed extend your cruise or whether you will have to turn round earlier than anticipated to arrive back at your hire firm's boatyard by the deadline.

Food

Your advance log completed, you can then turn your attention to what to take with you on your boating holiday. Storage space on hire craft is usually quite adequate but it is unwise to burden yourself with non-essentials. Food is an important consideration but it is certainly not necessary for you to transport bulk supplies for the entire holiday from your home. Most hire firms have arrangements with local shops for the boat hirer's order to be delivered to the hire craft on the day of departure and payment is conveniently by cheque. Some hire firms automatically supply printed order forms from the shops while others make a small charge for completing your shopping for you.

The idea is not to order stores for the entire cruise as shopping along the waterside and in strange towns and villages, particularly on market days, is all part of the fun of a boating holiday. We usually order through our boat hire firm only enough food and drink to keep us going for three or four days at most. As you usually start your boating holiday at a weekend when few shops are open and as shopping facilities can be few and far between along the waterways, you should start off with at least the essentials.

We take very little in the way of food from home but have learned that a cooked ham, turkey or a couple of chickens are most useful to have over the first weekend when the crew is settling in and cooking aboard is not convenient. It is not always possible to shop for fresh milk every day and indeed fresh milk is not always easy to obtain when wanted. We therefore order a tin of powdered milk and take a few cartons of 'Longlife' milk with us for emergencies. A large easy-pouring plastic container of salt and a pepper mill also goes along with us. Most items of food and drink can be obtained during the boating holiday. If you have noted in your advance log where specific shopping facilities are, it is a simple matter to coordinate shopping so that it does not interfere with your holiday plans. According to what is needed, I arrange to moor near the most appropriate facilities. If it is raining no one will want to walk to a village general store a mile or more away when by cruising on for a few more miles a waterside shop or a town providing all services is available.

Handy items

One of the most useful items on a boating holiday is a

collapsible shopping basket on wheels. We usually take two and a real boon they are. Another handy item for shopping convenience is a half-gallon plastic container, which we use to collect draught beer, draught cider or milk. It is much easier to carry than a number of bottles.

If you check your hire craft inventory you will see that it provides for most essentials. However, no inventory will cater one hundred per cent for everyone's particular wishes. Few hire firms include a large tray yet this item is invaluable for luncheons eaten under way or for drinks on deck. When placed on top of the Calor gas stove (unlit!) it provides an additional draining board for washing up.

We also take our own large cast-iron frying pan or a large non-stick one as it seems that food almost invariably sticks to strange frying pans. If a large casserole dish is not in the inventory, we take one of these, and as we are partial to salads we take a large salad bowl too. Being inveterate coffee drinkers one of our twelve-cup coffee pots is taken also. A knife sharpener or stone can also be invaluable.

Other items we gather in a 'boat box' are a 12–15 ft length of clothes line or $\frac{3}{4}$ in nylon or manila rope to use as a breast rope and to secure the gangplank firmly. We include a ball of stout cord and a sharp pocket or sheath knife. We take a ground sheet or tarpaulin, which is easily stowed under a mattress, to use on picnics ashore or if the superstructure of the craft is leaking. Another wet weather aid is a small rubber mat. Borrowed from your car and placed on the cabin floor just inside the entrance to the boat it will save a lot of mess and cleaning. A torch or two, depending upon the size of your crew, is really essential, as a number of overnight moorings are likely to be in remote places along a towpath.

A basic first aid kit to cope with headaches, cuts, bruises, abrasions and burns is a must, and a thermometer is useful if you have small children with you. We regard insect repellent and sun tan oil as part of our first aid kit.

Cameras and film should not be forgotten and the crew will get a good deal of pleasure from a pair of field glasses. Bird and flower fanciers may want to include suitable reference books, and a pack of playing cards will help to while away rainy spells.

You will see that in your hire craft inventory there are normally three blankets per berth and one pillow; sheets and pillow-cases are either included or provided for a small supplementary payment. On our first boating holiday we discovered that blankets take up a lot of room during the day and that dismantling and making up beds each day seemed an unnecessary chore. We subsequently asked the hire firm to supply one blanket per berth plus pillows and pillow-cases, and took sleeping bags with us. These can be rolled up compactly after airing and are more easily stowed than several blankets.

If you take your dog with you, you will be asked to keep him off berths and boat blankets and you will be warned that you are liable for any damage he may cause. We take a heavy-weight rug for our dog, and this goes on the cabin floor at night and over a lower berth by day.

Linen table cloths and napkins are unsuitable and we find paper napkins more convenient. You will find a heavy-duty floor cloth useful, and also a couple of spare good-sized bath towels.

Jewellery and expensive watches should not be taken; nor should transistor sets unless the boat is not equipped with a radio. For my advance log notebook I take a ball-point pen with a clip and use the back of this notebook to jot down captions for all the photographs taken. You will find it is impossible to identify every one taken unless you caption them at the time.

Clothing

Most boating holidaymakers take far too much clothing with them and then grumble that there is not enough storage space. Of course it is never possible, even with long-range forecasts, to be sure of your holiday weather and boat crews have to be prepared for anything. Informality should be the keynote and above all clothing should be serviceable. Very little tidy clothing is necessary. A drip-dry dress and cardigan or a drip-dry blouse, skirt and cardigan for the ladies and a pair of slacks and sports jacket or blazer for men is all that you will need for social occasions.

Clothing will get dirty and drip-dry material is most suitable in shirts, sports shirts, blouses, sun-tops, and socks. I have a pair of drip-dry lightweight trousers and a pair of jeans for chilly weather. Ladies will find that trousers and shorts are better than skirts for getting about boats and lock-sides, and shorts and jeans are most suitable for youngsters of both sexes.

Everyone will need rubber-soled shoes, which all hire firms insist upon. Tennis shoes will do admirably, or you can buy economically from ships' chandlers proper boating shoes which are much the same style but come with blue canvas uppers. These will inevitably get wet so you will want a spare pair, even though tennis or boating shoes can be dried out reasonably quickly in a Calor gas oven. Every crew member will want a pair of walking shoes, preferably with rubber soles. Ladies would be well advised to leave high-heeled shoes at home.

I always take a pair of short calf-length rubber boots for use in wet weather instead of a second pair of boating shoes. These together with waterproof trousers and jacket enable me to stay at the wheel or work locks in the heaviest of downpours without getting soaked. These boots are ideal for walking along towpaths after rain or in heavy early morning dew. Children will find ordinary Wellingtons useful for towpaths and for walking across fields, but they should not be worn on board. Although it rarely happens, it is possible for a child to fall overboard and these boots are a handicap in such circumstances.

Waterproof jackets and trousers are relatively expensive and an ordinary good raincoat can be substituted. In any case raincoats will be necessary for shopping and sightseeing, or if cruising in lighter rain or drizzle. Tunnels frequently leak badly and when at the wheel or working locks in the rain, it is a good idea to wear shorts underneath your raincoat or to roll up your trouser legs.

Even when cruising at the height of summer you will want warm clothing, and every crew member should have a heavy pullover, preferably with a roll neck. We have found the most useful garment is the hooded anorak which not only sheds water but is cosily warm. It is much more practical than a smart jacket for men, women and children.

Items like dressing gowns are superfluous. Wear pyjamas and use your raincoat as a dressing gown if you consider one necessary. Provided the crew has anoraks, bulky topcoats or duffle coats take space and are never really needed. The usual underclothing, toilet articles and make-up will be needed and for the ladies a head scarf is useful. While all waterways are not suitable for swimming, there are many swimming pools to be found and in any case you will need swim-wear for sunbathing.

All crew members should make out a clothing list and then ruthlessly prune it to essentials. Mothers will of course allow for the ability of young children to soil clothing rapidly.

Most of the crew's clothing will be stowed away in drawers under bunks. Hanging cupboard space, except on larger craft, is at a premium and is usually only enough for the crew's tidy gear, and perhaps raincoats.

You will probably think of other things, such as games to amuse the children, reading material and so on. Avoid the temptation to overload your boat. You can easily buy paperbacks *en route* and children will find more than enough to keep them amused during the holiday. You may also find that you make a surprising collection of souvenirs while shopping in strange places and will take home with you many items from antiques to clothes.

CHAPTER 5

OUR WATERWAYS STORY

EVER SINCE man discovered that a log would float, there has been boating of a sort. Britain's natural rivers were the chief means of both transport and communication from the earliest times until a few centuries ago. The Romans and other invaders like the Vikings established their sway in these islands by following the then wild and perilous tidal courses of the major rivers inland. Building stone and other necessities were soon moving along the dangerous rivers as settlements along waterways evolved into communities and castles, monasteries, churches and manor houses sprang up. The River Thames became London's life-line to the sea and in medieval times the Severn became the busiest river in Europe, apart from the Meuse. River traffic was erratic, however, for the rivers were untamed and afflicted with devastating floods in winter and extended droughts in summer. As industry slowly developed, and consequently the demand for reliable transport, the rivers were gradually improved for navigation, the only alternative being the costly and slow pack-horse train, for roads capable of accommodating wagons had yet to be constructed. The muddy tracks of the time could scarcely be called roads.

Progress in improving river navigation was painfully slow, for Britain of the sixteenth and seventeenth centuries was short of capital for such projects and possessed no engineering talent to speak of, while vested interests like millers and fishermen did not want their waters tampered with. The major engineering achievement of this period was the drainage of the Great Level of the Fens, carried out by Holland's Sir Cornelius Vermuyden with the backing of Dutch labour and finance. Even this project was primarily undertaken for the purpose of land drainage and reclamation, with benefits to navigation, the canalised river channels and artificial 'cuts' coming as a by-product.

Artificial waterways were not then completely alien to Britain. The Romans had made a start in East Anglia many centuries earlier. The Fossdyke Canal, for example, from Torksey on the River Trent to the Witham River at Lincoln which flows into the Wash, was dug by the Romans as early as A.D. 120, and Henry I was wise enough to deepen and improve it in 1121. The Exeter Canal from the River Exe estuary to Exeter was completed in 1566 and, although only five miles long, was also demonstrably practical and useful.

It was not, however, until the demands of a mushrooming industrial revolution became urgent in the middle of the eighteenth century, that any serious consideration was given to creating a national network of waterways. Vast areas of the country were still remote from river communication and cried out for an effective means of obtaining cheaper raw materials and distributing manufactured goods.

Although not the first man to build a canal in Britain, Francis Egerton, third Duke of Bridgewater, can fairly be said to have initiated the canal era in Britain. At the age of eighteen, in the course of an educational tour of Europe, he came across and was greatly impressed by Louis XIV's 150-mile Languedoc Canal, now known as the Canal du Midi. With his tutor Robert Wood young Egerton bumped by coach along the course of this unique waterway, which, completed in 1681 and still operational today, links the Atlantic at Bordeaux with the Mediterranean at Sète.

Within five years of the young duke's 'discovery' of the Canal du Midi and other canal engineering feats in Europe, he had obtained in 1759 the first of several Acts of Parliament authorising him 'to make a navigable Cut or Canal' in Lancashire. In its way the Duke's canal, first opened to traffic in 1761 and linking the family coal mines at Worsley with Manchester, was more revolutionary than Louis XIV's canal connecting two seas.

When the 'Sun King' built his canal, inland waterway navigation was already well established in France and Europe. When the 'Canal Duke' carved out the Bridgewater Canal with the help of his able agent, John Gilbert, and an almost illiterate millwright imbued with engineering genius, James Brindley, he had few precedents. The Roman navigable channels of East Anglia were little more than simple drains, John Trew's Exeter Canal was a miniature endeavour. One Henry Berry, with the blessing of the Liverpool Corporation, a few years before the Bridgewater Canal got underway, had begun the building of the St Helen's Canal running from Earlestown, near St Helen's, some eleven miles to the River Mersey estuary. The Duke no doubt picked up a few tips from Berry's efforts, but while Berry's canal improved the course of a stream, the Sankey Brook, the Duke's waterway, nearly three times as long, was independent of any river bed and was supplied with water from the soughs. It combined an underground mining canal and an open canal, the first of its kind in Britain and the world.

The Duke's canal was an instant success, the foundation of the famous 'Bridgewater millions'. More important, it was directly responsible for immediately halving the price of coal in Manchester, and coal, with water, was the basis of the Industrial Revolution. Brindley's ingenious Barton aqueduct, which carried the Bridgewater Canal over the Irwell River, was regarded by many at the time as 'the greatest artificial curiosity in the world' and demonstrated both that canals could be made to travel almost anywhere and that canals were superior to the old river navigations.

By 1767 the Duke's grand design was completed, over twenty-eight miles of main-line canal, several branch canals as well as some forty-two miles of underground canal, and Manchester had been connected with Liverpool and the open sea. But even before all was completed James Brindley had conceived a brilliant idea of a 'cross' of canals to link the Rivers Trent, Mersey, Thames and Severn, and had begun work on the Grand Trunk or Trent & Mersey Canal which was to open up a navigable waterway from the upper Trent via the Duke's canal to the Mersey.

The canals of this country were promoted primarily by local interests and enterprises, manufacturers, mine-owners and merchants. The Trent & Mersey Canal was fostered by a group of pottery manufacturers led by Josiah Wedgwood. These entrepreneurs, and others who followed them, often faced considerable opposition from certain landowners, mill-owners, road turnpike trustees, land carriers, coastal shipping interests and others who feared that their existing prerogatives, trade or livelihood would be adversely affected.

But at the same time the Duke's Bridgewater Canal had fired the imagination of the country and the nation's 'canal mania' was as catching as the 'tulipomania' that swept Holland some 150 years earlier. The press of the day reported on and speculated about canals and what they could contribute to the country and the people. Everywhere there was talk of canals, in inns, offices, manufactories, shops and homes. Of course it was the nobility, the landed gentry and 'big business' of the time that subscribed most of the capital for the construction of canals, but many professional people like doctors and lawyers and clergymen, and many small shopkeepers, tradesmen and craftsmen put what money they could scrape up into canal ventures in the hope of making quick profits from the most exciting projects of the period.

For it had dawned on the country that cheap and dependable transport of coal and raw materials would not only serve mines, supply factories, power steam engines, facilitate the building of houses and roads, enable agricultural land to be improved and bring warmth to the homes of even the poor, but that it would also expedite the distribution of both agricultural produce and manufactured goods to ever widening markets. With canal boats superseding pack-horses and cumbersome wagons, and with steam augmenting and supplanting water power, the whole pattern and pace of life would be changed and the country and its people could come into the greatest prosperity they had ever known.

Over my study desk at home is a framed map of 'the New Intended CANAL to join the Rivers Severn and Trent' with a cutting taken from an eighteenth century issue of the *London Magazine*, which reflects something of the enthusiasm and hopes of the canal age. The cutting describes the proposal for the canal advanced by one Dr Thomas Congreve and claims that although

this navigable communication will cost a very large sum, that the carriage of goods will, thereby, be made vastly cheaper, and that 71 market towns and cities may trade by this canal; to which we shall add, that such inland navigations might be made a support for our seamen in time of peace, if a law was made, that in time of peace, it is hoped it will be agreeable to the people; and having such a supply always ready at command upon a sudden rupture, would encourage the government to engage in every undertaking for increasing and extending our navigable communications.

The Staffordshire & Worcestershire Canal, or the 'Wolverhampton Canal' as it was originally known, was engineered by James Brindley and opened to traffic in 1772. Brindley, in fact, found himself engaged in a number of major canal projects at the same time. He and other engineers like Thomas Telford, John Rennie, William Jessop, Thomas Dadford, Samuel Simcock, Josiah Clowes and James Green designed and drove canals over one watershed after another, in the course of which they put civil engineering on the map with their locks, bridges, aqueducts, tunnels, inclined planes, canal lifts and what Dr Johnson called 'great efforts of human labour and human contrivance'.

So one canal led to another, for as canal mileage increased more industries were launched which in turn created the need for yet more canals. In the hey-day of the canal era, in 1793-4, Parliament authorised the construction of no fewer than thirty canals. Within eighty years of the initiative of the Duke of Bridgewater's canal, by the late 1830s, there were over 4,000 miles of navigable inland waterways, the vast majority of the canals forming a network centred on Birmingham and linking together the rivers and ports of the country. Other canals created time-saving short-cuts across the countryside, or connected other cities and towns directly with the sea. Some 2,600 miles of waterways had been added to the inland navigations of Britain between 1759 and 1840, and few towns were more than 15 miles from a navigable waterway. According to Rennie, craft could safely ply over 2,236 miles of improved river navigation and 2,477 miles of canals in Britain with sixty-nine rivers and eighty-six canals available in England and Wales alone.

Cities, towns, villages, industry, trade grew apace. Then, just as the canals augmented and in many cases superseded the old river navigations, the railways came, first to feed and then to throttle and eventually supersede the canals. Canal mania was quickly converted to railway mania as the success of this new form of transport became apparent. There was bitter rivalry between canal and rail, the effects of which linger with us to this day. The decline of the canal industry, involving in 1840 over 100,000 direct employees alone, was as rapid as its swift rise to prosperity.

The citizen of the 1970s can be forgiven for assuming that it was the steam locomotive that killed commercial transport on the canals. Certainly the locomotive made the transport of passengers by horse-drawn canal boats and, indeed by horse-drawn stage coach, obsolescent almost overnight. But as you cruise the canals and rivers you will see that water transport possessed and still possesses a number of advantage over rail and road as far as the carriage of heavy goods is concerned. That it did not and does not survive except in a few areas was and is due to a number of causes.

When the canals were built they were essentially constructed to meet local needs at different periods and, more often than not, were planned without taking into consideration that they might eventually form key links in a trunk route. This is one reason why they are so interesting to holidaymakers today for there is no uniformity of width, depth or gauge of locks, not only between different canals but even on the same canal. The railway builders were blessed with more foresight; with only one exception Britain's major railways were built to a standard gauge.

The canal companies were handicapped by generations

of neglect of old river navigations with which their canals connected and upon which they often heavily depended for much of their traffic. It was not until the nineteenth and twentieth centuries that badly needed major improvements were carried out on the Thames, Severn and Trent rivers, to name but a few, to advance navigation much beyond archaic medieval standards. Had new locks and other improvements been installed on these rivers before or even when the railways were introduced, the connecting canals could have given the railways a good competitive run for their money on through traffic. While the canal companies had no control over the river navigations, it was certainly their own fault that they exploited their monopoly position by charging often extortionate tolls and so foolishly competed instead of cooperating with each other.

The canal companies were further handicapped because they were merely toll-takers and not carriers like the railways. Carrying on the canals was handled by many canal carrying companies, many of them in a rather small way of business, who operated over particular waterways. This meant that the canals could not effectively speed through traffic along the inland waterways or indeed easily quote through-rates. While the railways first concentrated on passenger and parcels traffic to oust the canal packets and the stage-coach they soon, in the face of competition from each other, moved into the heavy freight field. This precipitated a freight rates war between canals and railways, and with drastically reduced revenue the canals became ripe for what we today would call 'take-over bids' by the railways. Some canals were bought up and converted into railways. Many coming into railway control were, with rare exceptions, run with the deliberate intention of reducing and ultimately killing competition. Every weapon at the railway's command was used to discourage freight

carrying on the canals they had taken over—maintenance
was neglected, water supplies were diverted, tolls were
raised, Sunday and night working prohibited, powered
craft banned, and they even stooped to closing waterways
for lengthy periods on the pretext of making repairs to
locks, bridges or canal sides. Between 1845 and 1847 alone
nearly a thousand miles of inland waterways became the
property of railway companies, and because these and
other waterways subsequently taken over included primary
trunk routes the prospect of the remaining canal
companies coming together to form a coordinated system
of inland waterways to compete with the growing domi-
nance of the railways was most effectively demolished.

In the century that followed the birth of the railways
few improvements were made to the canal system. There
were many 'committees' and proposals of all kinds and
many good intentions but precious few results. Lack of
traffic and neglect closed many canals, yet quite a number
of independent canal companies continued to carry heavy
traffic into the twentieth century and continued to operate
at a profit. In 1905 the canals were still carrying over 42
million tons of freight, but by 1924 the figure had fallen
to under 17 million tons and by 1938 to under 13 million
tons.

Early in our own century a Royal Commission spurred
by a revival of interest in canals recommended extensive
canal development, but its recommendations were never
implemented and the First World War then intervened.
Between the wars a number of improvements were put in
hand, primarily on the broad canals of the North-East
which continue as busy commercial waterways today.
Further south a group of canals were amalgamated to
form the Grand Union Canal Company and thus to unify
routes between London, Birmingham, and Nottingham.
The new company then carried out an extensive widening

scheme by constructing no fewer than fifty-one new broader locks between London and Birmingham.

These were moves in the right direction and prospects for the canals at last looked a little brighter. But with road transport added to rail competition canal modernisation was on too small a scale and what was done was heavily outweighed by neglect and abandonment on other routes. Then another war intervened. Wartime controls were scarcely lifted when in 1948, some 1,600 miles of the waterways network was nationalised. This 'takeover' was not as disastrous as the railway takeover a century earlier, but virtually nothing was done for the canals by a series of custodians until the British Waterways Board was given control in 1962 and the Government, jogged by the persistent Inland Waterways Association campaign and clear evidence that the public was increasingly using the waterways for pleasure, published a White Paper, *British Waterways: Recreation and Amenity*, in September 1967.

Legislation has since created a new charter for the inland waterways as far as the public is concerned. Over 1,400 miles of nationalised waterways have been designated 'cruiseways' and along them there are literally thousands of bridges, well over 1,000 locks, more than 275 aqueducts and upwards of forty tunnels. The system goes from sea level to a height of 518 feet and forms an interconnected 'grid' stretching from London and Sharpness in the South to Skipton and Selby in the North and from Wales in the West to East Anglia. In addition to this network there are some picturesque lengths away from and separated from the others, like the Lancaster Canal and the Crinan and Caledonian Canals in Scotland.

The Government has yet to take action to reclaim derelict canals and to foster and encourage commercial traffic on the canals, which if it did nothing more than relieve road congestion would be worthwhile. All that recent legislation has done is to designate less than a dozen canals and navigations as commercial waterways. These will add tremendously to your cruising pleasure, for pleasure craft are permitted to join working boats on such fascinating waterways as the Aire & Calder, Calder & Hebble, Caledonian and Crinan, Sheffield & South Yorkshire, New Junction, Trent, Weaver and Weston, Severn, Gloucester and Sharpness and Lee waterways. On some you will encounter traditional narrow boats, on others not only craft large enough for the coastal trade but vessels that venture to and from major European ports.

And quite apart from the waterways under control of the British Waterways Board there are even more miles of waterways open to you which are under the jurisdiction of other authorities. Many are connected with the Board's waterways, like the Bridgewater Canal which inaugurated the canal era, the River Thames, the Lower Trent, Humber and Yorkshire Ouse, the River Nene and River Avon. Still others like the Norfolk Broads, the Great Ouse and its tributaries and the Middle Level of the Fenland waterways and the River Medway provide easy access and additional scope and opportunity for holidays.

CHAPTER 6

THE FETCHING FENS

DURING OUR boating holidays over the years we have met hundreds of first-timers on the waterways and, while there have been some calls for practical assistance or advice, by far the majority of crews brought conversations around to what other waterways had to offer. I make no apologies, therefore, for the boating adventure tales that follow. They are a compilation of experiences on our inland waterways and reflect an enthusiast's determination to make the most of opportunities that both present themselves and must be ferreted out. They are set down in the hope that they will help you cater for the particular interests and tastes of your own crew and encourage you to seek out and exploit others.

There is no doubt that the one aspect of boating holidays which causes concern among beginners is the navigation past weirs and through locks. Yet locks and associated weirs are not difficult to navigate and most first-timers have little or no trouble with them. They can be forbidding and wearying, however, if beginners try to tackle too many in a single holiday.

My advice to those who have never been on our waterways before is to select those that have relatively few locks, and locks that work easily. I can think of no better area for beginners than the South Level of the Fenland waterways of East Anglia.

Fenland is a unique, low-lying district of some 2,500 square miles stretching to the west and south of the Wash, from south of Lincoln to Suffolk and from King's Lynn to St. Ives. There is something for everyone in Fenland, for the explorer, the naturalist, the antiquarian, the angler and for those who just want to relax. Even the history of this seventy-five-mile-long by thirty-five-mile-wide area is reflected in the continuing tenacious opposition to the various drainage schemes in succeeding generations.

Frequent flooding has been caused in the Fens by the coincidence of high spring tides and rivers swollen with water drained off the land. The system of sluices, closed at high tide, keeps the sea water from entering the rivers but likewise prevents the river water from escaping to the sea. The consequent piling up of fresh water strains the banks and flooding follows. There have been a number of disastrous floods since the early drainage works were constructed, but none so terrible as the flood of March 1947 when damage was estimated at over £20 million. On the night of 31 January/1 February 1953, a gigantic North Sea tidal surge caused further trouble and loss of life in King's Lynn and district.

Today, however, nearly half a million acres of the finest agricultural land in England are protected from flooding by the Great Ouse Flood Protection Scheme, completed in 1964, an ingenious £11 million project involving the South Level. This is the area to the east of the Hundred Foot River, through which the rivers are carried high above land level in embanked channels.

With no need to worry about a repetition of the disastrous floods of the past, the idea of boating through Fenland, where little windmills still occasionally dot the flats and where that old English dye-plant, woad, still grows, appealed to us. As it is impossible to cover all the Fens in a single holiday we chose first to do the South Level, comprising the Great Ouse, the Cam, the Little

Ouse, the Old West, the Lark and the Wissey rivers with the Burwell and Reach lodes.

The 300-odd miles of navigable waterways in the South Level will take you to five counties—Bedfordshire, Cambridgeshire, Huntingdonshire, Norfolk and Suffolk— and provide as pleasant cruising on gently meandering non-tidal streams as almost anywhere on Britain's inland waterways. The tributaries probe to within fifty miles of the popular Broads, yet Fenland has remained comparatively undiscovered. You will meet plenty of other craft but you will never feel crowded or rushed, for everywhere there is a predominant mood of peace and tranquillity. Many may imagine that the Fens are flat, dull and monotonous but this is not so. The range of scenery along the rivers is as varied as anywhere in England and there is a kind of medieval attraction about the Fens that is easier to sense than to explain.

Although the authorities, as throughout the Fens, are primarily interested in drainage rather than in navigation, there are few hazards and only fifteen locks, including the tidal lock at Denver, making the South Level a boon to novices, particularly as all but seven of the locks are manned. Boats up to 100 ft in length and 14 ft 6 ins in beam can traverse some sections of the South Level waterways, but the maximum size craft which can navigate the entire system can be no longer than 45 ft, with a beam of 10 ft 3 ins, draught of 2 ft 3 ins and freeboard (fixed height of craft above water level) of 6 ft 6 ins.

Our crew of five with our golden Labrador and current pet hamster boarded our comfortable and well-designed 36 ft x 9 ft 8 ins bridge-deck hire cruiser *Invader* from Banham's boatyard in Cambridge one Saturday afternoon in August. Banham's, who have built many a Cambridge 'eight', can be highly recommended for their hire cruisers. Of course there are other boatyards on the South

Level, among them Elysian Holidays of Ely, whose recently introduced glass fibre craft have particularly impressed us.

It was pouring with rain as we stowed our gear aboard but as we collected our dinghy and set off, the sun burst happily through the clouds. Despite our previous experience we welcomed the short trial run, as every craft we have ever hired has had some differences in controls and instrumentation and the time to become familiar with these is at the start of a cruise.

As my wife's family lived near Cambridge we knew the city well and did not explore it, but those of you who are not familiar with it will find a day reserved for sight-seeing most rewarding. The best mooring for this is below Jesus Lock on the left bank, as power craft are not welcomed above Town Quay at King's Hill.

We were surprised to find the reach of the Cam from Banham's to Baitsbite Lock, half an hour's cruise downstream, a direct antithesis of the slum-like conditions of the Thames riverside at Oxford. This reach is used by Cambridge University and Town Rowing Clubs and a section of it on either side of the Plough Inn at Ditton is the only one where cruisers are requested to reverse the 'keep right' rule. The notice boards are easy to spot. The Plough Inn, much favoured by undergraduates, offers good moorings, food and drink. It is only one of the scores of pubs, all friendly to the boating fraternity, along the South Level waterways. Half a mile beyond the Plough Inn is Baitsbite Lock and your first lesson in operating locks.

By now you will begin to appreciate having your advance log and chart of the South Level waterways at hand to alert you to points of interest. The Cam is already very pretty. After leaving Baitsbite Lock the river flows through an avenue of trees and osiers, dominated on the right bank by Horningsea's thirteenth-century church. Another half-hour of cruising brings you to Clayhythe

Bridge and the good moorings and food of the Bridge Hotel. The village of Waterbeach is within easy walking distance of the bridge. Watch carefully for sailing craft between the bridge and Bottisham Lock. Once through Bottisham Lock you can cruise for 130 miles if you wish without going through another lock, for the next locks are at Denver on the Ouse, Hermitage on the Old West and Isleham on the Lark.

You will find the scenery changing now to more open Fenland countryside. A few miles along on the right, some eleven miles from Cambridge, at Upware, we would recommend leaving the Cam to pass through the electrically operated lock gates at Burwell Lock to explore the Burwell and Reach lodes. Return passage through the lock will cost 3s, but this investment is small enough for the pleasures it opens up to you and your crew. Although the Lord Nelson Inn at Upware was destroyed by fire many years ago it carried a tablet on its wall with a brief legend all boaters would do well to think upon. It said simply : 'Five miles from anywhere—No hurry'. This is a motto or slogan for all boating holidays everywhere.

After leaving the lock you will come to a wooden bridge on the left bank. You can moor virtually anywhere on either side of this bridge which leads to Wicken Fen, now a National Trust Nature Reserve. It is one of the oldest and in many ways one of the most important in Britain, for it has preserved many of the plants and animals characteristic of the ancient Fenland before drainage and agricultural improvement changed the landscape.

When the drainage of the Cambridgeshire Fenland was begun in the seventeenth century the folk of Wicken managed to keep undrained an area of nearly 250 acres close to the village, which would permit them to continue gathering reed and sedge for thatching and digging peat for fuel. Because of their stubborn insistence on their rights to take these raw materials they preserved the flora and fauna which drainage banished from the rest of the Fenlands. Wicken Fen today remains the home of over 5,000 species of insects including over 700 kind of butterflies and moth and nearly 200 kinds of spiders. There is a vast variety of birds and something like 300 species of flowering plants as well.

The National Trust acquired the first strip of Sedge Fen in 1899 and since that time many donors have added to the original holding so that not only the Sedge Fen but another 400 acres of St Edmunds Fen and the bordering North Adventurers Fen on the other side of the lode are all part of the Trust property. Admission to Wicken Fen can be obtained from the keeper's house, a pleasant walk along the narrow Wicken lode beyond the footbridge.

Just past the footbridge you will come to a fork in the main waterway. Bearing left is the Burwell lode and to the right the Reach lode. The upper ends of both lodes are narrow and shallow but we took them gently to visit the tiny hamlets at the ends of each. The hamlet of Reach, where the Iceni under Boadicea built the Devil's Dyke, is perhaps not as attractive as Burwell but you will enjoy the lovely water-lilies on the Reach lode. We enjoyed rootling among the antique shops in Burwell, buying some of the best sausages we ever tasted from the butcher near the church, and visiting the church itself with its notable brasses.

Back on the Cam once more, two miles of cruising below Upware brings you to Pope's Corner. The Fish and Duck Inn stands on the left at the junction of the Cam, the Ely Ouse and the Old West. The old white painted inn has recently been rebuilt with greatly improved facilities, and remains a popular port of call.

Continuing straight on and using the 215 ft high West Tower of Ely Cathedral as a landmark you will find the river now widens. As Ely is approached the high banks give way to meadows and as the course bends to the left there is a low railway bridge and the Cutter Inn comes into view. There is a little ferry here which shunts back and forth across the river. You will get a friendly reception if you moor at the Riverside Boatyard of Elysian Holidays which incorporates the fleet of Appleyard Lincoln & Co., a name well known throughout the South Level. This is a well equipped and handy service centre and the atmosphere of the Cutter Inn is most pleasant. Round the next corner you can moor at the attractive U.D.C. moorings on your left, just a short walk to the shopping centre and cathedral.

Ely, so-called because of the abundance of eels in the river, has a fascinating history which can be traced back to A.D. 673. It ranks as a city because of its cathedral but is really quite a small town, albeit one with particular charm. The splendid cathedral itself dates back to Norman times and is the third largest in England. It stands at the top of a hill and below it is a collection of both ancient and modern buildings. Do not overlook the monastic buildings, the quaint old shops and inns, Steeple Gate, Goldsmith's Tower and Sacrist's Gate, the fifteenth-century Palace and the park known as Ely Porta. Ely queens it over the Fens and rightly so.

Continuing downstream you may meet some barge traffic from the local sugar-beet factory. These barges sweep very close to the banks here and mooring along this section is unwise. Your next landmark is the Queen Adelaide Bridge, the start of the 'Adelaide Course', a three-mile stretch used for the Cambridge trial 'eights'.

You will shortly spot the entrance to the River Lark on the right. This attractive little river is navigable for some ten miles, flowing through the villages of Prickwillow and Mildenhall. There is only one lock near Isleham, with a resident keeper. Prickwillow, which derives its name from the old 'pricks' or skewers which were made from willow, is about four miles above the entrance to the Lark, and the only accessible village on the river. In spite of its pretty name, frankly we found the village disappointing.

The bridge over Isleham Lock is rather low and it may be necessary to lower the canopy and screen. You can cruise on safely for two miles to Judes Ferry, and the inn there marks the site of a useful turning point. It is possible to row a dinghy to Mildenhall but there is too little water to take a cruiser beyond Judes Ferry.

Returning to the main river the next landmark is Sandhill Bridge and there are moorings on the left bank for Littleport. Some 3½ miles downstream you will reach the junction of the Ouse and the Little Ouse or Brandon Creek. On the corner stands the Ship Inn, with a convenient water hose, a well-stocked kiosk, meals, snacks and drinks. There are moorings here, just round the corner on the right by the inn. Hire craft on the South Level are equipped with insulated cold boxes, and ice packs can be changed at all boatyards, stores and inns which you will find listed in the cruising guide. These boxes are most useful for perishables in hot weather. The Ship Inn can usually supply frozen foods and fresh bread and milk.

The Little Ouse is navigable for some twelve miles to Brandon Railway Bridge, and is as attractive as the Lark, with interesting walks to Hockwold cum Wilton and Brandon. Along this river you will find Cross Water Staunch which is no longer used and has but one channel, clearly marked. It looks narrow but there will be no difficulty in getting through. There are a series of meres as you cruise on to Wilton Bridge, with good moorings in the wide pool just before the bridge, and the craft can be turned with ease. The footpath to Hockwold cum Wilton is on the left bank and you can walk along the river to

Brandon which has a good shopping centre; here also is the Flint-Knappers Inn. Until a few years ago the ancient craft of flint-knapping was carried on behind the inn, the last surviving centre of an industry which produced the firing material for flintlock guns. We were fortunate enough to find the last of the flint-knappers still at work but he told us that with the decline of his last substantial trade with Africa he had decided not to continue. The site remains but there are no longer any flint-knappers. The flints themselves came from Grimes Graves, some four miles from Brandon, and this is an excursion you will find fascinating. The mines made by Neolithic Man in excavating flints for making his primitive implements are kept open to the public by the Ministry of Works and both the mines and the countryside surrounding them are more than just interesting.

Turning right out of the Little Ouse and heading north there are few landmarks but conditions are excellent for sailing all the way to Denver. Some four miles down-stream of the Ship Inn on the right is the entrance to the Wissey River, the narrowest, wildest and loveliest of the three eastern tributaries of the Ouse. The entrance is deceptively narrow and it is wise to stay in midstream unless you are passing other craft. In less than ten miles of the Wissey there are stretches of open meadowland, bird-filled reeds and wooded country. We were much taken by the little village of Hilgay with its pleasant moorings just beyond the bridge on the right, friendly shops and All Saints Church. In the churchyard is the grave of one of Lord Nelson's school friends, Captain George Manby, inventor of the rocket life-saving apparatus. The idea of developing the rocket lifeline came to Manby at Yarmouth where he saw a seaman die as a result of being stranded on a wreck close to the shore. Local legend has it that he used All Saints Church tower for experiments with his invention.

It was at Hilgay that we met one of those unforgettable characters surprisingly frequently found along the waterways. We first sighted him riding a bicycle along the river bank and it was he who hailed us with an offer of fresh vegetables and fruit from his garden. When he came aboard with the supplies we offered him a drink and learned that his name was Albert Armsby, and that he had been a mole-catcher for over thirty years. He entertained all of us with fascinating tales of the mole's way of life. Little is known of the voracious and restless mole because he lives entirely in the dark in burrows and is one of the few creatures which cannot be kept in captivity. We did not realise at the time that Armsby, who has spent his life trapping moles both for their valuable pelts and to prevent damage done by their tunnellings, is an international authority on moles. Several years ago I read in *The Times* a report that he had been summoned to Holland to advise the Dutch on trapping moles. He presented me with a monogram on the subject written by him and published in 1952. This is among the most treasured of our waterways souvenirs. The text is not only informative and interesting but is filled with delightful sentences such as:

He has vocal chords and can be heard making snuffling noises and slight squeals and purring as he plays moley games with his friends.

The river broadens into a small lake beyond Hilgay and the countryside is wooded all along the upper reaches. The Bull Inn, with good moorings and a friendly landlord, is the limit of navigation. A short walk to the village of Stoke Ferry will supply basic stores, petrol and water.

Returning to the main river again, turn right for Denver

Sluice, a mile away. This is the guardian of the Fens and the key to the drainage of the South Level. It is the limit of navigation for hire craft although boatyards will occasionally permit experienced crews to lock through Denver to make the return trip via the New Bedford or Hundred Foot River. This is as straight as a Roman road and uninteresting, and the depth of water can vary considerably. The river below Denver is tidal, of course, and dangerous for beginners. In any case there is little of interest between Denver and King's Lynn. Even experienced skippers can come to grief on this tideway if they encounter the bore which can produce a fast-moving wall of water up to 3 ft and more high, or if they navigate the tideway at the wrong state of the tide.

While at Denver you can see the new head sluice of the Flood Protection project to the east of the Denver sluice and the junction of the new Cut Off and Relief channels. Perhaps of greater appeal to most of the crew, however, is the Jenyns Arms, just west of Denver Sluice. This pub is reminiscent of a coaching inn and here you can obtain refreshments, stores and water. Downham Market, where Lord Nelson and Captain Manby went to school together, is within walking distance of Denver and from Downham you can take a bus to Hunstanton or to Sandringham.

From Denver we returned to Popes Corner and the Fish and Duck Inn, mooring along the way as fancy dictated. At Popes Corner you can turn right into the Old West river, for eleven miles of delightful cruising. The river is narrow and shallow despite considerable recent dredging and should be taken slowly. There are bridges with blind approaches and it is impossible to see round some bends because of high banks. But the Old West will give the novice no trouble if navigated at reasonable speed.

The scenery along the Old West is all rural and you

may well find cattle straying into the river. The engine house between the road bridge carrying the B1085 over the river and the Wooden Bridge contains a most impressive 1837 Boulton and Watt beam-engine still in perfect working order, a reminder that steam provided the power to drain the Fens. An inspection can usually be arranged with the pump-man, who lives in the house adjoining the engine house.

Little more than a mile beyond the Wooden Bridge there is a large basin with good moorings hard by the Royal Oak, a favourite rendezvous of anglers. The bridge here carries the A10 and as you pass under it there is a sharp bend to the left and the river becomes narrow as it flows along for some distance parallel with the highway. The next road bridge is called 'Twenty Pence Bridge' and on the right bank stands the Bridge Inn. The river continues to wind its way through pleasant rural countryside with here and there a glimpse of a farm or pumping station. As you come within sight of Hermitage Lock, on the right bank is a recently established boatyard of Elysian Holidays.

Once you have passed through Hermitage Lock which was rebuilt in 1968 the river is tidal for the short stretch to Brownshill Staunch. There is no danger here, but when mooring do leave the ropes slack enough to allow for a rise and fall of water of up to 4 ft. The normal summer rise and fall rarely exceeds 2 ft 6 ins. At low water this reach is inclined to be shallow, and care should be taken. As you leave Hermitage Lock you will see the New Bedford or Hundred Foot River entrance to your right and almost immediately beyond this the mooring for the Crown Inn followed by the Quiet Waters Boatyard of F. W. Carrington, which is in a backwater above the Crown. You can moor at either place. Carrington's provide the usual boatyard services, petrol and water. Earith is a pleasant little

village with good shopping facilities. It is but 20 minutes
from Earith to Brownshill Lock and on your right before
the lock is Bury Fen, where the National Ice Skating
Championships are held. There are shoals at the approach
to the lock almost in midstream so check the chart and
proceed carefully. The lock-keeper's house is hidden behind
a high bank on the left and you may have to tie up to the
landing stage for a bit while a member of the crew fetches
him to work the lock for you.

From Earith there is another thirty miles of cruising on
the Ouse with nine locks to Tempsford Bridge, the current
limit of navigation for cruisers, and it is all most attractive. Beyond Brownshill Lock you will find the pretty
Pike and Eel Inn on the right bank, set among weeping
willows. A little further along the river is the village of
Holywell. We found it enchanting with its thatched cottages, one of which housed a poodle parlour, ancient church
whose tower was once a beacon for ships, historic well
which accounts for the name of the village, and 'Ye Olde
Ferry Boat Inn', part of which, like the church, dates back
to A.D. 890. Here, where Hereward the Wake fled across
the river from William the Conqueror, we dined superbly
one evening. Here too, we watched the reed cutters at
work. It is wise to book meals in advance at the Ferry
Boat Inn (telephone St Ives 3227). When sitting in the
bar, enjoying a drink, ask the landlord to tell you the tale
of Juliet Tewsly, whose 900-year-old ghost is said to
appear at the inn on St Patrick's Day. And ask him to
show you the grey granite slab which once marked her
grave and which is now incorporated in the bar floor.

From Holywell to St Ives the water is rather shallow
in places and careful navigation is required. The approach
to the lock should be taken with caution if the sluices are
running, for the water from them creates a strong eddy
and tends to run a cruiser into the lock. Once through the

lock, avoid the piles on the right and turn left into Staunch Haven, the L. H. Jones boatyard, for water if you did not fill up at the lock, or just to visit the ship's chandlers.

St Ives, which appears as Slepe in the Domesday Book, and is named after the Persian bishop Ivo who died at Slepe about A.D. 600, is a picturesque halt, and mooring is available at the town quay on your right before the bridge or at the Waits Quay above the bridge. For overnight mooring the town quay is ideal, and convenient for shopping. The medieval bridge at St Ives is lovely and quite remarkable in that it still retains a chapel built upon the middle of it and dedicated to St Ledger. It is one of the few bridges with chapels now left in Britain. It is interesting to note too that the arches nearer the town are pointed in the Gothic style while the ones on the opposite side are round.

The Dolphin Hotel is at the waterside and the town is good for shopping. There are many old houses and a statue of Oliver Cromwell in the Market Place. Cromwell was born at Huntingdon but farmed at St Ives and lived at Old Slepe Hall, near what is now known as Oliver Cromwell Place. The most interesting place in St Ives, we thought, was a rope factory where our children were shown how ropes were made before modern machinery took over.

The scenery between St Ives and Hemingford Lock is glorious. Hemingford Lock is the first of the unmanned locks and here you will be able to try your hand at operating a lock. The chart will reveal a shoal in the middle of the pool at the approach to the landing stage for the lock. As you leave the lock you will see a boathouse to the left with a licensed restaurant. St James's Church with its peculiar truncated spire stands between the boathouse and the lock. Hemingford Grey is a real beauty-spot with many

lovely timbered houses and thatched cottages. Just round
the bend in the river from Hemingford Grey there is a
backwater to the left. This is only navigable to the Bailey
Bridge but is a pretty diversion, heavily carpeted with
water-lilies. Close to the entrance to this aptly named
Sleeping Waters is Hutsons boatyard and nearby is
Hemingford Abbots.

Houghton Lock and Mill, next upstream, are owned by
the Society for the Protection of Rural England. The mill,
a seventeenth-century timbered building, is used as a
youth hostel. There is a particularly beautiful stretch of
river past ancient Hartford church to Huntingdon, but the
water is shallow in places.

Huntingdon is linked to its neighbour Godmanchester
not only by river but by a raised road known as the
Causeway. To visit Huntingdon, moor at the Huntingdon
boatyard on the right bank, just before the bridge, at
the Old Bridge Hotel hard by the bridge, or above the
bridge on the opposite bank at another Elysian Holidays
boatyard. Godmanchester lock is not far away and on
locking through a backwater round to the left offers excellent moorings from which to explore Godmanchester,
which has the distinction of being the smallest borough in
England. While Huntingdon has two inns of interest,
some ancient churches and chapels, and the house where
the poet Cowper lived for a time, Godmanchester, which
obtained its first charter from King John, boasts many
beautiful old houses and an excellent pub, the Black Bull.
Shopping facilities are adequate.

After Brampton and Offord locks, the latter set in
between wooded banks, you will come to the two villages
of Offord Cluny and Offord D'Arcy, once noted for lace-
making. These are on the left and in Offord Cluny you
will find the Swan Hotel less than 200 yards from the
river. There are several islands in the reach to St Neots

Lock and your chart of the South Level is invaluable here. It is a help to keep the chart in use folded to the relevant section beside you in a plastic envelope, weighted down by something heavy. This keeps it dry and prevents it being blown overboard.

Beyond the lock the approach to St Neots is by several more wooded islands which open up to a very wide stretch of water bounded by pleasant meadows on both banks. There are scores of mooring places on this reach and while our dog dug for moles we tried a little fishing. The Great Ouse is one of the most popular rivers in England for coarse fishing, and bream, chub, dace and many other kinds can be caught, even trout. Fishing from the banks requires a permit from the riparian owners, but fishing from the boat needs only a licence from the Great Ouse River Authority. We did not on this particular occasion fish for very long for our youngest daughter managed to imbed a fish hook in her leg so effectively that she had to be taken to the local doctor in St Neots to get the hook removed. St Neots, named after St Neot, a monk of Glastonbury who, with St Swithun, educated King Alfred of 'burnt cakes' fame, is a charming market town with one of the largest market places in the country and a fine church. Shopping facilities are excellent and we enjoyed the fair held there during our visit.

There is still another hour's cruising to Eaton Socon lock and mill at Tempsford Bridge, the head of navigation until such time as restoration, now well under way, is completed to Bedford. These upper reaches are lovely although there are very few ports of call other than the Kelpie Marine Boatyard and the Anchor Inn near Tempsford Bridge.

We shall never forget our return journey from Tempsford to Cambridge. On the morning of our departure, a heavy mist was hanging over the river so that visibility was similar to that from an aircraft flying through wispy white clouds. As the sun burst through, it created a kind of halo over the river and this peculiar light effect produced yet another perspective of the Fenland waterways.

We cruised over 300 miles on thirty-nine gallons of petrol in a fortnight, which gave us more than adequate time to explore most of the countryside. Yet we feel we scarcely scratched the surface of the beauty, peace and delight the Fenland rivers offer. We remember many of the interesting people we met, the picnic lunch in the meadows near St Ives, the beer gardens at the Three Jolly Butchers at Wyton; indeed, each member of our crew, despite the many boating holidays we have enjoyed since our discovery of the South Level, still occasionally comes out with a 'do you remember' question about the Fetching Fens. You and your crew will experience many of these and other pleasures like the memorable view of Hemingford Grey church from upstream and you will regale your friends with tales and photographs of your adventures, explaining to these landlubbers how, for example, you quickly mastered that guillotine gate at Hemingford Lock.

Like us, you too will have some experiences you will not talk too much about. Although we returned the *Invader* in good condition there was one little bit of damage. One night we put our hamster's cage a little too close to a curtain and in the morning found that he had literally eaten the bottom half of it. Banham's thought this hilariously funny when we showed them the neatly bisected curtain, but perhaps this was due more to my embarrassment than the damage. They did not want to make a charge for the damage but when I insisted upon it they finally accepted the princely sum of 1s 6d.

CHAPTER 7

THE 'LITTLE MED'

WE CALL the River Medway, which separates the Men of Kent from Kentish Men, the 'Little Med' because, like the vast Mediterranean Sea it offers, albeit on a small scale, a great variety of holiday pleasures. The estuary, from the River Thames to the tidal lock at Allington a short distance downstream from Maidstone, is no place for novices, but the Upper Medway Navigation is as perfect a waterway for beginners as can be found anywhere.

From the tidal lock at Allington to Tonbridge Great Bridge, the head of navigation, is little more than eighteen miles, but the Upper Medway Navigation packs more scenic beauty, rustic charm and historic association into its short course than many rivers ten times its length. The countryside through which it flows has appropriately been named 'the Garden of Eden'—a sweeping panorama of meadows, orchards, hopfields and woodlands. Studded sporadically throughout this garden like jewels in a treasure-chest are impressive memorials of Kent history—castles and churches, manor houses and moated homes, ancient bridges and picturesque villages, to say nothing of strangely-shaped oasthouses and charming pubs. We were, in fact, amazed to find that apart from a short stretch of river round the country town of Maidstone this beautiful navigation was almost completely rural. The river tends to lose itself in the countryside and in history.

Our short holiday on the Medway, shared with our

friends, Dr Roger Pilkington of the 'Small Boat' series
fame and his wife, Miriam, was squeezed into an already
full cruising programme on the *Thames Commodore* on
the Continent, and on hired narrow cruisers on Britain's
canals.

Yet our first taste of the Medway that May weekend
so whetted our appetite for the river that we have subsequently returned for more of the same, and have brought
the *Thames Commodore* from Teddington Lock on the
Thames through the Medway tideway right up to Maidstone Bridge, which is as far as a craft of her dimensions
can venture.

Beginners who have only a week or two to spare will
find the Medway an ideal waterway on which to start
messing about in boats. And experienced boaters who have
overlooked the Medway will find it charmingly different
from any other waterway they have explored.

Allington Lock, with its unusual Victorian-Gothic lock
house, is located at the end of an attractive, curving reach
of river which is under the authority of the Medway
Lower Navigation Company as far as the College Garden,
Maidstone, little more than a fifth of a mile south of
Maidstone Bridge. The remainder of the non-tidal navigation is controlled by the Kent River Authority which
deserves to be congratulated on its superb maintenance of
the waterway. There are only nine locks on this, the Upper
Medway Navigation, each capable of taking craft up to
80 ft long and 18 ft 6 ins beam, and almost any craft
drawing 4 ft or less with freeboard of no more than 8 ft
6 ins can cruise right to Tonbridge without a qualm. Unlike the Thames and most other rivers in Britain and
abroad, there are refuse disposal arrangements at every
single lock and we saw no litter anywhere. All locks were
in first-class condition and we found it possible to moor
virtually anywhere along the navigation. The London and

Home Counties Branch of the Inland Waterways Association have seen to it that there are landing stages at each lock, fresh water taps, a public mooring at Tonbridge, and they publish a most useful handbook or guide to the river, complete with handy chart of the Upper Medway navigation.

There are a number of hire firms on the Medway, including Hire Cruisers (Maidstone) Ltd at the Tovil Bridge Boatyard where we found an excellent choice of craft. The four-berth, 24 ft x 8 ft *San Diana* with a draught of 2 ft and headroom of 5 ft 11 ins was spotlessly clean and well equipped when we took her over that sunny Friday afternoon in May. Our golden Labrador, Wiggers, who has become a sea-dog of great discrimination, approved of the standard of comfort and found the modest vibration of the Stuart Turner diesel much to his liking. If you take a dog on a boating holiday you may find that he will spend a good deal of time lying directly over the engine. I have never discovered whether it is the vibration or the warmth of the engine that appeals to dogs because Wiggers will lie over the engine both in cool weather and in blazing sunshine.

We cruised first from the boatyard to East Farleigh Lock, some twenty minutes upstream, to collect our lock key as arranged by Derek Salmon. He, as honorary secretary of the London and Home Counties Branch River Medway Sub-committee, also gave us a special I.W.A. lock pass for a fee of £2. This enabled us to pass through all locks between 8 a.m. and one hour before sunset and permitted us to work the locks ourselves. Until recently locks on the Upper Medway Navigation were worked by lock-keepers and the upper six locks, Sluice Weir Lock to Tonbridge Town Lock, could only be navigated at fixed times with craft in convoy unless skippers held an I.W.A. pass. In 1968 the London and Home

Counties Branch succeeded in getting all restrictions on locks lifted and you can now operate them yourself.

Cruising back from East Farleigh to Allington Lock we skipped Maidstone and made directly for the Malta Inn at Allington, an absolute 'must' port of call on the Medway. Originally a bargeman's inn, dating back to the late eighteenth century, it has in recent years been extended and 're-done' and unfortunately nothing now remains of its old character; it can best be described as 'plush popular', but the food, wine and service is of high standard.

We set off next morning for Maidstone, passing cruising clubs and marinas, a string of moored sailing barges converted to houseboats but no moving craft. Through the trees was a glorious view of the moated, medieval Allington Castle, now a retreat centre run by the Carmelite Order. The river all the way to Maidstone is wide and fairly deep and with luck you will meet tugs and lighters carrying paper pulp or coal to the paper works at Tovil or the gas works at Maidstone. Once past Allington Marina you come to industrialised riverside waterworks, engineering works, sweet factories and the like, as well as relics of the old waterside at Maidstone. This industrialised shabbiness lasts for only half a mile to Bazalgette's Victorian Maidstone Bridge with its wide granite arches. Through the bridge you will find moorings at a low wharf beneath the splendid Archbishop's Palace and high-towered All Saints Church, the largest parish church in Kent. The county town of Kent looks little more than an ordinary shopping centre by road, but it is extraordinarily rich in fine old buildings and such treats as the remains of a fascinating eighteenth-century water-pavilion, the Chillington House Museum and Art Gallery and the Coach Museum founded by Sir Garrard Tyrwhitt-Drake. Nearby the moated Leeds Castle stands romantically.

From Maidstone to Tonbridge there is a continuous towing path for those who enjoy pleasant waterside walks. Between Maidstone and Tovil there is a little more industry but above Tovil Bridge the river narrows and winds through woodlands to East Farleigh Lock. Just above the lock you will come to the first of the many superb medieval bridges on the Medway. East Farleigh Bridge, in my view, is the finest of them all and one of the most beautiful in England. Its four rather flat pointed arches are separated by massive cut-waters both up and downstream, and though the roadway is a scant 11 ft wide, there are no recesses for pedestrians. The bridge is also the worst navigational hazard on the Upper Medway, for the navigation arch and lock are well out of line and a dead slow angled approach from the lock to the bridge is essential. Craft have come to minor grief here through excessive speed and carelessness.

On a hill above the bridge on the south bank sprawls a large hopfield with its forest of poles and wires strikingly topped by the broach spire of St Mary's Church. There is a memorable view of the river from the top of the hill. East Farleigh village has a grocery shop and is a quarter-mile from the lock.

The wide two-mile reach to Teston Bridge and Lock is typical of the rural charm of the entire river to Tonbridge. There is the timber-built Kettle Bridge whose piers are encased in concrete, the soaring spire of Barming church rising above green orchards, and hop gardens on sloping hills. We were told that fishing is excellent and we spotted wild mink swimming as we approached the rushing waters of the wide weir beside Teston Lock. Behind it, nestling in the hillside, you will see the ivy-covered remains of an old linseed mill, to add one more delightful touch to one of the most attractive spots on the river. Teston (pronounced Teeson) boasts a bridge that runs East Farleigh's a close second for beautiful simple lines and it does have handy pedestrian recesses.

Kent, of course, is the home of cricket and at Teston village cricket and hockey balls have been made since 1808. We cruised on through open fields and patches of woodland falling gently to the banks, to the distressingly modern Wateringbury Bridge. You can get a bus from the village crossroads at the top of the hill for a visit to nearby Mereworth Castle which is open to the public.

Leaving Wateringbury behind, you will come to a straight reach and will soon see Nettlestead church and the 'big house' on a hillside to starboard. This is Nettlestead Place but is not open for inspection. St Mary's Church can be reached via a narrow footpath from the mooring just below Nettlestead Place. This church is fascinating for the half-dozen great fifteenth-century windows of the nave and similar but smaller windows of the chancel, designed as frames to exhibit the skill of the craftsmen in painted glass of the period. Enough of the glass still remains to make one bemoan the loss to posterity.

From Nettlestead the river bends sharply and there are some high banks where it divides, swinging to port to become the main channel to Twyford Bridge. Although a dead end it fully repays exploration and there is ample room to turn round. There are glorious views along this wide reach bordered by meadows and with the Beult and Teise streams flowing into it. Back at the junction, taking the right-hand channel and moving slowly through the narrow cut will take you to Hampstead Lock, where the towpath changes to the left-hand bank. This lock, built in the eighteenth century at the end of an artificial cut to save travelling round the big Yalding bend in the river, is the second deepest lock on the river and is certainly deep enough to use the hanging chains in the chamber.

At the upstream end of the narrow cut, just round a

bend, is a small drawbridge which is quite simple to operate with your windlass. You can get water from a hosepipe here. Immediately beyond the drawbridge you will find the ancient thatched Anchor Inn with moorings on the wall opposite.

From the moorings here you can walk half a mile across the fine Twyford Bridge, with its massive pointed cut-waters, and the pleasant Lees to Yalding. In this most attractive village with its ancient cottages, pretty timbered and Georgian houses, a smithy and at least five pubs, we discovered in one of these latter a pre-1912 wall pinball machine which proved great fun and rather profitable. Medieval Yalding Bridge, a scheduled monument like the old bridges at Twyford and Laddingford on the Teise, is distinctly different from all the other ancient bridges on the Medway, for it is really a stone causeway some hundred yards long with seven arches and showing signs of having been widened on the upstream side.

From the Anchor moorings and the big automatic sluices nearby, the river makes a right-angle turn, an area popular with swimmers. After two more bends you will be in pretty open countryside again with trees overhanging the banks of the river.

The nine locks on the Medway give a total rise of 58 ft 6 ins and the six remaining locks to Tonbridge from Hampstead Lock were ten until 1914, for in the 8½ miles of river involved, the rise is well over 30 ft. Extensive work by the Kent River Authority has made four of these locks unnecessary. However, you can still see the remains. There are only two main bridges over this stretch and five minor ones, so that the entire course to Tonbridge is un-spoiled valley and weald. The river above Yalding is somewhat shallower than below but will accommodate craft of under 4 ft in draught.

The river, now banked by woodland, narrows above the

angled Branbridges Bridge and becomes shallower with
the banks being noticeably gravelly and high. There are
a number of sharp bends and because of the shallowness
you should steer round the outside of the bends, keeping
well away from the banks. There are more shoals at the
approach to Sluice Weir Lock than anywhere else on this
river, I would say, yet the lock is the deepest on the Upper
Medway. Once through the lock you will note that the
valley begins to open out again and soon you will pass
the mouth of the River Bourne, another of the Medway's
many tributaries, to reach Oak Weir Lock, beautifully
situated in a setting of trees.

Above the lock the banks are wooded for a short stretch
but you will reach open countryside again before Ford
Green Bridge. There is a pleasant picnic mooring spot
where the river widens into a pool below the bridge. More
hop-gardens and meadows appear as the scenery almost
constantly changes. Where the river divides you should
take the left-hand channel to East Lock about a quarter of
a mile further on. There are many footpaths leading to
little hamlets like Tudely Hale and Golden Green, and
such inviting names made us regret we had so little time
on the Medway.

The towpath changes from the left to the right bank at
East Lock and at Porter's Lock you will find a most beautiful and peaceful setting. Below it, beside the towpath,
you can search for a weathered milestone marking the
distance up from Maidstone. The next reach, a mile long,
with woodlands to port and meadows to starboard, will
seem so isolated and quiet that time almost stands still.
From this reach you can see 'May's Folly', a peculiar
Victorian-Gothic erection some 150 ft high, dominating
the countryside. It was built at Hadlow in 1810 by a
Barton May, ostensibly to permit him to see the sea, but

it was not quite tall enough and later the slender top storey was added.

At Eldridge's Lock in surroundings of open fields and orchards, we saw some youths clowning with a canoe, which we later discovered had been stolen. This is the only instance of theft we have encountered on the waterways in over a decade, either in Britain or on the Continent. Although you are now only little more than a mile and a half from Tonbridge, you will find the river bordered by farmlands, water meadows and willow trees. We reluctantly ignored the many tempting moorings along this reach which twists and turns on its way to Cannon Bridge, where the gasholder inevitably blots the horizon, and Tonbridge Town Lock, nearly 60 ft above Maidstone. It is not wise to moor on the high brick wall below the lock. Lives have been lost scrambling between boats and the top of the wall. There is another drawbridge at Town Lock, from which you can see the excellent I.W.A. mooring on the left.

The Great Bridge just beyond the I.W.A. moorings is the official head of navigation, but smaller powered craft which require only about 5 ft clearance can cruise slowly for another two miles upstream to Lucifer Bridge.

Tonbridge, a Medway crossing from pre-Saxon times, home of an ancient public school, a centre of printing and a bustling market town, is rich in history. You will enjoy viewing the ruins of the moated castle high on a 60 ft mound beside the Great Bridge. The gardens are particularly colourful. There are fine half-timbered houses in the High Street, not least of these The Chequers, the oldest pub in Tonbridge, which has very pleasant bars.

Tonbridge, perhaps more than any other town on the river, was transformed by the opening of the Medway to commercial traffic. It was King Charles who started the move to make the Medway navigable in the 1660s, but

nothing was achieved for some seventy-five years and the
river was not opened for traffic to Tonbridge until 1741.
The then unimportant town, so poorly served by roads,
quickly became a thriving commercial centre. Coal, timber,
stone, iron, lime and other cargoes were first bow-hauled
by men and then drawn by horses in increasing quantities.
The town's whole appearance changed as imported building materials replaced the local timber and the new
Georgian-style architecture became fashionable.

Monopoly of carriage on the river coupled with the
coming of the railways affected trade from the 1850s and
the conditions on the river progressively worsened. Despite
the establishment of a new authority and the complete
remodelling of the navigation above Maidstone to enable
the reopening of the river to commercial traffic in 1915,
this traffic never returned. We mused sadly on this as we
cruised peacefully back to the Tovil Boatyard in the warm
sunshine. Commercial traffic will never conceivably return
in force to the Upper Medway but Kent and England has
a grand and beautiful waterway that must be preserved
at all costs.

We find ourselves returning again and again to the
'Little Med', sometimes by boat, sometimes by car for
lunch at a waterside inn and sometimes just to walk along
a stretch of towpath to exercise our dog and feast our
eyes. There remains much more for us to see and we
want to delve one day into the story of the oasts. A complete stranger I met on the towpath was telling me only
the other day that hops were reputedly cultivated in Kent
in the 1520s to provide beer for Flemish weavers who had
settled there. The secret of success in processing hops is
apparently in the drying, and the picturesque Kentish oast
gradually evolved into its present form from replicas of
oasts used in Flanders. Circular oasts with revolving

draught cowls were the brain-child of one John Read in the 1830s and are still in use today. It is boating holidays with towpath encounters like these that rouse one's curiosity and open up new fields of interest. You cannot help but enjoy such a beautiful little river as the Medway remains to this day.

CHAPTER 8

THE NOWHITHER NENE

IT WOULD be misleading and unfair to suggest that it is mandatory to introduce yourself, your family or friends to boating holidays on navigationally easy waterways with only a few locks. There is no reason why more active and energetic first-timers on the waterways should not holiday on our many artificial cuts or canals, or indeed on a combination of rivers and canals, as long as excessive ambition in respect of locks is curbed and ample time is allowed.

While holidaying on the South Level of the Fenland waterways we had met a craft from the River Nene which had come from Peterborough to Hilgay via the Middle Level, and the owner of the converted lifeboat and his wife had raved over the beauty of the Nene. While the Nene had certainly caught our fancy we also had a yen to try out tiller steering and after some debate the vote was to try to combine the two. We were fortunate to find very quickly at Bletchley on the Grand Union Canal the tiller-equipped *Suzybelle S.3*, a comfortable and suitable 6-8 berth 41 ft x 6 ft 10 ins narrow cruiser with a draught of 1 ft 10 ins, which would take us anywhere on the waterway network. It was a simple matter to work out the lock mileage from Bletchley to Peterborough and return, and to calculate that the 180 miles and 128 locks of the round voyage could be covered in a fortnight by averaging an easy 22 lock miles per day.

By early February we had booked the *Suzybelle S.3* and

completed an advance log based on available charts and relevant literature.

Until modern engineering brought it under control in this century, the Nene was a terrible rogue of a river, dealing out death and destruction after heavy rain or quick thaw. The fear in which the Nene was held for centuries is reflected today in the way towns and villages were defensively built on spurs of high land at the sides of the broad valley, two miles wide in places. The sites chosen were close enough to the river to use it for transport and power but high enough and distant enough to avoid the floods, damp and fog of bygone days. The history of the Nene is a fascinating story worth delving into, but you will be more interested in what it is like today. The Nene rises in the Northamptonshire uplands, one branch near the battlefield of Naseby, the other from a spring near Borough Hill, the site of the B.B.C. Daventry station. The streams join forces and then the Nene proper flows through the outskirts of industrial Northampton and back into open country at Midsummer Meadow, where some 500 years ago thousands fleeing from the battle of Northampton were drowned.

The valley broadens out almost immediately into a flat expanse of lovely meadows which continue to the outskirts of Peterborough. Northampton is only forty miles from Peterborough as the crow flies, but what we have dubbed the 'nowhither Nene' loops so much that there are some seventy miles of wild and unspoiled river between these two towns. This is referred to as the Middle Nene, for it only becomes a big tidal river in the lower reaches stretching a further twenty-odd miles from the Dog-in-a-Doublet lock to the Wash.

We all hoped there was a little madness left in the Nene as we took over the *Suzybelle S.3* from the Bletchley boatyard one Saturday afternoon. It took a few miles as we cruised north along the pleasant and rural Grand Union for all the crew to get the feel of tiller steering, much more direct than the wheel steering we were accustomed to. It was strange standing at the tiller instead of sitting on a high stool by a wheel. A folding deck chair did not quite provide comfortable steering as the tiller arm was too high and the frame of the chair got in the way every time a sharp turn had to be made. It took us some little time to discover that the most comfortable way to steer with a tiller for any length of time is to straddle the arm. This enables you to steer with the inside of your legs and to shift your weight from one leg to another. This is useful on long pounds, but when approaching badly angled narrow bridge holes and locks it is wise to return one hand to the tiller arm and use the other to manipulate the throttle and gear lever.

You will enjoy the gentle lock at Fenny Stratford on the Grand Union with its swing bridge and a fall of only a few inches.

The lock marks the beginning of the eleven-mile Fenny pound, nearly three hours cruising without having to work a lock, and goes through the pretty valley of the Ouzel. Canals are like this. You will find pounds unobstructed by locks for twenty miles and more, and then on the same canal there is a succession of locks or even flights of locks within a distance of a few miles. Most canals take full advantage of the contours of the land but many have to be taken over watersheds and through hills, thus the necessity for locks and tunnels.

The Grand Union Canal was built only after the completion of the Midlands canals made a direct link by water with London imperative. The thriving Oxford Canal was not really satisfactory because it connected the Midlands waterways with London via Oxford and the Thames, a roundabout route which meant higher shipping costs. Several schemes for new canals were mooted and in 1793 the Grand Junction Canal, stretching from Braunston high up on the Oxford Canal to Brentford on the Thames, was authorised by Parliament, today the longest section on the Grand Union system.

The Grand Junction took twelve years to complete and must have nearly driven the noted canal engineer, William Jessop, to distraction. By the time it was finished in 1805 Jessop had successfully locked over the Chilterns and had driven two long tunnels through the tough ironstone outcrops at Braunston and Blisworth. The latter, the longest navigable tunnel on our waterways today, was a particular problem and delayed completion of the Grand Junction for all of five years. Between 1800, when the rest of the waterway was opened to traffic, and 1805, goods had to be transhipped into horse-drawn wagons and hauled over Blisworth hill on a plate railway.

Despite setbacks, the Grand Junction was an immediate success, substantially speeding up and reducing the cost of shipping goods between the South and the Midlands. It was even used for troop movements, and as the news-papers of the day reported that this not only saved time but made for the arrival of troops in fresh condition, you can imagine how dreadful the roads must have bee a: the beginning of the nineteenth century.

As you cruise along the Fenny pound, with luck meeting a few working narrow boats, it will be difficult for you to imagine that this quiet canal was once the waterways equivalent of the M1 motorway. Only over a relatively few miles will you hear or catch glimpses of roaring road traffic, and you will be smugly satisfied that you are idling along on the water while so many others are cursing con gestion and delays on the roads.

Work on the Grand Junction continued sporadically over the years until 1883 when the last of eight arms or branches was completed. It was not until 1929, however, that the present name of Grand Union Canal was adopted after amalgamations. In 1948 the Grand Union was included in the nationalised waterways and has been operated by the British Waterways Board since January 1963.

On the Grand Union there are certainly more pubs than service areas along our motorways. Near Bridge 83 the Barge Inn at Little Woolstone specialises in country wine and chicken on the spit. By Bridge 77 you will find the Old Wharf Inn and still another pub in Lindford village, a short walk along the road to the left. And at the next bridge, No. 76, stands the Black Horse Inn and a café. The bridges along the Grand Union are eye-openers. You will find, quite apart from the marks of old tow lines, graceful architecture to admire and beauty of line.

Cosgrove Lock and the end of the eleven-mile Fenny pound comes almost immediately after the short Wolverton aqueduct. The derelict Buckingham Arm is on the left above the lock, which takes you up a bare $3\frac{1}{4}$ ft to the next pound, some five miles long. There is a watering point and moorings at the lock, but to visit the village you should moor by the Barley Mow Inn, which sits back from the left bank of the canal in a little hollow. The church repays a visit if only for the lovely view from the tower. There is a good grocer near the church.

The Stoke Bruerne flight of seven locks, like other flights, may sometimes be padlocked at 7 p.m. While there is good mooring below the bottom lock, Stoke Bruerne is a long walk up the flight, which raises your craft some 56 ft to the Boat Inn. It is advisable therefore to time your arrival before 7 p.m. With the locks against us we have taken as long as an hour and a half to lock through this flight. By lock-wheeling, however, you can easily do it in under an hour. Unless there are pressing reasons it is foolish to rush through locks and smart and steady winding is the least tiring; windlasses with sleeves on the handles are more efficient than the old type of lock handle without a revolving sleeve.

The Stoke Bruerne flight is itself very pleasing to the eye but the scene at the top is a gem lifted as it were from centuries past. The village of Stoke Bruerne with its Norman church and thatched cottages nestles snugly by the canal, and the canalside itself—with the Waterways Museum depicting over two centuries of canal history, the Old Boat Inn, the cottages of canal employees with their gaily painted doors, an early traditional narrow boat, boat-weighing machine and a pair of cast-iron lock gates among outside exhibits in a natural setting—is the showplace of British Waterways.

The Museum, which is open daily including Sundays from 10 a.m. to 8 p.m. except for meal breaks, is a treasure trove of relics of a most colourful industry. There is a model of a giant brush with which tunnels were cleaned, traditional boaters' clothing and cabinware, paintings, brasses, documents, photographs, a full-size reconstruction of a decorated and fitted out butty boat cabin, and even 'legging' boards on which boatmen lay to propel their craft with their legs through nearby Blisworth Tunnel.

Blisworth and Braunston Tunnels on the Grand Union, like many other canal tunnels, were constructed without towing paths. In the early days when commercial craft were bowhauled by their crews or towed by horses or pairs of mules, an alternative method of propulsion was necessary in these tunnels. The solution was 'legging' and teams of 'leggers' were based at the tunnels. From 1805, when Blisworth Tunnel was opened to traffic, to 1850, when steam tugs took over, 'leggers' took craft through the 3,075 yard long tunnel. 'Legging' boards were placed across the bows of craft and two 'leggers' positioned head to head on the boards with their feet projecting over the sides of the boat literally walked or 'legged' along the sides of the tunnel. It was a dark, cold, wet, tiring job and long tunnels like Blisworth must have seemed endless. The 'leggers' reigned at Blisworth for forty-five years while the tugs maintained their sway for eighty-four years, until 1934, by which time virtually all craft were motorised and able to navigate the tunnel unaided.

There is picturesque mooring for scores of craft at Stoke Bruerne and you will certainly decide to linger here to water, replenish stores, refresh yourself, do some sight-seeing, take photographs and obtain items of 'canalia' from the little souvenir shop beyond the inn. You'll find retired boaters here too and both the lock-keeper and attendant at the museum enjoy chatting and filling you in on Stoke Bruerne's way of life in its hey-day.

Blisworth Tunnel is just round the bend from Stoke Bruerne. Although it looks very narrow and gives delusions of curving away, it is actually fairly straight with good headroom and ample space for two narrow boats to pass with care. The tunnel is in good repair and there are seven air shafts, five original shafts and two added later, all of which drip and in a wet season provide free showers. This was our first canal tunnel and we took over an hour getting through. On subsequent journeys, after discovering the advantage of turning on all cabin lights as well as our searchlight, we have navigated the tunnel in under twenty-five minutes.

You will blink as you leave Blisworth Tunnel and reach bright light once again. Woodland, cottages and rose gardens are in strong contrast to the darkness and clammy atmosphere you have left behind. Another mile along and some $23\frac{1}{2}$ miles out of Bletchley boatyard, you can swing $90°$ to starboard into the narrow, somewhat weedy North-ampton Arm, leading to the River Nene.

We are early risers and when cruising there is normally

someone astir by 6.30 a.m. We use all the daylight available and are generally tucked in our sleeping bags by 10.30 p.m. Of course it is quite possible to lie abed in perfect peace and quiet and I suppose most people do, judging by the number of craft we pass in the mornings still moored with no sign of life; lying-in undisturbed may be one of the advantages of boating holidays that I have failed to point out.

As you gain experience you will acquire a remarkable knack of estimating accurately how long it will take you to travel from one place to another. My wife had become accustomed to accurate forecasts and when we moored above the Top Lock on the Northampton Arm for lunch on this cruise, I recall being nicely chided for being ten minutes late and responsible for the fact that the roast beef was slightly overdone.

Not a single craft was moving on the Northampton Arm and we could well believe that only two boats had passed through in the fortnight before our arrival. The lock paddles were so stiff that only my son Paul was strong enough for the role of lock-wheeler and he was therefore pleased when the lock-keeper appeared on his bicycle at the seventh lock and kindly took over. No charts exist to my knowledge of this short Arm. There are seventeen narrow 7 ft wide locks in five miles as well as a number of drawbridges providing just as tight a squeeze. We found five broken or malfunctioning paddles and one balance-beam rather less than 18 ins long, but fortunately not on one of the single top gates. The Arm is rather hard work and understandably frustrating and wearying for beginners. But it need not be. More extensive use by boats would ease the stiffness of the paddles and lead to better maintenance. The views from the top of the locks are glorious, the surrounding countryside is unmarred except for one major road bridge, and passing through is great sport, especially when a heavy dog and heavier crew leap off the bows with a flourish as you enter locks two inches wider than the beam of your craft.

We were through the Arm in under three hours, thanks to noble work by the lock-keeper who, when we thanked him in approved fashion, tipped us off as to the hazards on the approach to Northampton Lock No. 1. The stretch immediately after the Arm's bottom lock is a disgrace to the city of Northampton, which has conversely done so much to make Midsummer Meadow so appealing. The river is badly silted here and chock-a-block with weed and debris, while the banks look rather like a slum. Once under the road-bridge we were greeted by a splendid stretch of quayside to port but we had to avoid weeds and debris and run on for several hundred yards past the toll house before we found enough water to moor safely. This is a typical example of the wisdom of obtaining and paying attention to the advice of local lock-keepers, for we could easily have gone aground in a dozen places.

Our keys to the Nene locks were awaiting us at the toll house as previously arranged with the Welland and Nene River Authority at Oundle. If you hire a craft on the Nene these keys are available from the boatyard and you need not concern yourself with navigation tolls. But as we had come from the nationalised waterways and our craft was not licensed for the Nene we had to pay £2 17s plus £2 returnable deposit on the two keys to navigate the thirty-seven unmanned locks between Northampton and Peterborough. There was also a small insurance premium of 10s to cover possible damage to river controls. On writing to the Engineer's Office at North Street, Oundle, you will receive an application form with several sheets of instructions regarding navigation of the Nene. These instructions include directions for operating what I must frankly admit are the stiffest series of locks on any inland waterway in Britain. The operation of the locks is simple enough but they are hard work, despite the fact that they are modern and in good condition. All the locks are fitted with timber pointing doors upstream similar to those on most canals and rivers but have vertical steel 'guillotine' gates at the lower end. Unless otherwise instructed you must leave locks with the pointing doors closed and the vertical gate raised, and it is the raising of these gates that sets every muscle in your body grumbling. These gates have to be operated with care. There may have been unauthorised interference with the balance weights and at the first operation you will always have to take the weight of the gate carefully, using both hands. Nor can you get away with only partially raising the gate. The river foremen insist that gates be left raised to the fullest extent to ensure that the next craft entering the lock does not sustain damage. I am told, incidentally, that the gearing on these vertical steel gates has been purposely made stiff to prevent rapid opening of the gate and possible damage to craft, but that does not account for the fact that gates supplied by one manufacturer are much harder to work than those supplied by the other.

Once you have your keys to the padlocks on the vertical gates and paddles on the pointed doors of each lock, put them on a long cord and carry them round your neck, as they are so easily dropped into the river. The locks are all 83 ft 6 ins long and 15 ft wide and we calculated a total fall of 189 ft in the sixty-nine miles of the non-tidal Nene. The River Board do not guarantee any fixed water levels and care must be taken when approaching river controls with a rapid flow on the river. The river foremen are quick to come to your aid if you experience any difficulty due to lack of water or in operating locks but they can become justifiably annoyed when someone sabotages their vital water levels. We had no difficulty at all in navigating the Nene and found plenty of headroom under all but half a dozen of the sixty-six fixed bridges. You may find more adverse conditions in times of flooding but they are unlikely to worry you, for craft up to 78 ft long 13 ft in beam, with a draught of 4 ft and headroom of 7 ft 3 ins are always permitted on the river.

Your lock keys will not, however, fit the padlocks on Northampton No. 1 lock, which is set in a lovely park superbly equipped with sports facilities. The lock-keeper who lives in the toll house on the quayside will operate this lock for you and guide you to the best moorings for your visit to Northampton. This is a sizeable community of over 100,000 people and the shopping centre is within minutes of the moorings. You will find a gem of a market square and a host of friendly shops like the specialists in leather we discovered with the finest collection of leather goods we have seen anywhere in the world. Places like St John's Catholic Church, built as a hospice in 1140, are delightful and the parks of the city are an eye-opener. A chatty park superintendent proudly told us that North-ampton has more parks than any other town in Britain and we did not doubt him for a moment.

The whole of the Nene lay before us, shimmering in the sun. No river anywhere presents such a winding course through such pleasant pastoral countryside. Apart from short industrialised stretches at Northampton and Peter-borough and the rather 'niffy' sewage farm at Irthling-borough the Nene presents an almost uninterrupted panorama of meadows, woodlands, lovely stone and thatched villages and picturesque mills and parklands. Although you will find remarkably few inns along the riverside, there are more than enough within a short distance of the banks to keep the thirstiest of crews well fortified.

The river winds through large bends out of Northampton to Rush Mills Lock, which is one of the three on the river with radial shutters instead of guillotine gates. A great variety of wild flowers and wild life decorate the river. With the help of a reference book we identified over thirty different types of birds and I am sure we missed many others. Abington Lock is only a mile from Rush Mills, indeed in the fourteen miles of river between North-ampton and Wellingborough, the next sizeable town, there are twelve locks.

The countryside becomes more glorious as you go on through Rush Mills and Weston Favel locks to Clifford Hill Lock and charming backwater moorings. A footpath from the right bank can be followed for a pleasant one-mile walk to Little Houghton, a village of unspoiled stone dwellings.

Billing Lock, under a mile away, has little to commend it as a scenic attraction, but just beyond the lock on the left is the entrance to Billing Aquadrome with moorings for visitors who want to have a meal or to entertain the younger members of the crew at a fun-fair and other attractions available here. There is more than a mile of lovely countryside before Cogenhoe Lock is reached. Moor well below the lock, as there is a rather dirty camp site and chalet village almost on top of the lock-side. The little village of Cogenhoe is reached by climbing half a mile up the steep hill on the right. Shopping is good here and your shopping basket on wheels will be a help.

You will find pleasant and peaceful scenery as you cruise to Whiston and White Mills locks. There is an inn a few hundred yards along the road to the right which also leads to Castle Ashby village and Castle Ashby House, the seat of the Marquis of Northampton. The house is open to the public on Thursday and Saturday afternoons and on Sundays in June, July and August. It is reached by a path through a mile of park, containing big lakes, and the stone houses of the village are tucked away below the terraces of this stately home.

This ornate and beautiful sixteenth- to eighteenth-century house is famed as being the scene of the 'bride in a basket' legend. The first Earl of Northampton having been refused the hand of Elizabeth Spencer, daughter of the wealthy Lord Mayor of London, posed as a baker's boy and carried his bride-to-be from her father's home in a bread basket. They married against the will of Sir John Spencer and Elizabeth was disinherited. Queen Elizabeth intervened and 'ordered' Sir John to adopt a child in place of his disinherited daughter. As the baby proved to be his grandson the tale has a happy ending. As you will have to walk nearly two miles from the lock if you visit Castle Ashby, it is worth stopping to see the handsome fourteenth- to fifteenth-century church as well, with its unique brass in the chancel floor.

Following the road from the lock in the opposite direction for a mile will bring you to Earls Barton, a large village, so called because it was the site of the Earl of Huntingdon's barley farm. The church here is still as it was over a thousand years ago, richly ornamented.

Bird lovers will admire a water-fowl sanctuary to port along the reach to Barton Lock, an excellent use for old gravel workings. Doddington Lock quickly follows. You may think it worth taking pictures here for the lock is beautifully situated and the Mill House is charming. The Mill House at Wollaston Lock is occupied and the boating enthusiasts who live here will provide water if you need it, and we found them very friendly.

The navigation deteriorates beyond Wollaston Lock and the run to Irthlingborough is rather less interesting than the previous countryside. From Upper Wellingborough Lock you are likely to run into weeds. Weed-cutting is normally in progress on the Nene from spring until the autumn and an eye should be kept open for the weedcutters. The weeds cut during each day are allowed to float downstream to a rope or line of timbers across the river, prior to removal. These obstructions are visible some distance ahead, and at times are indicated by floating red markers. The cutters will always release the ropes or timbers on request to permit the passage of your craft but they need a little time to clear a way for you.

Shortly above the lock you will come to the low Wellingborough bridge and pleasant boulevard moorings to port for Little Irchester. If you cross the river bridge and old railway crossing, a few minutes walk will bring you to the Cottage Inn where you may well meet barge crews who deliver grain to the nearby mills. You can get a bus to Wellingborough, a mile away on the other side of the river, for excellent shopping, a visit to the zoo, the famous public school or perhaps a meal in the handsome old Hind Hotel overlooking the market square. The parish church with its medieval tower and a vast fifteenth-century tithe barn are among the other worthwhile sights in this town which is so clearly fond of trees.

Bridges are all rather low in this area and there are a number of shoals at the approach to Lower Wellingborough Lock, and also in the next few reaches. Ditchford Lock is another of the radial-type locks, and is just fifteen miles by river from Northampton. Higham Ferrers bridge, about half-way to Higham Lock some two miles distant, is one of the most dangerous on the river, not only because of low headroom but because it straddles a bend in the river and there are timber baulks jutting up under both sides of the arch. The best moorings are above the bridge for Higham Ferrers, which stands high on a hill to your right. This is a delightful small town which should not be missed despite the uphill walk. The ancient church with its lovely spire has a cluster of ecclesiastical buildings round it that are reminiscent of corners of Oxford and Cambridge. You will not want to moor for the night near Higham Ferrers bridge, however, as the town apparently holds the record for polluting the Nene.

The next bridge on the river is the lowest of the entire sixty-six and should be navigated with great care. After passing through Higham Lock you will quickly come to a railway bridge and viaduct after which you will find moorings for Irthlingborough. This sprawling village has little noteworthy to commend it to the visitor except for its church and the Railway Inn, which can be reached from your moorings across a couple of footbridges. It is a tiny inn which may not be rated highly among the most picturesque inns of England but it is the home of the 'Irthlingburger'. This is an inexpensive, tasty and filling concoction consisting of fried bread and a hamburger topped with a fried egg, worth every penny the landlord charges. Since our discovery of this simple local dish we have duplicated it both at home and aboard our holiday cruisers time and time again.

Once past the tannery and sewage farm nearby you will notice that the locks are more widely spaced and it is over two miles from Irthlingborough Lock to Upper Ringstead Lock. There is a path here leading from the left bank to the village of Great Addington, which stands proudly on a hill dominated by a fourteenth-century church.

From Lower Ringstead Lock the Nene now loops back on itself as you cruise on to Woodford Lock. At the sharp bend before the lock a footpath leads over the fields to Woodford village and the Duke's Arms. Keep clear of the piers of the railway bridge as you leave the lock as there are a number of underwater stakes. Where the river forks at the approach to Denford Lock keep to the left hand channel.

You will probably not want to visit every village along the way, particularly those which involve longer walks, for some have little of special interest to offer. We have found that if neither shopping nor visiting a particular place is contemplated, it is pleasant to moor as fancy dictates and then explore along one bank on an outward journey and on the other on the return trip. We have discovered many charming spots not mentioned at all in guide or reference books, and there must be many more. Sometimes disappointment is inevitable, but footpaths and country roads make pleasant walks and if you take a dog he will welcome the exercise.

By all means, however, moor above the bridge on the next reach between Islip and Thrapston. Islip is a pretty village of stone houses and cottages on the left, and the Woolpack Inn close to the river serves excellent meals. This is one of the Washington villages and as an American I was, of course, drawn to the elegant fifteenth-century church with its monument to Mary Washington, a great-grandmother of the first American President. We also walked nearly a mile into the market town of Thrapston, which despite the loss of its castle and with its modernised church we found most attractive, with good shopping and a well-stocked antique shop. The rector of the parish church of St James kindly took us over the church and showed us the arms of Sir John Washington on a stone tablet in the church. From the stars and stripes in the arms, the American flag stems.

After another two miles of pretty river you will reach Titchmarsh Lock and the new headquarters of the Middle Nene Cruising Club, which used to be located just above the bridge at Islip. Members are most hospitable and helpful and we learned a good deal about the Nene from a talk with two of them.

You will find the Imray, Laurie, Norie and Wilson chart

of the Nene most useful. It includes public footpaths which enabled us to visit the twin-churched village of Aldwincle, little more than half a mile from the river. Aldwincle All Saints and Aldwincle St Peter's are linked by a long street with delightful groups of grey houses set among trees. The poet John Dryden is said to have been baptised at the 600-year old font in All Saints Church and St Peter's Church is claimed to have the finest broach spire in all of Northamptonshire. You will like the 450-year old Rose and Crown too, and find it worth the walk. The footpath leads surprisingly through vast fields of grain and meadows, one of which happened to be stocked with bullocks. Catching sight of Wiggers they mounted a charge, but our crew must have been more frightening than frightened for we all shouted at the top of our voices and waved our walking sticks with such ferocity that the herd turned aside a dozen yards from us. Since that day we have always made a point of looking into fields before striking across them.

Thorpe Waterville, once a Danish settlement, lies on the right bank of the river, just five minutes from the bridge. It once had a fine castle built in 1300 but the walls were destroyed in the Wars of the Roses and all that remains is the great banqueting hall with a kingpost roof, which today serves as a barn. Good grills can be obtained at the attractive Fox Inn.

The Nene now takes on a new beauty in a rather weedy narrow reach to Wadenhoe where there are moorings at the King's Head. The lovely village with its ancient mill lies near the river and a steep winding footpath leads to its saddleback-towered church standing on a lonely knoll. From Wadenhoe it is little more than two miles to Lilford Lock, which we believe is the prettiest on the river, with a background of a charming stone flying bridge, woodlands, Lilford Hall farm and deer park.

A few miles of idyllic river will bring you to the first of the Barnwell Locks. After the lock on the left is a sharply angled channel into Oundle Marina, created from old gravel pits by J. T. Newington. This marina is splendidly laid out and set in woodland with the noble spire of Oundle's church in the background. A well-stocked chandlery can be found here and a fleet of hire craft. Until Newington introduced hire craft to the Nene in 1963, none were available on this river. He has shown how it can be used for holidays and his hire craft can be recommended wholeheartedly to anyone who wishes to explore the Nene.

Beyond Lower Barnwell Lock the river winds and curves back on itself once again *en route* to Ashton Lock and pleasant backwater moorings. Once through the lock there is a footbridge with a path leading on the right to Ashton, a village owned by the Rothschilds, and noted as the venue for the annual All England Conker Championships. The footpath to the left leads to Oundle with its famous public school, and to one of the most interesting churches along the river, and the old Talbot Hotel. While shopping and sightseeing in Oundle my wife discovered that she had left her purse in Thrapston's antique shop. By telephone we learned it was being held for us, so we hired a taxi whose driver insisted on giving us a free tour round Barnwell Castle, home of the Duke of Gloucester. Although it is not open to the public, our driver knew his way about and we much enjoyed the drive.

Cruising on through looping river you will come to Cotterstock Lock and Mill with a grand view of Cotterstock Hall from the distance. The attractive village of Tansor follows on the right but moorings are difficult to find as the water near the bank is very shallow. After another mile of open country the oddly named Perio Lock is reached. It has been impossible to find out how this lock came by its name for no one seems to know. From the lock the splendid tower of the Collegiate Church of Fotheringay can be seen. Good moorings can be found here and the church and bridge both merit inspection. Two booklets can be bought at the church giving historical notes; Richard III was born in a castle of which only a grassy mound remains, and Mary Queen of Scots was imprisoned and executed here. There are many delightful buildings in the village, a good shop, and the friendly Falcon Inn.

Beautiful as Fotheringay Bridge is, make sure you strip your decks and take the centre arch, as many craft have been damaged here.

We found people along the Nene very friendly and helpful. At Elton a householder invited us in for tea, the publican at the Crown delivered supplies to our craft, we were shown over Elton Hall although it was not officially open, the couple who run the general shop and post office provided us with produce from their garden and even cashed cheques. Fishermen use this village a good deal and fishing is very good indeed. Many size-able fish are frequently caught, we were told, and there are pike, tench, chub and many other kinds for those with patience and skill. It is not noteworthy for trout but it holds so many different kinds that few but the trout specialists will mind. It can be fished in most places and day tickets are available from local angling clubs.

From Elton there is a long three-mile reach past the village of Nassington on the left with backwater moorings by the Queens Head, to Yarwell Lock which has a low guillotine gate worth watching. Yarwell is only a wide loop of river away from Wansford Lock and then in a few minutes you will be in Wansford-in-England. The river itself is not so beautiful here but the village is charming despite the nearby highway. It reminds one that the Nene valley is rich both in history and folklore. We enjoyed our stay because we knew one version at least of the legend of 'Drunken Barnaby', and how the village obtained its name. This genial character was sleeping off the effects of too much drink in a haycock one evening when the river rose in flood and carried haycock and Barnaby to Wansford. On waking up, he was fearful that he had been washed out to sea. Even on being told he was at Wansford, he shouted, 'Wansford where?' The reply was 'In England', hence the present-day name.

The lovely old Haycock Inn at Wansford-in-England serves a good country tea. We happened to arrive in the midst of a wedding celebration, and one chap, who reminded us somewhat of Barnaby, insisted on giving the entire crew, including our dog, champagne.

After Wansford there is nearly four miles of cruising through wooded countryside and past the villages of Stibbington and Sutton, facing each other across the river, to Water Newton Lock. Here there is a mill and a church surprisingly close to the river banks. You will cruise now past the site of Roman potteries and indeed the old Roman town of Durobrivae, and a footpath from the left bank will lead you into the village of Castor, one of the most important of all our Roman settlements. There are still Roman remains to be seen; the church is one of the most beautiful ever built by the Normans who used stones from an earlier Saxon church and convent; there are two pleasing inns, and two lovely old houses. Milton Hall is a handsome Elizabethan house in a park of some thousand acres, one of the seats of the Fitzwilliam family.

Further along the river on the right is Peterborough Cruising Club, with good moorings and a watering point. We found our I.W.A. pennant was a kind of passport on the Nene to the four motorboat, cruising and yacht clubs on the river. A warm welcome, ready assistance, and yarn swapping was automatic as soon as the pennant was spotted. While moored for the night at pretty Alwalton Lock just beyond the Peterborough Cruising Club—the sunsets here are glorious—we were hailed by the commodore of the Cruising Club who was on his way to evensong at Alwalton church. He stopped to chat and missed the service and indeed the licensing hours at the Wheatsheaf Inn as well. This kind of thing happens frequently and we revel in the little parties we give aboard our hire cruisers. The commodore had led fifty to sixty craft through the Middle Level navigation from Peterborough in 1965 in a bid to keep this little used system of waterways open, and we were interested in his experiences. The system consists of some ninety miles of almost lock-free 'navigable drains' lying between the Nene and the Great Ouse. The area is for the most part below sea level and the channels run between high banks and pass through or near the towns of Chatteris, March, Whittlesea and Ramsey. Cruising here is not what one would describe as gloriously scenic and there are few villages to be found on Middle Level drains, but I can confirm that they have a charm of their own. The countryside is wild and remote, nature in the raw so to speak, and the most peaceful and quiet you will find anywhere. Coarse fishing is reputedly excellent here, and bird watchers will have many a rewarding day. It is not possible to enter the system much after mid-June because of heavy weed accumulating in the approach channel, but for an off-beat spring cruise really to get away from it all, the Middle Level is the answer to a prayer.

One more huge loop and the river at last reaches Orton Lock and the approaches to Peterborough. Despite its proximity to the cathedral city, this reach is glorious with delightful 'lynches' or wooded banks. Orton Lock is the last on the non-tidal Nene and you are soon in Peterborough, which sprawls across the river. There is a town quay, a good shopping centre, a fine Guildhall and busy market place, to say nothing of the impressive cathedral which is considered to be among the grandest in Europe. Care should be taken when mooring, for there is little water by the quays and often quite a number of barges about. The banks opposite are shallow and stony too. Just beyond Peterborough there is a channel which goes under a railway bridge to the right, past two boatyards to the lock leading into the Middle Level. By taking the left-hand channel there is some five miles of Fenland cruising to the electrically operated Dog-in-a-Doublet sea lock, worth inspecting if you have never seen one, but you will not be permitted to take your craft into the tideway and The Wash. If you visit one of the local inns and watch the antics of the tide, the flotsam and jetsam and the mud banks, it makes you appreciate all the more the beauty of the non-tidal Nene which you will explore further on the return to your boatyard.

CHAPTER 9

ON TO THE 'GRAND CIRCLE'

To COMBINE both river and canal on a boating holiday and thus to enjoy the different beauties of both and the varying pleasures which each affords is rather like having your cake and eating it too. Even though, as on our River Nene holiday, you spend but a few days on relatively short sections of the Grand Union Canal, you become vividly aware of the contrasts.

The first holiday on which we felt we had broken out of the rank of beginners was our cruise round the 'Grand Circle' in the brand new narrow cruiser *Aylesbury Golden Eye,* recently re-named the *Flying Mexican.* In twenty-one days we chalked up no less than 367 miles and 235 locks from the canal basin at Aylesbury to the Grand Union at Marsworth, to Napton at the junction of the Oxford Canal, to Oxford on the Thames and thence to Lechlade before returning downstream to Teddington, out on the tideway to Greenwich Pier, into the Regent's Canal Dock, through London to Uxbridge and back along the Grand Union and Aylesbury Arm to the canal basin. We averaged just under 29 lock miles per day over the total 602 lock miles at an average speed of 4·77 miles per hour. Our total cruising time was 126 hours or approximately six hours a day.

Having stowed away our stores, our own gear from home, a 56 lb anchor for use if necessary on the Thames tideway, and checked to see that we had all the appropriate maps and booklets, we left Aylesbury one Saturday afternoon late in July. The Aylesbury Arm is rather shallow and one has to go slowly, which gives a good opportunity to get the feel of the boat. As all locks have to be emptied after locking through and you are locking up on this Arm, it takes about four hours to cover the 6¼ miles and sixteen narrow locks to the junction with the Grand Union Canal main line at Marsworth. No chart exists of the Arm, the locks are fairly well spread out and preclude lock-wheeling, and although narrow and shallow the canal is surprisingly weed-free and passes through pleasant farming country for most of its length.

The Arm was so attractive and isolated that we have subsequently walked its towpath from Marsworth to Aylesbury with our dog on a number of occasions in the spring, enjoying a good lunch at the Bell or Bull's Head in the market square.

Passing by a working pair moored at Marsworth we picked up speed in the Grand Union, despite occasionally churning up mud from time to time. We were quite content to moor at Ivinghoe Bridge at 8 p.m. as it was raining hard, having covered ten miles and twenty-one locks.

With bright sunshine next day we were all astir early and underway before 7 a.m., having breakfast while on the move. Everyone was in a gay mood and we negotiated one lock after another to reach the twin towns of Leighton Buzzard and Linslade before 9 a.m.

As my wife and I had frequently joined Dr and Mrs Roger Pilkington both on the *Commodore* and the *Thames Commodore* on Continental waterways, we invited them to join us on this voyage. We arranged to meet 'any time on Sunday on the Grand Union north of Marsworth' and agreed that I would chalk our locking-out time on one of the balance beams. The lock-keeper wondered what it was all about when I wrote '1038' on the balance beam but grinned when I explained. The

Grand Union in this area is very rural. There is a delightful towpath walk between the Globe Inn with its unusual bar on the canal side near Linslade and the inn beside the Three Locks. The villages near the canal are worth exploration as all have some attractive features. From Bridge 106 you can walk half a mile into Stoke Hammond and then four miles through hilly Bedfordshire landscape to the Duke of Bedford's scenic and amusing Woburn Park.

Topping up our water tanks at Fenny Stratford gave us an excuse for a pre-lunch drink at the canal-side Rose and Crown. During the afternoon the heavens suddenly opened and as we locked damply through Cosgrove Lock, I had some difficulty in chalking our time on the wet balance beam. It was pelting so hard as we approached Bridge 57, near Grafton Regis, that we could hardly see our friends who were huddled under the bridge. We found the *Golden Eye* a marvellous craft for entertaining and after a pleasant meal we heard Dr Pilkington's hilarious description of their attempts to find us. He was able to estimate exactly where he could encounter us on the canal but the road system in this area is confusing. However, they had waited only five minutes for us at the bridge. Normally the best way of arranging for guests to join you *en route* is to work out when you will reach a convenient railhead near the waterway on the day agreed and set a tentative meeting place and time. It is usually easy to telephone the day before and confirm existing arrangements. One of the great joys of boating holidays is the mere fact that you do not have to keep to a timetable but can dawdle along as you will. We often get a day or two ahead or behind our planned voyage. Some stretches may be less interesting and we cruise on with few halts, or we may decide to moor for the better part of a day to laze about, or to visit a place nearby.

It was great fun for us all to revisit Stoke Bruerne, and the Waterways Museum never fails to provide new interest and new people to chat to. We had the pleasure of leading a convoy of six craft through Blisworth Tunnel, all of which had waited for a boat to lead them through. Just after passing the Northampton Arm leading to the Nene river, the wash of three working pairs of hurrying narrow boats put us temporarily aground.

You will see the radio masts of Daventry on the horizon as the Grand Union sweeps wide round the town. As you come to the Weedon Beck aqueduct over the Nene, on your left is an enchanting view of what we call the 'church-in-the-hollow' standing well below the canal. There is a farm beyond the aqueduct with fresh eggs for sale. You will find many pleasant moorings from which to explore pretty villages like Everdon, Fawsley, Nether Heyford and others, some immortalised by Gray and Dryden and also those associated with the Washington family.

The seven Buckby locks mark the end of the long sixteen-mile pound from Stoke Bruerne, and Buckby top lock provides splendid overnight moorings. There is a well stocked shop and a useful grocery store beside the New Inn on the canal side. We were amused when the grocer locked his store, walked to a door at the back, stepped into the pub and then, functioning as the publican, opened for business. Here we met a family of boaters, who rarely talk to amateurs, but this family was an exception. They told us that they always started at first light and kept on the move until dark, but despite the meagre living, hard work and long hours, and living in cramped conditions they would not wish to live on land. The Grand Union, they said, is not what it used to be. Now they could only carry 20 tons in the boat and 25 tons in the butty, because the canal was no longer kept dredged to its normal depth as in the old days. Their young daughter, just in her teens, did not approve of the life and wanted a 'proper house' and 'fun'.

The Leicester Arm branches off to the right and the route to Braunston is straight on from Buckby along the two miles of the Braunston Summit on the great divide of the Midlands, rising to over 600 ft. Braunston Tunnel, like Blisworth, has no towpath but it is much shorter, 2,049 yards, and not quite as wet. There is a flight of six locks, descending to Braunston village, a centre of boat-building and decoration for many years. There are watering points at both top and bottom locks, and moorings at the Blue Line boatyard and marina. Full marks must be given to Michael P. Streat, managing director of Blue Line Cruisers, for what he has done not only to develop Braunston boatyard into one of the finest in England, but to popularise pleasure cruising and to maintain commercial carrying on the canals.

After shopping in the village we lunched at the Rose and Castle on the canal side and then took the wooded five-mile reach to Napton Junction. Dozens of traditional narrow boats, gaily painted, are usually moored at Braunston Junction, which marks the southern end of the Northern Section of the Oxford Canal. You are on the Oxford Canal rather than the Grand Union until you reach Napton Junction and the northern end of the southern section of the Oxford Canal. It is unusual to find that such an essential link in a main line canal route is actually part of another canal. This entire reach is a haven of peace and beauty.

At Napton Junction turn left into the southern section of the Oxford Canal, one of the earliest to be built. By 1790 this canal, with the Coventry Canal, linked the Thames with the Trent and Mersey, and for fifteen years saw very heavy traffic. However, in 1805 when the more direct route was opened between Braunston and Brentford via the Grand Junction, which also connected to Napton and Birmingham and the Warwick canals, the southern section below Napton lost the bulk of its traffic and was not improved or straightened like the northern section between Napton and Hawkesbury. Thus the southern section is still the original contour canal planned by the famous James Brindley. It is this which gives it its river-like character and the well-deserved reputation of being one of the loveliest of our English canals. Its entire fifty-mile course from Napton to the Thames is virtually un-spoiled and rural, truly idyllic. Its thirty-eight locks (thirty-nine including the lock in Duke's Cut leading to the Thames) will take craft no larger than 7 ft in beam and 70 ft in length, and because of the many low bridges and lift-bridges will take craft with no more than 7 ft headroom. It is also very narrow and shallow and it is wise to keep dead centre while under way. Even so we went aground twice. We noticed workmen hedging and ditching, thus keeping the towpath clear, but dredging is all too infrequent as a single dredger has to be shared with the Northampton Arm.

Two miles from Napton Junction there is a sharp 90° bend, an attractive bridge, and Napton Bottom Lock, the first of a flight of nine. Although the locks on the Oxford Canal are operated by users, there is a lock-keeper on duty at Napton Bottom Lock, but his major task seems to be issuing warnings about the proper use of the locks. A fortnight before our arrival a working pair had slammed through the flight, twisting two lock gate rails, breaking two paddles and cracking a balance beam. This is all lovely countryside and after passing Napton on the Hill you will see very few dwellings and will hardly believe that throughout its length the canal is within easy reach of so many attractive villages, parks and interesting churches. This is Civil War country, rich in the history of the Cavaliers and Roundheads.

There will inevitably be days when the weather and everything else seems to go wrong, and our next day was dark and overcast, cheered only by a few bursts of sunshine. The water pump failed to switch itself off but a one-notch adjustment put that right. Then the sink became blocked. However, we found that by taking our coil of water hose, inserting it in the sink drain outlet just above the water line and giving a few hearty blows it was cleared. This is a very simple method and most effective. A 60 ft length is not necessary, a yard-long piece being sufficient, and should be taken as useful equipment.

Soon you will cross the Warwickshire-Oxfordshire border where the local brownstone gives villages a Cotswold-like appearance. From Bridge 135 a three-quarter-mile walk will bring you to Wormleighton and into Tudor England, with a lovely manor house, a 700-year-old church, and thatched cottages. This is a delightful hilltop village where stands the great gateway, gatehouse and cottages built for John Spencer in the reign of Henry VIII.

Fenny Compton is a little over a mile beyond the canalside George and Dragon but we found its name more attractive than the village itself. The canal now enters a cutting, still called the 'Tunnel', although the former tunnel was opened out as long ago as 1868 to save its being rebuilt. This is the longest straight stretch on the southern section and very pretty.

We were down the five Clayton Locks in under half an hour and in the next two miles went quickly through Elkington's, Varney's, Broadmoor and Cropredy Locks. There are many pleasant villages near the canal, including ancient Chipping Warden with its Roman remains and a church containing a 'leper squint'. Cropredy must be seen, however, and you can fill up your stores at the pretty village shop, obtain water at the coal yard, and wander through the village to look at the church which commemorates the Civil War battle of 1644 by displaying a collection of relics such as suits of armour and weapons. It also has a fine brass globe and eagle lectern.

The channel from Cropredy to Banbury is extremely shallow and although we eased off to almost crawling speed we went aground just above Bridge 157. However, some energetic poling soon had us off.

We arrived in Banbury by dinner time and found rather miserable moorings. What a pity that the town council filled in the canal basin to make a parking place, for it could have become the most attractive feature of the town. We felt that the once lovely town square had been ruined by modern shop fronts and that the local authorities made a mess of a town long famous for its Cross and its cakes. In 1790 the town blew up its ancient church rather than repair it and replaced it with a sombre substitute. Even the famous Cross was destroyed and the present one dates only from 1858. British Waterways is trying to improve facilities at Banbury by the construction of a marina there, part of the new Amenity Service Division's plans to develop the canals for pleasure in conjunction with private enterprise.

From Banbury the canal continues to be very shallow and we grounded above Grant's Lock. All the locks now have single gates in contrast to those above Banbury which have single top gates and double bottom ones. From Tarver's Lock a footpath leads to pretty Adderbury, a village with a sturdy church and a large medieval tithe barn close by. The Cherwell flows along the canal for miles south of Banbury and the countryside is mostly lovely meadows.

Aynho Weir Lock is an unusual diamond shape. We had

come across this type of lock before on the Lower Avon Navigation. The width is double that of the narrow boat lock and is built only where the rise or fall is small. The object of such a shape is to equate the amount of water passed with that of the ordinary deeper locks above it. Aynho Weir Lock has a fall of little more than 8 ins while Nell Bridge Lock above it falls 8 ft 8 ins and Somerton Deep Lock below it has a fall of 12 ft, the second deepest canal lock in this country.

The village of Aynho is most attractive with its typical Oxfordshire cottages and there is a beautiful view of the surrounding countryside from the church tower. We ran into weed beyond Aynho Weir Lock, near Somerton. This village keeps its church constantly locked and to get in you have to collect a huge key fastened to a massive truncheon from the local shop-cum-post-office opposite the church.

The thirteen miles from Somerton to Bridge 220 hard by Hampton Gay are the most beautiful along the entire canal with pleasant pastures and fields which were ripe with grain. There are delightful villages set back from the canal with fascinating names such as Steeple Aston, Fritwell and Duns Tew. At drawbridge 205, the only iron drawbridge in England, stands Heyford Mill, mentioned in the Domesday Book. Rebuilt in 1800, it stopped milling only after the Second World War. Eel-traps can still be seen here, for it once supplied the local manor with hundreds of eels. Both Upper and Lower Heyford are worth visiting for photography and shopping alike. Rousham House and Park, the gardens laid out by William Kent, and Blenheim Palace and Park, which needs no recommendation, are the next features of real merit along the canal.

Almost immediately after Baker's Lock, the Cherwell joins the canal for about half a mile and here the water is deep indeed. All too soon you will come to Shipton Weir Lock, another diamond-shaped one with a fall of little more than 2 ft.

Hampton Gay has a lonely church set in a field of buttercups, lit by candles and containing one of the few real barrel organs in the world. On the final stretch to Oxford, the canal is lovely right up to the British Waterways Juxton Road Wharf, where we reluctantly had to disembark the Pilkingtons who were going off to continue their cruise on *Thames Commodore* on the Moselle.

There are two ways to enter the Thames from the Oxford Canal. The shortest, easiest and prettiest is via Duke's Cut below Bridge 231, which brings you into the river above King's Lock; the other is the more difficult and exciting route via Isis or 'Louse' Lock, and a railway swing bridge below Fiddler's Island. This latter entry is three miles further on, may involve some delay and is little used, but there is a right of navigation which we, as a matter of principle, usually decide to exercise.

The Thames is broad and beautiful as you pass from the railway swing bridge into this once royal river at its downstream junction with the Oxford Canal. To traverse one of the loveliest of England's canals and one of the loveliest of her rivers in one cruise is perhaps the single most delightful aspect of the Grand Circle Tour.

The beauty and charm of the Thames, navigable for over 215 miles from Lechlade to the sea, lies in the eye of the beholder. This truly national river has a claim on the affections of the English everywhere as it has on all visitors and expatriates like myself who inevitably succumb to its lure. The Thames is all things to all men, its appeal is many-sided for it serves the varied interests of artists and writers, antiquarians and historians, naturalists and anglers, boaters and ramblers, swimmers and campers and others involved in specialised sports as well as those who, far from being marine-minded, nevertheless obtain enjoyment from just sitting in their cars along its banks.

We cruised briskly up to Godstow Lock and bought a return lock pass from Godstow to St John's Lock, near Lechlade. Next to the Norfolk Broads, more pleasure craft ply the Thames than any body of water in Britain, and as this was the high season we had decided to spend our weekend on the little used upper reaches. These lie above the ugly steel Osney Bridge, the lowest bridge anywhere on the Thames, with a headway of only 7 ft 7 ins at summer water level, thus precluding many craft from these lovely waters.

There are excellent moorings for the night just above the mellow stone Godstow bridge to port, almost opposite the Trout Inn with its peacocks and its fish leaping for tit-bits in the weir stream, and only a few steps from the ruins of Godstow nunnery. There is no point in casting off until shortly before 9 a.m. in the mornings for the manned locks do not open until then. We greatly enjoyed our run along the twenty-eight miles of rural Thames and ten locks to Lechlade, despite an incessant downpour. We stopped only once—for lunch at one of our favourite pubs, the Rose Revived, just downstream of Newbridge. Above King's Lock the river narrows considerably, is very winding with a number of horseshoe bends, and completely rural with only a few houses and pubs in view from the water. Its beauty is beyond description even through misty fog-like conditions. We had the river almost to ourselves for we passed fewer than half a dozen craft on the move and all under 25 ft. There are good and extensive moorings at Lechlade. Apart from its dominating church spire there is little of interest other than 'Halfpenny Bridge', an attractive stone structure built by an Act of Parliament in 1792, and so-called because of the toll levied here.

Although barges once made their way to Waterhay

Bridge the stream is now navigable only for canoes and skiffs as far as Cricklade. Experts still argue over whether the true source of the Thames is Seven Springs, at the head of the Churn, or the spring at the base of an ash tree in a pleasant meadow some three miles from Cirencester. Be that as it may, the willow-fringed rustic stream that is the Thames above Lechlade is well worth exploring on foot to find charming spots like Ashton Keynes with its host of little bridges.

It was a gloomy Sunday morning when we began our 155-mile cruise down the Thames to Greenwich Pier. Half a mile downstream we came to St John's Lock and Bridge, hard by an old riverside inn, the Trout, whose garden is constantly under attack from the weir stream. Soon we had bright sunshine, giving quite a different look to the pastoral scenes stretching for miles beyond each bank. Fishermen were more numerous than cattle and from the number of fish we saw landed it must have been a most successful day for them too. The next lock, Buscot, is one of the deepest on the river, some 9 ft with a charming Cotswold cottage for a lock house, leased to the Thames Conservancy by the National Trust. The river meanders peacefully along, scarcely 30 ft wide, through winding reaches, continually building up shoals which are more or less marked by floating buoys. Lonely isolated Grafton Lock stands amid flat green fields, the only sign of civilisation being the lock-keeper's house.

After another mile of lovely river on which stands Kelmscot Manor, the home of William Morris, Radcot Bridge appears, spanning two arms of the river. This is actually two bridges, the one over the former main stream built in 1200 being the oldest on the Thames, and the second over the current navigational course built in 1787 to span the newly dug channel. Alongside the newer bridge is the delightfully unspoiled Swan Inn, noted for its fine collection of fish decorating the bars, all caught locally, and for its beautiful garden.

At Radcot Lock, half a mile below the bridges, is the first of the Thames Conservancy Sanitary Stations. Many locks and some boathouses have these facilities, which are largely responsible for the absence of flotsam and jetsam and litter on the non-tidal Thames. The Thames Conservancy which is responsible for over 135 miles of river from Cricklade to Teddington and its catchment area (nearly 2,500 miles of tributaries and subsidiary streams) does an excellent job. The waters within their jurisdiction are beautifully clean. Boaters are not allowed to use flush toilets or even drain washing-up water into the river. While slightly inconvenient this is a splendid measure appreciated by all who live beside the Thames or use it in any way.

Below Radcot Lock the gaunt Old Man's footbridge straddles the stream, marking the site of a former flash weir of the same name. At Rushey Lock there is a splendid garden kept by the lock-keeper. The lock garden competition, with the Sir Reginald Hanson Challenge Cup as the prize, is indeed an inspiration contributing greatly to the natural beauty of the river. You will soon pass Tenfoot Footbridge, which apparently leads to nowhere in particular, and the village of Chimney on the left bank, once called Chimley, which explains why some country folk still mispronounce the word. There are suitable lunch-time moorings in the lovely cut leading to Shifford Lock. Although the lock and cut were built comparatively recently, in 1896, nature has healed all the scars and created worthy scenes to admire. Newbridge, actually one of the oldest, dating back with its name to the thirteenth century, is the next identifiable spot, site of the attractively named The Rose Revived, and boasting a second inn, the Maybush, on the opposite bank. Find a bridge on the

Thames and you will usually find a pub, sometimes two or more. Just above Newbridge the River Windrush adds its waters, and scarcely a mile away is Ridge's footbridge, marking the site of Hart's Weir. In the upper reaches, we are told, footbridges inevitably indicate that weirs once existed on the site.

At the next lock, Northmoor, the weir adjoins the lock and provides a unique opportunity to look at the construction and operation of a weir. A weir is an artificial dam built across the river to maintain its water at a certain minimum height, known as head water level. This is done by means of weir tackle at the top of the dam, regulated according to the flow of water. Some two pretty winding miles beyond Northmoor Lock stands the Chequers Inn and here is the last ferry on the Thames, Bablockhythe Ferry, big enough to transport cars and yet operated by chain, pulled by hand. This chain stretches taut across the river when in use and is lowered to the bed of the river when the ferry is not working.

The scenery now is hilly as the river curves to Eynsham (Swinford) Bridge, with Whitchurch, one of the last two toll bridges remaining on the Thames, and Eynsham Lock. There are excellent moorings here for the Swan Hotel and Talbot Inn and shopping in Eynsham. For a modest fee the Thames Conservancy allows camping on the lock island here and at four other lock sites, Pinkhill, King's, Godstow and Day's Lock. With extensive woodland on your right you will soon reach an island, and the Thames has more lovely islands than any other river in the country. Mooring once again above Godstow Bridge we calculated actual cruising time from Lechlade to be just under seven hours, every moment of it thoroughly enjoyable.

From Godstow Lock, where we bought a lock pass to Teddington, there is a lovely view of the spires of Oxford across Port Meadow, which is seemingly oblivious of time.

This broad reach is a favourite one for sailing and rowing. As you come to the little village of Binsey and the Perch Inn you now follow the main stream to the right of Fiddler's Island, the left branch leading to the main entrance of the Oxford Canal. Beyond the low Osney Bridge there are moorings convenient to the market and the railway station, and from here you can easily explore the many famous sights of Oxford. Between Osney and Folly Bridges the Thames is undoubtedly sordid. Oxford, one of the most interesting and beautiful cities in Britain, should be ashamed of its treatment of the Thames, which is frankly disgraceful.

Once Folly Bridge is passed, the river comes to life again. From the remaining wharf and boathouses it is evident that commercial traffic once heavily plied the Thames. Salter Brothers boatyard and offices are here and have run a seasonal river steamer service between Oxford and Kingston since 1888. The new university boat houses are splendid and the river looks lovelier than ever as you cruise on past Christ Church Meadow, the entrance of the Cherwell river, and past the remaining college barges to Iffley Lock.

Hire cruiser yards now appear on every reach. After Sandford Lock, the deepest on the river with its paper mill and nearby King's Arms Hotel, you will come once again into open country. You can ease off as you pass Nuneham Park to watch the deer. There are pleasant moorings between two willows on the right bank above Abingdon Bridge, hard by the municipal swimming pools and the remains of Abingdon Abbey. The delicate spire of St Helen's Church and the surrounding almshouses are beautiful and you will find Abingdon well worth the hours you spend there. The Crown and Thistle, dating back to 1605, is an enchanting creeper-covered hotel with a delightful courtyard in which to enjoy a tankard.

A little further downstream the River Ock joins the Thames very near the one-time entrance to the derelict Wilts & Berks canal, which once passed by Wantage, Swindon and Calne to join the Kennet & Avon some twelve miles east of Bradford. The short Culham reach soon branches left into the long and narrow Culham Cut leading to the lock, while the weir stream, well worth visiting, flows along to the pretty village of Sutton Courtenay to fall over a series of modernised weirs into beautiful Sutton Pools. At Clifton there is a similar long lock cut and the reaches become increasingly lovely. Beyond Clifton Lock, a red brick bridge, once a toll bridge for the old toll house which can still be seen on the right, leads to Clifton Hampden and the Plough Inn on the left, and to the half-timbered, thatched-roof Barley Mow Inn of *Three Men in a Boat* fame.

There are now open meadows and woodlands as you pass Burcot. The wide sweep of the river as it approaches Day's Lock make the Sinodun Hills, or Wittenham Clumps as they are called locally, look as if they are on the move. From Day's Lock there is a pleasant mile-long track skirting the ancient Dyke Hills to Dorchester, a delightful town with an Abbey church as interesting as its coaching inns. The lovely reach between Benson's and Cleeve locks is the longest on the Thames, some $6\frac{1}{2}$ miles, and then the first really attractive Thames-side houses appear on the short half-mile reach between Cleeve and Goring, one of our favourite stretches of river with lovely wooded islands. Goring and Streatley are twin villages, joined by a bridge, with the attractive Swan Inn on one side and the historic Miller of Mansfield on the other. The Lower Hartslock woods are decidedly impressive on their hilly site and Whitchurch Lock is very pretty indeed, looking much as it did in etchings in books published over a century ago. The second toll bridge on the Thames just below the lock links Whitchurch and Pangbourne, the former peaceful and picturesque, the latter bustlingly commercial. The little islands in the next 2½ miles long reach are clearly popular with campers. Mapledurham Lock, the first to be mechanised on the upper reaches, is electrically operated and we were through in less than three minutes, compared with an average of eight minutes for the locks upstream. Historic Mapledurham House, the mill and a church used for both Protestant and Roman Catholic services, are the highlights of the area. After more pleasant riverside houses and gardens, industrial Reading rears its ugly head, as if to vie with Oxford.

However, the beauty of Sonning makes you quickly forget Reading and the lock garden backed by trees is enchanting. Sonning is almost invisible from the river and a charming port of call. The path to the Bull Hotel leads through a churchyard, the best kept we have seen anywhere, and the church itself has a lovely carved wooden entrance porch. The reach to Shiplake is like an oasis of peace with views of pleasant fields and gentle hills. Near Shiplake a series of wooded islands adds to the charm. This lock works hydraulically, a system which is proving superior to electricity. Moorings can be found at the George and Dragon at Wargrave, whose inn sign is surprisingly the work of two Royal Academicians.

Another chain of attractive eyots lies in the reach to pretty Marsh Lock, and it is only a fifteen-minute run to Henley on a wide reach dotted with more islands. There are good Council moorings above the five-arched Henley Bridge with its two sculptured heads of Isis and Father Thames and also at the Angel Hotel which, with the church tower, dominates the left bank by the bridge. The town's long main street is almost as attractive as the river here and useful for shopping.

The famous Henley Regatta course, dead straight for

a mile and a half between Phyllis Court and Temple Island, was deserted except for Canadian geese as we cruised by in the early morning. After a very sharp right hand bend we were at lovely Hambleden Lock with its beautiful weir stretching back to the white mill in a wonderful play of falling water. The 3½ mile reach to Hurley Lock is also one of our favourites, beautifully wooded, dotted with islands with overhanging trees and crowned by the picturesque Medmenham Abbey. What an ideal spot Sir Francis Dashwood and his Hell Fire Club chose for their orgies. There is a glimpse of chalk cliffs before the entrance to Hurley Lock cut and another typical Thames view unchanged in over a century. Here half a dozen islands provide peaceful moorings from which to visit the famous Olde Belle.

Twenty minutes more of blissful cruising brings you to Marlow with its recently rebuilt suspension bridge. This bridge with the tall spire of Marlow's church on one side and the Compleat Angler and vast curving weir on the other, makes Marlow one of the most delightful spots on the Thames. Just above the bridge is Meakes Boatyard and chandlery, one of the best in the country. There are now a succession of delightful reaches and locks, Marlow, Cookham, Boulters, Bray, Boveney, Romney and Old Windsor, to good overnight moorings at the Bells of Ouzeley. Cliveden reach, between Cookham and Boulter's locks, is the loveliest of them all.

We felt inclined to carry on and did so, feeling that this is one of the nice things about a boating holiday. We by-passed Maidenhead which we have never found particularly interesting, and even Windsor, which we decided to reserve for a return visit next morning. Windsor has unfortunately become a 'tourist trap' with only the castle and park attractive. There were far too many shoddy souvenir shops for our liking.

Beyond the Bells of Ouzeley, whose original bells were thrown into the river at the Dissolution and eventually replaced with bells of Bristol glass now on view in the bar, is Magna Carta island and Runnymede with its hill-top R.A.F. memorial and, at the foot of Cooper's Hill, the American memorial to the signing of the Magna Carta and the British Memorial to President Kennedy. Factories straddle the riverside through Staines, but just before Rennie's bridge, on the left bank in a recreation ground a few yards from the river, stands the famous London Stone, surrounded by railings, and marking what was once the upstream limit of jurisdiction of the City of London before the Thames Conservators took over in 1857. This most historic stone bears a worn inscription— 'God preserve the City of London A.D. 1280.' It functions today as a mark for the upstream limit of free fishing. From Staines into London the river becomes rather heavily populated with houses and bungalows in almost every conceivable type of architecture. Penton Hook Yacht Basin on the right bank is without doubt one of the finest and best equipped inland harbours in Britain. Over 500 craft can be moored in its eighty acres of sheltered water connected to the river by a deep channel. Good use is made of the islands on the pleasant reach to Shepperton Lock for there are communities of bungalows and weekend cottages here, all tidily kept and clearly enjoyed. This lock and the entrance to the pretty little River Wey below it delights the eye and makes an ideal overnight mooring.

The river now is not as scenic or appealing as the upper reaches but there are some rather charming spots, such as Sunbury, and also Hampton Court. The run through Kingston brings civilisation but in contrast a regatta was under way as we approached Teddington Lock, the end of the non-tidal Thames and snug overnight moorings.

CHAPTER 10

LONDON'S WATERWAYS

TEDDINGTON LOCK is something of a misnomer for there are actually three locks—a large barge lock, 650 ft x 24 ft 9 ins, a launch lock, 177 ft 11 ins x 24 ft 4 ins and similar in size to the upriver locks, and a 'coffin' lock, 49 ft 6 ins x 5 ft 10 ins for small craft.

Teddington marks the limit of the tidal waters of the Thames. Above the locks the river is placid and quiet, while below the locks tides are as relentless as time and it is evident that anyone who ventures on to a tideway in a small boat must have his wits about him.

Hire firms will normally allow amateurs to take hire craft through Teddington Lock for some four miles to Brentford, opposite Kew Palace, where locks lead into the Grand Union Canal. The use of the lock at Brentford Dock is regulated by the state of the tide and you should consult the lock-keeper at Teddington or the British Waterways Board at Brentford (01 560 8941) to ensure that you arrive at this lock at the right state of the tide. High water here is one hour later than at London Bridge and the locks operate a few hours before and after high water.

If you buy Stanford's Chart of the Lower Thames and follow the course duly marked on it carefully, you should have no difficulty with this stretch of the tideway. On your first experience of a tideway, never attempt to moor. A wall which looks perfect for mooring when you see it at high water may have 20 ft less water beside it when the tide goes out. Always give a wide berth to other craft on the move or at anchor as well as to bridge arches, for you can be sucked against them if you go too close. A good rule for beginners on a tideway is to keep six feet away from everything except when entering or leaving a lock.

Passing through Brentford Lock, the Grand Union will take you through eleven more locks, including the Hanwell flight for six miles to the Bulls Bridge junction with the Paddington Arm which in turn gives access to the Regent's Canal. This is the simplest and easiest way to explore London's own canal from the Thames. We had special permission to take the *Golden Eye* through the heart of London and into the Regent's Canal from its other end at Regent's Canal Dock, some eighteen miles downstream of Teddington. We can strongly recommend this itinerary to any enthusiast with sufficient practical experience.

However, there are complications in using this route. The distance between Teddington and Brentford is so short that you can leave Teddington on the tide and have ample time to get into Thames Lock No. 101 before it closes. Even if you have to cruise the four miles against the tide it is no problem. But as Regent's Canal Dock is much further than this and high water is over an hour earlier than at Teddington, it is impossible for a slow-moving small craft to catch the tide and arrive at the Dock in time to use the tidal lock there. In order to arrive when the lock is in operation means bucking the tide and making a much slower journey with greater fuel consumption.

To benefit from the tide involves arranging overnight moorings at Greenwich Pier (which are very bumpy) and passing through both Regent's Dock Lock and Regent's

Canal next morning; intricate calculations are necessary to make sure timings are accurate.

On the Brentford route the best time to leave Teddington is shortly after high water there, which will enable you to by-pass the half-tidal Richmond Lock, used only between half-ebb and full flood. Soon after the water reaches the half-tide mark patent sluices stretching across the river beside the lock are drawn and boats can pass freely until about two hours after high water. The tide will increase your speed by two to three knots and you will be exhilarated by the surge before you pass the obelisk on the Surrey shore, 300 yards below Teddington Lock, which marks the beginning of the jurisdiction of the Port of London Authority, stretching ninety miles to the sea. Here, 136 miles from the source of the Thames, the Port of London somewhat surprisingly encroaches. We had always assumed it began at London Docks, near Tower Bridge, the furthest upstream of the five great dock systems owned by the P.L.A. But this body controls the whole of the tidal reaches, handles all matters relating to navigation on the tideway, the licensing of wharves and structures extending into the river below high water mark, and the maintenance of the broad approach channel from the estuary into the heart of the port.

It is Britain's premier port and one of the busiest in the world with something like 100 million tons of shipping passing through annually, with cargoes totalling upwards of 60 million tons. Apart from the five great dock systems on both sides of the river, there are many hundreds of privately owned wharves and factories, power stations, gas works, oil depots, sugar refineries, cold stores, granaries, barge building yards, dry-docking facilities and so on, which play an important part in the trade of the port. It is constantly changing, indeed facilities are moving closer and closer to the sea, as the use of large containers and other modern developments alter the pattern and nature of water transport. However, in spite of modernisation, the river banks through London remain overcrowded with history.

The water is dirty and brown as compared with the upper reaches and vast quantities of debris drift along at the whim of the tide. Evasive action must frequently be taken to avoid damage to propellers. But the river has a stark beauty of its own. You will notice that the Surrey shore is still pleasantly rural while attractive gardens and houses can be seen on the left bank. Past Eel Pie Island, once famous for its eel pies, you will see yacht clubs, cruiser clubs and boatyards as you approach Richmond Bridge and the open sluices under the narrow footbridge. Past Isleworth Eyot you may get waves from cheerful crowds taking the sun by the old London Apprentice, one of London's most charming riverside pubs. Syon Reach is as beautiful as any upstream with the gardens of Kew stretching almost to Kew Bridge, while on the left Syon House still stands majestically in its park, followed all too quickly by the Brentford entrance to the Grand Union Canal. Turning left here brings you to new locks which were mechanised and enlarged in 1962 to take barges of up to 175 tons. It is wise to keep an eye open for commercial traffic and the lock-keeper will tell you what to do.

The Thames down river of this point is a tremendous thrill which you can look forward to seeing another time. Every reach and bend provides a unique glimpse of what London once was and what it is today. The blending of old and new along the river is by no means incongruous and provides an unusual history lesson. We were surprised to find that London's bridges varied so much, being built of stone, iron, steel or concrete, some with only three arches and others with seven, some ornate and colourful and others plain, and with clearances at high water ranging from 14 ft 3 ins at Hammersmith to 140 ft 9 ins at Tower Bridge with the bascules up.

Towering concrete and glass skyscrapers vie with the Gothic Houses of Parliament and ancient Lambeth Palace; pleasure gardens compete with power plants; modern Festival Hall and the South Bank contrast strangely with ageing warehouses beyond Blackfriars. Cleopatra's Needle, St Paul's, the Tower of London and Tower Bridge stand out in all their splendour from the river while picturesque Wapping Old Stairs, the Angel and the Prospect of Whitby can really be appreciated only from the water. And then there is the clutter of shipping of all kinds from all parts of the world, dashing trip boats and ferries, fast-moving P.L.A. and police launches along with tooting tugs towing nests of lighters. Dockland with its batteries of cranes is nothing short of spectacular, an education in itself. From Teddington to the dry-docked *Cutty Sark* at Greenwich Pier took us just $3\frac{1}{2}$ hours at one-third throttle, an afternoon one can never forget.

The Thames was as busy as Hyde Park Corner at rush hour with scores of tugs and lighters on the move, huge freighters and even a Wilson Line ocean-going vessel when we left Greenwich Pier as *Gipsy Moth IV* arrived that August Monday. We bobbed about like a tiny cork in the cross wash over the two-mile run and after twenty exciting minutes we swung to starboard up to Regent's Canal Dock and heaved lines over our heads to the bollards on the quayside. The dockmaster, Mr McLean, gave us priority treatment and we locked through with a timber barge in under fifteen minutes. Few people are aware of the huge basin inside the locks which will take craft up to 300 ft in length, 45 ft beam and 16 ft draught. From the basin there was, until recently, a regular service of ships to and from the Continent.

We had to wait for about fifteen minutes while two workmen pushed and shoved half a dozen timber barges out of the way so that we could lock into the Regent's Canal. The lock-keeper quickly ushered us through and as we thanked him a colleague set out along the towpath on a miniature tractor to prepare the next locks for us. This was a most unusual and unexpected service, performed most cheerfully. Beyond the first four locks, on the starboard side, is one of the shortest canals in the world, the Hertford Union, only $1\frac{1}{2}$ miles long. Also known as Duckett's Canal, after a previous owner, it was completed in 1830 to link the Lee Navigation and the Regent's Canal, which technically is an arm of the Grand Union. Duckett's Canal has three locks and for most of its length borders on Victoria Park, one of the East End's largest public parks. It is inevitably filled with timber barges. For this reason we had chosen the Regent's Dock entrance instead of the adjacent Limehouse Cut or Bow Creek entrance, $2\frac{1}{2}$ miles downstream. Today Limehouse Cut is abandoned but a new arm leads from Regent's Dock basin into the Lee Navigation.

The East End and City sections of the Regent's Canal are like something out of another age, comparable to entering a familiar home through an untidy and unfamiliar back door. It has to be seen to be believed for even Londoners are largely unaware of its existence. After City Road Basin comes Islington tunnel, which passes under the Angel at Islington. This is a narrow tunnel without a towpath, just 960 yards long, and the first of four on the run to Braunston from the Thames. Just beyond St Pancras Lock—and how different this part of London looks from the water—is British Waterways' St Pancras Yacht Basin, on the port side and skirting the marshalling yards. Once used for unloading coal it was allowed to become derelict and then wisely, in 1958, was reconstructed as a permanent harbour for pleasure craft.

Kentish Town and Hawley Locks follow, both original examples of the double locks on this canal. The narrow boat *Jenny Wren*, which takes both adults and school children on educational cruises, is moored below Chalk Farm Road bridge. At Hampstead Lock, the last on the canal, the original lock-keeper's house still stands in proud and arrogant neglect. Beyond it a green cast-iron tow-horse bridge swinging diagonally across the canal is yet another tribute to the elegance of canal architecture. Then at a sharp right turn under a bridge lies Cumberland Basin, near the Regent's Park Zoo. The manager of the Barque and Bite, an excellent floating restaurant permanently moored in the basin, was most helpful in hauling on ropes to enable us to berth in the space normally used by a 15 ft launch.

That night we had a party with some seventeen friends joining us for cocktails aboard the *Golden Eye* in the basin. As the party warmed up everyone insisted on a short cruise, so we had a hilarious three-mile run past the Zoo to Little Venice and back during which we passed the famous *Jason* and the Zoo waterbuses, and explained to our guests why the iron bridge at North Gate, Regent's Park, is called 'Blow-up Bridge'. Fifty-four years after the canal was completed in 1820, a boat laden with gunpowder blew up under the bridge. The tree at the southeast corner of the bridge still bears the marks of the explosion. The original bridge, together with the boat and boatmen, was destroyed by the explosion, but the iron stanchions were salvaged and used again, and were erected back to front. Towline marks are still visible on the 'wrong' sides of the stanchions. Since 1874 boatmen have always called this 'Blow-up Bridge'.

The Regent's Canal is only a little over eight miles long and it is the last mile to Little Venice that is the most attractive, taking you through the Zoo and under Maida Hill tunnel, unexpectedly topped by houses. The canal in its present state is hardly a holiday venue but in recent years a number of voluntary bodies, local authorities and groups of enthusiasts have been campaigning for a 'face-lift' for the Regent's Canal and the Paddington Arm. More recently still, the London Chamber of Commerce, in its official journal, added its influential voice to the demand for urgent action to improve these waterways, insisting that London could have stretches of canal as beautiful as those in Amsterdam if only more attention was paid to them. Westminster City Council and the G.L.C. have taken some steps to improve some areas of the canal but there is tremendous scope for further action. A Thames barrage to exclude the tide and danger from flooding has now been suggested and this would transform the Thames through London. Welcome as piecemeal improvements are, it is, however, high time that London began seriously to consider the needs that increasing leisure will demand. Our London waterways taken together offer most promising and rewarding prospects for meeting at least a part of these needs.

Swinging hard to starboard at Little Venice you enter the Paddington Arm of the Grand Union, $13\frac{3}{4}$ miles long without a single lock to Bulls Bridge, where it joins the main line of the Grand Union Canal. This stretch is dingy, dirty, and bordered by slum housing, coal and timber yards, rubbish dumps and run-down factories relieved only by Sudbury Golf Course and the odd pub like the Black Horse at Old Field Lane Bridge.

There is a completely different atmosphere after you pass under a humped towpath bridge and turn sharp to starboard at Bulls Bridge into the Grand Union main line. From Denham Lock it is well worth visiting the delightful old-world village here, with its fine fourteenth-century church, pleasant inn and lovely houses. The canal side becomes attractive once more and along these pounds you will come across names like Benbow Way and Black Jack's Lock, inexplicable links with the sea. Black Jack's is pretty but the next lock, Copper Mill, is lovelier still for here the River Colne makes one of its junctions with the canal.

Through a weedy section of canal to Rickmansworth, and then comes Cassiobury Park. Here Watford maintains some 900 acres of enchanting parkland. The park was once the home of the Earls of Essex and has long been a beauty spot on the banks of the River Gade, which flows alongside the canal. There are children's playgrounds, a paddling pool and miniature railway in the park and in fine weather this is a superb place for a picnic. The Gade flows into or alongside the canal all the way to Hemel Hempstead and there seems to be a glut of weirs. The locks become more numerous as they form a long flight of steps carrying the canal over the Chiltern Hills. The Fishery Inn at Bridge 149 near Boxmoor is a good place to stop for a 'bargee sandwich', a triple decker filled with bacon, egg, cheese, tomato, lettuce, mayonnaise and pickle. This inn combines beauty with good service and reasonable prices.

The canal then goes through pleasant countryside to the swing bridge hard by the Three Horseshoes, and then the pounds become shorter and shorter as the ascent through the Chilterns grows steeper. There are in fact eighteen locks in under seven miles but the hard work has its compensation in the beauty of the wooded rolling countryside, and pleasant moorings at the Cowroast at Lock 46. From here it is only a five-minute bus ride to Tring for shopping and sightseeing. The Rothschild collection of crustacea, reptiles, fish, moths, butterflies and rare insects at Tring is one of the finest in the world and is open to the public. There are interesting medieval earthworks at Berkhamstead near the castle, as well as ancient inns and homes dating from the fifteenth century. At Northchurch, a mile from Berkhamstead and connected to the town by the ancient and mysterious rampart known as Grims Dyke, is one of the oldest and most delightful churches in the world, dating from Saxon times. A walk into the countryside from here will give you splendid views of the Chilterns.

This is one of the three summit levels, some 400 ft above the level at Brentford. There are now very pretty tree-shaded stretches and within an hour you will reach the disused Wendover Arm and the Marsworth Seven, the last of the locks before the junction with the Aylesbury Arm. The Marsworth Seven is a place for bird watchers for all along on the left are reservoirs populated by many rare species. From here Ivinghoe Beacon can be visited where you will find some of the most beautiful views in the country.

Next morning we reached the *Golden Eye*'s base at Aylesbury and the crew all agreed that the 367 miles and 235 locks of the 'Grand Circle' had been a wonderful experience.

CHAPTER 11

LOOPING THE MIDLANDS LOOP

THE COTSWOLD glass swing door between the dining room and kitchen of our new home in Highgate has on the dining room side a huge wooden handle into which has been carefully embedded and covered with plexiglass an irregularly rectangular piece of slate about 12 ins x 3½ ins. It is one of the most unusual door handles in the world, for this particular piece of slate was picked up high in the Welsh hills near the magnificent Pontcysyllte Aqueduct on the Llangollen Canal about dawn one morning a few years ago by Dr Roger Pilkington in the course of a pre-breakfast walk. On this piece of slate he inscribed:

> MS Aylesbury Golden Eye
> Captain—Fred Doerflinger
>   July—August 1967
>
> Market Harboro'
> Anderton
> Ellesmere Port
> Pontcysyllte
> Autherley
> Leicester
> Market Harboro'
>   RP

This slate briefly outlines a wonderful 700-lock-mile holiday cruise which we refer to as looping the Midlands loop of waterways. Your inland waterways map will show you that this journey forms a massive irregular figure '8' over the Midlands on to which is added the wide sweeping curve of the Llangollen Canal probing into Wales. It embraces eight canals and three river navigations in no less than ten counties and covers $428\frac{1}{2}$ miles of waterway with 268 locks, the only waterways lift in the country, as well as the most spectacular aqueducts and tunnels anywhere in the world. The enthusiast could happily plan three to four separate holidays over this journey, yet the full itinerary is a realistic target with three weeks to a month to spend on it. Our total cruising time was 176 hours and 51 minutes and we averaged 3·93 lock miles per hour for a normal cruising day of 8 hours and 25 minutes.

As we did not want to repeat the familiar Grand Union run from Aylesbury to Braunston, we arranged to board the *Golden Eye* at the basin boatyard at Market Harborough instead of its then home port of Aylesbury Basin. The pretty little town of Market Harborough lies at the end of a completely rural $5\frac{1}{2}$-mile long canal arm with no locks. At first the tortuously winding arm is shallow and a bit weedy but it widens after Bridge 13 and you can cruise at normal speed past glowing fields of grain and along quiet wooded stretches of waterway.

There is pleasant mooring above Bridge 3 at Foxton for a visit to the village where John of Gaunt was once lord of the manor. A hillside church commands a view of cottages and orchards but the village has only one claim to fame, the nearby Foxton Flight, one of the outstanding engineering triumphs of the nineteenth century. We moored for the night in the large basin below Foxton Bottom Lock as we wanted to pass through the flight of ten locks, which has a rise of 75 ft, in daylight. Built on the Brindley pattern, arranged in two staircase formations, and numbered 8-17, each 7 ft wide lock has its own side pond and there is a meeting pond between locks 12 and 13 which allows craft to pass each other. It normally takes about ninety minutes to lock up, but if the lock-keeper helps, you can, as we did, navigate the flight in under the hour. This is admittedly tiring and because of this in 1900 an ingenious lift was constructed alongside the locks on an inclined plane to reduce passage time to only twenty minutes. This inclined plane was 300 ft long with a rise of 75 ft, having twin tanks or caissons running on rails. The two tanks, connected by a wire rope, each taking two narrow boats or a barge, ran sideways on eight sets of wheels carried on four pairs of rails. It cost just under £40,000 with the land and was of the counter-balanced type, using a steam-driven winch to overcome friction. Opened for traffic in July 1900, it was sound enough in principle but was built before its time in the sense that only steam power was then available to operate the winch. This meant keeping steam up on the boiler continuously, and with commercial traffic falling off, this soon proved uneconomic. By November 1908 it was decided to rein-state the locks, originally built in 1812, to pass traffic at night when the inclined plane was not working. Two years later it ceased operation and all traffic has since used the locks. The machinery of the inclined plane was allowed to rust away until 1926 when it was dismantled and sold in 1928 for only £250. Nature was then allowed to reclaim the site and today you would never dream that one of the wonders of the canal system ever stood here. The Foxton Flight is as attractive a sight today as can be found on canals anywhere. The view from the top is one that you will never forget.

Once up the flight you are on the summit pound 412 ft above sea level. The Leicester section of the Grand Union Canal looks down on valleys dotted with farm houses, barns and grazing cattle in meadows between rolling hills. There is a wealth of bird life from hawks to warblers and finches. The reed-lined canal is rather weedy but there is ample water to maintain normal cruising speed. It takes a wide and gentle sweep around the hills, giving view after view, all unspoilt, for no villages lie on the canal at all, although many are within easy walking distance.

It is two hours' cruising with panoramic views all the way before you reach the 1,166 yard long Husband's Bosworth tunnel. Although completed in 1813 it has not a single drip to dampen your quarter of an hour passage through. The nearby village has both religion and witch-craft to commend it to history. It is the birthplace of Henry 'Silver-tongued' Smith, that most eloquent of Elizabethan preachers, and the home of John Duport, a local rector who was one of the makers of the Authorised Version of the Bible. At the same time the village is notorious for one of the cruellest and most tragic stories of witchcraft in English history. One morning in 1616 nine women were executed as witches because some poor boy had a series of epileptic fits. Six more women were convicted of being 'hostages to Satan' and provoking these fits, sentenced to death, but later fortunately reprieved.

Between Husband's Bosworth and the 1,528 yard long Crick Tunnel is another beautiful stretch as you pass the derelict Welford Arm and along an aqueduct over the River Avon. There are hours of peaceful chugging along, each bend bringing yet more delightful views. The first few hundred yards of Crick Tunnel leak very badly, and it has always been a problem. When the engineer, Benjamin Bevan, completed the Foxton Flight he found that the line of his proposed tunnel at Crick went through unfavourable strata including quicksand. A new line had to be adopted and the present tunnel was built at an extra cost of over £7,000.

Crick village and the Red Lion are within easy walking distance. This was the home for the last fourteen years of his life of George Smith of Coalville, a brickworker, born in poverty at Clayhills in Staffordshire in 1831. Smith did more for canal folk than any man in history. After little more than a year's schooling he was put in the brick-fields, working thirteen to fifteen hours a day for a meagre wage of 6*d*. His biographer, Edwin Hodder, describes his youth and early manhood as 'commonplace'. He married twice, had two sons, managed several small brickyards and made the first blue bricks and sanitary ware in his part of the country. This would have been George Smith's story had he not begun the series of one-man crusades to help under-privileged children. In 1868 he wrote his first letter to the newspapers about the plight of brickyard children. He kept up a constant bombardment of letters to the press and by 1871 had published *Cry of the Children from the Brickyards of England*. This forced Parliament to pass regulations concerning the employment of children in the nation's brickyards. He then turned his attention to the plight of gypsies and again got the government to take remedial action.

Smith's movement to aid the canal population began with a letter to the London and provincial press in October 1873. By this time he knew how to whip up public opinion and waged a nation-wide 'Letters to the Editor' campaign which he adroitly followed up by lobbying Members of Parliament and ministers. He alone was responsible for the Canal Boats Act of 1877 regulating boat-life and securing some education for the waterways children. In his fascinating book *Our Canal Population* he ruthlessly exposed the dreadful plight of canal folk, emphasising that in the 1870s over 100,000 men, women and children lived and worked on the 4,170 miles of river and canal network in a state of wretchedness, misery, immorality and cruelty. There were some 22,400 men, some working in threes and operating the fast non-stop 'flyboats', others who were traditional boatmen, and still others known as 'Rodneys' or 'loafers', that is helpers. There were over 22,000 women, of whom 13,000 were living with but were not married to the men whose life they shared on the waterways. Of the 72,000 canal children, some 40,000 were illegitimate and fewer than 2,000 went to school. Smith's figures may not have been completely accurate but they certainly represented the most intelligent estimate made at the time. None of these canal families had homes on land. The average family of four or five, and often as many as twelve, shared a narrow boat cabin only 6 ft x 7 ft 6 ins x 4 ft 6 ins or some 202 cubic feet in size. The cabins were 'damp, hot, stuffy, buggy, filthy and stinking holes', according to Smith, who walked and went on the boats on many stretches of canals in his investigations. One canal woman told him she had not slept on land for twenty years, another was quoted as admitting to giving birth to twenty-one children in the same cabin.

At that time a 70 ft narrow or 'monkey' boat cost between £100 and £130, could carry 30 tons and could be expected to last about twenty years. The average speed for these horse-drawn craft was a mere 2 miles per hour, and there were some 25,000 on the waterways network. Wages were low. The men earned between sixteen and twenty shillings per week and with his entire family hard at work they might get as much as twenty-three to twenty-four shillings. Over 95 per cent of the boatmen could not read or write, some 90 per cent could be classed as drunkards, and less than 2 per cent were members of a Christian church. In short, boatmen and their families lived and behaved almost like animals until Smith, a

pioneer of social welfare, succeeded in getting legislation
to improve their miserable and unhappy lot.

It is only a mile from Crick Tunnel to the graceful
Watford Flight. Here, within sight of the M1, are seven
narrow locks in under half a mile with a total fall of 52 ft
6 ins. Like those of the Foxton Flight they have side ponds.
Numbers 7, 2 and 1 are the usual type of locks with
individual top and bottom gates. Numbers 3 to 6 are
staircase locks which, it should be pointed out, share gates
so that the top gate of one lock is the bottom gate of the
lock above.

After leaving the long and lovely twenty-mile pound
between Foxton and Watford Flights, one of the highest
stretches of navigable waterway in Britain, you will be
360 ft above sea level for the final two-mile run to the
swing bridge at Norton Junction and the deeper water of
the Grand Union main line.

It is less than half an hour's cruise along the
Northamptonshire heights to the 2,042 yard, bat-
occupied Braunston Tunnel, another difficult feat of
engineering for the canal builders. Quicksand caused
delays and extra expenditure here too, added to which a
contractor made a miscalculation in direction so that the
tunnel, which was opened in June 1796, has a slight S
bend in it. I never travel through Braunston Tunnel without recalling 'Ben the Legger'. He was discovered by
George Smith in 1880, at which time Ben was in his
seventies. Smith reported that Ben had been legging boats
through the tunnel for over fifty years. 'He legged—lay
on his back upon a narrow board about 12 in wide and 3 ft
long, overhanging the side of the deck, called a "wing",
and worked a boat along with his feet between 50,000
and 60,000 miles, or twice round the world, through this
watery and ghastly cavern of black midnight darkness',
is how Smith succinctly summed up Ben's career.

It is six locks to Braunston Junction, the Blue Line Marina and the Rose and Castle. Here you turn right into the Northern Arm of the Oxford Canal and an important chapter of canal history. It took over twenty-five years to create the vast network of canals linking the major rivers of the country, of which the Oxford Canal is an integral part, and that great canal engineer, James Brindley, master-minded most of them, laying out no less than 523 miles of waterway.

But built over such a long period of time by different companies, employing different engineers, frequently hampered by lack of funds, subjected to alterations in line as still more canals mushroomed in the wake of changing trade patterns, the canals of the 'cross' were not uniform in gauge and some canals even varied in architecture from section to section.

As you cruise along the Northern Arm of the Oxford you will find it quite different from the idyllic, narrow and twisting Southern Arm. The canal is much wider and straighter for between 1829 and 1834 the contour route was shortened by $12\frac{1}{2}$ miles at a cost of nearly £200,000, while the declining Southern Arm which carried less traffic was left virtually untouched.

It is little more than twenty-two miles from Braunston to Hawkesbury Junction and the end of the Oxford Canal, but the landscape consists of hills and rolling fields and a few farm houses. Most villages, like feudal Barby, are well over a mile from the waterway. The first six miles to Hillmorton Locks crosses and recrosses the Warwickshire-Northamptonshire county boundary There are three pairs of locks at Hillmorton for they were duplicated in 1840 in order to speed up traffic. You can moor at Bridge 59 for Rugby, three-quarters of a mile to the left. Rugby is a pleasant town for sightseeing and shopping and is, of course, the home of the famous school founded by a grocer, Lawrence Sheriff.

Less than half a mile further on you will find pleasant moorings for Newbold on Avon, which stands on a hill between the canal and the looping River Avon. There is excellent shopping here and on the hill above the river you will see beautiful cottages, many of them centuries old, farms and a fifteenth-century church with very lovely porches. Near the church can be found the old tunnel through which the canal originally ran.

Newbold Tunnel beyond Bridge 50 is only 205 yards long, is bone dry and rather unusual in that it has two towpaths. There is a swing gate across the canal at the Maid Line Cruiser headquarters at Brinklow and a watering point. The manager of the yard advised against using the Coventry Arm which runs for 5½ miles from Hawkesbury Junction to Bishop Street, only a few minutes' walk from the new cathedral and shopping centre. The short arm is virtually lined along its entire length with industrial eyesores and is frequently used as a dumping ground for everything from old prams to parts of car bodies. To visit Coventry you can take a bus from Binley, not far along the canal from Brinklow.

There is now fairly flat country to Hawkesbury Junction along rather fine cuttings and embankments on the fourteen-mile pound from Hillmorton Locks. Near the junction you come into the sprawling outskirts of Coventry and the junction itself is rather dirty and neglected. After Lock No. 1, open at both ends, there is a 90° turn hard to starboard under a statuesque cast-iron towpath bridge, and once again a sharp 90° turn again to starboard—a virtual doubling back on your course—and you are in the Coventry Canal. This is not a canal on which to linger and because of the state of the navigation some hire firms no longer allow holidaymakers to take their craft on it.

There is little scenery to speak of and few interesting places at which to stop, but we found it both frustrating and fascinating. Immediately after Hawkesbury you pass the collieries of Bedworth and Nuneaton, and after about two miles you will reach Marston Junction. Here on the right is one of the loveliest little canals in the country, the Ashby-de-la-Zouche Canal. Although there is a stop lock beyond the bridge at the entrance, the canal has no other locks, and is the only lockless canal in Britain. It was completed in 1805 and was originally some thirty miles long, intended for carrying coal from the Leicester-shire coalfields at Ashby-de-la-Zouche and Moira to the canal network. Severe mining subsidence long ago forced the draining of the last seven miles and it is now navigable only as far as Ilott wharf, some twenty-three miles from the Coventry Canal. The canal-side scenery is exquisite along almost its entire length and you can spend a pleasant day or two on a side-trip along the Ashby Canal. About a mile beyond the entrance is the opening to the Griff Arm, a private canal built in 1787 by Sir Roger Newdigate to link his colliery, about half a mile distant, with the Coventry Canal. Coal has been carried on this short canal for nearly 175 years and traffic ceased only when Griff colliery closed down in 1961.

You will now notice that the water in the canal is red and dirty and that there are effluent pipes discharging constantly into the canal as you approach Nuneaton. Between Bridges 23 and 30 the canal is not only dirty and smelly but exceptionally shallow. We had great diffi-culty in navigating this stretch although we slowed down to tick-over speed to give our propeller the greatest possible clearance. Even so our rudder frequently bumped the bottom and on occasions we were literally ploughing our way along.

Typical of the attractive canal architecture are the

old workshops of the Coventry Canal Company at Harts-
hill by Bridge 32. Now part of British Waterways' maintenance yard here, they have a splendid clock turret. It
is only a few miles now to the Atherstone Flight of eleven
locks with a total fall of 80 ft, and as you near them the
water becomes cleaner and deeper. You will also notice
stone quarries near the canal from which roadstone was
shipped by water for many years. There are good moorings
and a watering point beside the King's Head five locks
down. Watling Street or the A5 crosses the canal a little
further on and it is only a short walk into Atherstone
from the bridge. There is a milestone in the town which
calls attention to the fact that Atherstone is 100 miles
from London, Lincoln and Liverpool. Although the canal
is shallow the surroundings suddenly become attractive.
As you approach Lock No. 6 you can see the turrets of
Merevale Hall on the left, jutting out of wooded hillsides. The remaining locks are now somewhat further
apart and soon you are at Bridge 52 at Polesworth. This
is a good centre for exploration of the North Warwickshire
countryside with is squat-towered churches and old
villages like Appleby Parva and Appleby Magna. The
canal continues to be shallow and there are vast tips along
the banks, some huge and so old that they are now screened
by trees and undergrowth, others startlingly red with
truncated tops.

At Fazeley Junction, you turn right into the Birmingham & Fazeley Canal to join the detached portion of
the Coventry Canal to Whittington Brook for the Trent
& Mersey Canal at Fradley. The whole of this stretch,
which is 209 ft above sea level, is quite attractive and
winds a great deal. There are no locks but we counted
over thirty bridges, about three per mile. Fradley Junction
is one of the most picturesque canal junctions in the
country and the Swan Inn just opposite the swing bridge

is a gem and is managed by Wilfred Bolley, an enthusiastic boater who cruised for many years off the Norfolk coast. He is very proud of the Swan, where he has been since 1961, and showed us over the old stables, built in 1763, where at one time as many as twenty-two towing horses were stabled. The inn, of white-painted brick, is as old as the stables, with relics of the days when it catered for working boaters and their horses. It has old canal maps and handwritten lists of subscribers to the Coventry Navigation dated 1767. There are several bars and even a basement bar which Bolley claims was once used by smugglers. You will find mooring rings on the quayside in front of the inn.

This section of the Trent & Mersey between Trent Lock and Great Haywood was the first to be built and was completed before Brindley died in 1772. There are three narrow locks in quick succession with woodland all along the left bank and the hills of Cannock Chase in the distance. At Bridge 54, some two miles from Fradley Junction, you can moor if you wish to visit Lady Godiva's home at pretty King's Bromley.

On the left as you approach Armitage Tunnel is a handsome collection of waterside buildings; the entrance to the tunnel is carved out of solid red rock, making it one of the most unusual anywhere on the canals. This tunnel was probably the first to be built with a towpath through it. The Trent & Mersey provides a series of contrasts. The attractive scene at Armitage Tunnel follows a factory-lined section of canal where peeping through the windows you can get a glimpse of the wide range of sanitary ware manufactured locally. Our youngsters nearly went into hysterics as window after window revealed lavatory pans of every shape and colour. Once through the tunnel you pass through massive coalfields with huge pithead structures competing with a new electricity generating station for attention. This panorama of power development may bring out the cameras for the massive wheels and huge towers make good subjects for photography. The River Trent twists its way along the canal and you cross over it at Brindleys Bank aqueduct a mile beyond Rugely, which lies on the edge of Cannock Chase.

Past Wolseley Park and Hall on the left, you will quickly come to Colwich Lock with hills soaring to over 500 ft in the distance. Haywood Lock follows and from here there are views of a conglomeration of bridges spanning the Trent & Mersey, the Staffordshire & Worcestershire as well as the Trent and Sow rivers. The marshy land around Great Haywood Junction is a haunt of wild birds and you will see many herons both here and for miles along this canal. Between Hoo Mill and Weston Locks stands Ingestre Hall in a majestic park designed by 'Capability' Brown. From Haywood Lock you are gradually rising with locks getting deeper and deeper as you go, with the River Trent rarely more than a few hundred yards away and the rolling countryside dotted with great houses and parks. The views across the Trent Valley are magnificent, particularly round Sandon. From here you can spot five hills, each decked with structures of one kind or another. One boasts a church, another a house, another a ruined tower and the other two monuments to Parliamentarians. A long straight stretch of canal brings you to Aston Lock, which we voted the prettiest of the seventy-six on the 93½ miles of the Trent & Mersey Canal.

The old and interesting town of Stone is little more than a mile further on, and both canal and river flow through it. The big basin at the bottom lock is shallow and there is better mooring above the first lock beside the Star Inn. The four locks of the Stone Flight take you up nearly 40 ft and there are a few more miles of lovely scenery before you begin to notice the potteries and power stations beyond the Meaford Flight of four locks. After Bridge 103 there are moorings for a visit to the famous Wedgwood Factory which can be seen from the canal. Josiah Wedgwood, who was born at nearby Burslem in 1730 and started his first works there, was a great canal enthusiast. It was a pamphlet of his published in 1765 which pointed out the advantages of a canal to link the Trent and Mersey rivers and thus the ports of Liverpool and Hull that sparked off the construction of the Trent & Mersey Canal, originally called the Grand Trunk. He even contributed handsomely to the cost of Brindley's survey of the line and actually cut the first sod of the new waterway at Burslem in July 1766.

Three more pottery-lined miles and the five locks of the Stoke Flight appear. The canal gradually gets dirty and rusty looking and we encountered considerable floating weed. Despite the museum at Stoke-on-Trent with its fine exhibition of pottery, the town from the canal is ugly, lined with factories and slums, and we hurried up the 50 ft flight to the summit pound above. The entire six miles of this pound is shallow, weedy and dirty as it wends its way through the heart of the potteries, but the exciting passage through the 2,919-yard Harecastle Tunnel is more than adequate compensation. The first tunnel which was 2,897 yards long was designed by Brindley and completed in 1777 and was the first tunnel over a mile in length to be constructed anywhere in the world, but it had no towing path and was subject to subsidence. The present tunnel beside it was built by Thomas Telford between 1824 and 1827 and is much larger and with a towpath. Mining subsidence made this towpath impassable at the turn of the century and electric haulage had to be introduced, a tug towing as many as twenty craft through at a time. Powered craft put the tug out of business and today boats move through the tunnel individually after first reporting to the tunnel keeper. You will see a gauge over the entrance as you approach and the keeper will insist that your craft clears this gauge before you are permitted to navigate it. This is simply because the walls of the tunnel have shifted from subsidence, making the tightest squeeze for craft of any tunnel on the inland waterways network. Most hire craft will go through but it is wise to check in advance that the boat you hire will meet the 5 ft 9 ins headroom specification of the gauge. This is, of course, one-way traffic only and it takes a good forty-five minutes to navigate. Many sections leak, there are numerous stalactites, and the walls appear to be buckling inwards in many places. Progress can be checked by the large painted numbers on the walls and the lowest part of the tunnel is from 15 for about 250 yards. Our handrail scraped on one occasion and you will have to be careful of sunken towpath sections, but your passage should cause no problem if you go cautiously.

The canal continues to be shallow and weedy for another mile to the Red Bull Flight of six locks which now take you down over 54½ ft. Just before these locks is the entrance to the Macclesfield Canal on your left, which will seem odd as the canal is actually on your right. This canal, 26½ miles long, connects the Trent & Mersey with the Peak Forest Canal high in the Pennines near Marple and the entrance to it is most unusual. It was designed by Telford, famous for his road and harbour engineering, and he devised a three-quarter mile branch canal to run parallel with the Trent & Mersey and then swung it over the latter on an aqueduct, the first 'flyover' canal crossing in the world. Incidentally, the Macclesfield Canal together with the few miles of the Peak Forest Canal between Marple Junction and Whaley Bridge is still open and provides some of the most wonderful canal scenery anywhere. A whole week can be spent dawdling along, exploring these two almost forgotten waterways, an experience never forgotten.

We continued along the Trent & Mersey, through the Red Bull Flight and into rural countryside once more. From Harecastle Tunnel twenty-four of the twenty-six locks to Wheelock are in pairs but some are derelict. Shortly after the Lawton Flight of six you will come to Upper Thurlwood Lock, one of the most unusual on our canals, a high and imposing steel structure. Special instructions on the site do not advise users to slide the long bar which releases the lower gate. We found three craft with very puzzled crews waiting to get through.

After Hassal Green with the Romping Donkey near Bridge 147 the Wheelock Flight of eight locks carries you down nearly 80 ft, and you will find there is steam over the canal all the way to King's Lock near the junction with the Shropshire Union Canal. The salt and chemical works here even turn Rumps Lock into a warm bath. However, from Crows Nest Lock there are delightful country walks to well-favoured villages like Warmingham. For overnight moorings we recommend the British Waterways hire cruiser base just beyond the junction with the Middlewich Branch of the Shropshire Union which links the north with the Midlands. Middlewich grew to prosperity on salt and the canals which carried it away to markets all over the country. The town is agreeable and excellent for shopping. The old stocks still stand outside the local church but of course have not been used for some long time.

After passing through the Middlewich Flight you will find Lock No. 75 which has double gates and is wider than the locks already navigated from Fradley. Both this lock and No. 76 are 9 ft wide. Lock No. 76 is near the top end of the Trent & Mersey before it flows through Preston Brook tunnel and links with the Bridgewater Canal. The

Trent & Mersey therefore has three different widths in its locks. From Middlewich to Dallow Lane Lock just beyond Burton-on-Trent the locks are 7 ft wide, their size being governed by problems of water supply and the width of the Harecastle Tunnel which would have cost a fortune to make wider. But the six locks below Dallow Lane Lock are all wide enough to take Trent river barges. When the canals were being constructed their builders had good reason for making narrow locks, such as water supply or lack of money, but eventually the variations in gauges from one canal to another made it much easier for the railways to supersede water transport.

The Trent & Mersey goes through lovely countryside all the way to the outskirts of Anderton, some nine miles from Middlewich. There are woodlands and meadows, wild flowers and birds, and from time to time the canal widens into large lakes, the biggest one being after Bridge 180 near Billinge Green. At Bridge 184 there is a handsome black and white pub called The Old Broken Cross, and there is a useful canal-side shop.

We had arranged to meet Dr and Mrs Pilkington at Anderton one afternoon for what we promised would be an incomparable adventure. This was to enter the Shropshire Union Canal from the top end at Ellesmere Port via the Anderton Lift, River Weaver Navigation and Manchester Ship Canal. While there is no reason why beginners should not navigate the Anderton Lift and even venture into the Bridgewater Canal, some experience in handling a boat would be useful before cruising on the Manchester Ship Canal and into Ellesmere Port. It is only a short run back to Middlewich and the convenient Middlewich Arm entry into the Shropshire Union Canal.

While waiting at Anderton we talked to the Fleet Superintendent of what was then the Willow Wren carrying company who bemoaned the decline of commercial traffic on the waterways. Since our visit the former North Western fleets of Willow Wren and British Waterways have merged into a single narrow boat fleet, operated by the Anderton Canal Carrying Company, which is now the largest in the country. Even so, this company began 1970 with only ten craft, and except for the transport of concrete piles, the company's activities are conducted solely between Preston Brook on the Trent & Mersey and Weston Point Docks. Much of their cargo is salt for export and the boats are often used as floating warehouses to save double handling. The reason for the company's survival in the difficult business of commercial narrow boats seems to be their ability to load or unload direct into ships, thus avoiding paying dock dues.

The seven-mile elevated run to the Bridgewater Canal through the crooked Saltersford, Barton and Preston Brook Tunnels, the first to carry canals through hills, is a delightful diversion. From Anderton you may also wish to visit nearby Marston, where salt has been mined for centuries. The village is built on pillars of salt which are slowly dissolving and much of it has been lost in the old brine pits. In 1958 a new half-mile section of canal had to be built and was opened within weeks of part of the old section of the canal collapsing into a mine shaft. In 1844 the Tsar of Russia came to visit Marston's famous Old Mine, one of the biggest in England, and dined in it with the Royal Society. Ten thousand lamps were used to illuminate the ancient mine, which is 360 ft deep and covers thirty-five acres.

CHAPTER 12

SENSATIONS AND SPECTACULARS

You WILL find many opportunities on inland waterways holidays to make gala occasions of certain runs. For our voyage from Anderton to Chester via the Manchester Ship Canal we arranged a little party, and our guest crew on this occasion included not only Dr and Mrs Roger Pilkington but also Dr and Mrs Lawrence Pilkington and the Lord Bishop of Chester, who had not yet seen his diocese by water, he said, and his son.

The River Weaver lies some 50 ft 4 ins below the Trent & Mersey Canal at Anderton and transhipment of cargoes from one waterway to the other was an expensive and time-consuming business until the massive Anderton Lift was opened in 1875. Although there are even bigger lifts on Continental waterways today, the Anderton Lift is the only one in use in Britain. Situated on an island in the river basin, this unusual structure is connected to the canal by a two channel aqueduct some 162 ft 6 ins long, each channel being 17 ft 2 ins wide. These lead to the two 75 ft x 15 ft 6 ins x 5 ft wrought iron tanks of the lift itself, each tank when full of water weighing 252 tons. For the first thirty years these tanks carried boats up and down hydraulically but in 1907 the main rams were renewed and the lift was electrified. Each tank is now suspended by means of wire ropes passing round large overhead pulleys. Counterweights consisting of 252 tons of cast iron hang from the free ends of the wire ropes, so that comparatively little power is needed to raise a tank, although the total weight moved is about 570 tons. Power is supplied direct to the pulleys by an electric motor of only 30 h.p.

It is a strange sensation to cross the aqueduct, enter the open water-tight doors of a tank, see them close behind you and then float almost silently in the tank as it moves slowly down between a vast network of girders, wire ropes and weights while pulleys whirr overhead, being lowered to the river over 50 ft below. The whole operation takes under 15 minutes and costs £2 single or £3 return. British Waterways supplies an illustrated souvenir ticket with pertinent statistics. Initially the lift cost £26,302 and modification costs were £25,000. An attendant is on duty from 8 to 5 on weekdays, 8 to 11 on Saturdays and occasionally on Sundays in summer. He will take you on a conducted tour of this enormous structure and its mechanics and you may be as lucky as we were in meeting a pair of narrow boats coming up from the river as you descend from the canal.

As you leave the lift a vast I.C.I. complex towers dead ahead. Turning left into the Weaver you can cruise for a few miles through two locks to the pretty Winsford Flashes, large lakes beside the river with access just above to Winsford Bridge. A right turn takes you to the Manchester Ship Canal. You soon come to lovely tree-covered hills and glorious views. The river is wide and deep and there are only five locks on the twenty-mile long navigation, each taking craft up to 130 ft long, 35 ft in beam and up to 10 ft in draught. Even so, we were surprised to see round the first bend after leaving Saltersford Lock a big Danish coaster bearing down on us at about 10 knots.

Despite some major industrial plants, there is magnificent scenery all along the Weaver. At Weston, some nineteen miles from Winsford, Marsh Lock gives access to the Manchester Ship Canal. This is a busy commercial waterway and pleasure craft must obtain written permission to use it from the Manchester Ship Canal Company. Our brief excursion on it cost us £5, involving us in obtaining £50,000 insurance cover and a certificate of seaworthiness for our craft, the acquisition of extra gear including a 56 lb anchor, and a fair amount of letter-writing to arrange a Saturday passage timed to fit in with the operation of the Anderton Lift and entry into Ellesmere Port.

The Ship Canal, which runs from Eastham Locks some thirty-six miles to Manchester, is not what one can describe as scenic for it has high banks depriving anyone on a boat of all but rare glimpses of the surrounding countryside. It is nearly as broad as the Thames through central London and considerably deeper. There are lights and signposts all along the canal, and Ince Low and High Cuttings are clearly cut out of solid rock. We saw many huge tankers discharging, and two of them pulled out of their berths within a hundred yards of us, swinging across the canal seemingly oblivious of our presence.

All boating enthusiasts have their favourite spots on the waterways. One that comes most frequently to my mind is Ellesmere Port, which links the Manchester Ship Canal to the former Ellesmere, now the Shropshire Union Canal. Ellesmere Port has both striking beauty and repulsive dilapidation. It recalls bygone architectural and engineering genius and reflects current regrettable negligence. It tells the whole tragic story of the rise and fall of this country's canal system. The modern and mechanised facilities for the Ship Canal here are excellent, but the nearby 'Shroppie' Cut facilities which brought growth and prosperity to the former group of tiny villages, are by comparison an incongruous island of decay.

As we swung up to the large tidal lock we noted on the

north pier a gem of a miniature red brick lighthouse, 35 ft tall with a graceful lantern. Dating back to the opening of the Ellesmere Canal or Wirral Line from Chester in 1795, it guided vessels coming to the port from the Mersey tideway before the Ship Canal was completed in 1894. The vast outer basin here contained a motley collection of shabby craft and as there were at that moment dark skies overhead, it gave the atmosphere of a 'ghost port'. We turned under a warehouse arch to zig-zag our way through obstructions jutting out of the water into an inner basin, filled with a mass of floating rubbish. The narrow locks were derelict and the water in the wide locks, in the short pound between them and in the canal above was a bleak panorama of duckweed and floating clumps of reed filled with old oil drums and an appalling collection of flotsam and jetsam as far as the eye could see. The padlock on the lock gates had to be sawn off after the lock-keeper dropped the keys in the lock, either by accident or threw them away in disgust. As the locks filled a great cascade of green descended and we went ahead very cautiously indeed. Then we had to hook the biggest and heaviest of the debris away from the top gates. Even then there was so much left on the 4 ins thick bed of duckweed along with wriggling elvers that we had to plot a course out of the lock. Although the weed thinned gradually the waterway was almost totally green with it to Stoke Bridge, some three miles distant. Never before in all of Europe's waterways had any of us encountered so much weed that our wake was completely undetectable. There is only one thing to be done under such conditions, other than turning back, and that is to proceed gently. Attempts to get through quickly will only damage your craft.

The first real development of Ellesmere Port was inspired by my favourite canal engineer, Thomas Telford, whom I have already mentioned. The Wirral Line was Telford's first canal enterprise and the transformation of Ellesmere Port his last. When in 1835 he began the construction of new sea and canal locks, docks and warehousing, Ellesmere Port consisted only of a pub and a few small cottages. He died before his last great contribution to the nation's canal system was opened with great ceremony and noisy celebrations in September 1843. After an expenditure of some £100,000 Ellesmere Port was now geared to deal with any coastal trade and canal traffic and could boast over seventy houses, a church and church school, and three inns. The crowning glory then, as today, is the unique main warehouse to his design to facilitate transhipment from river to canal. This warehouse, standing in mellowed beauty today, is four storeys high. The bottom floor is level with the docks and the third floor on the canal side is on a level with the canal. Adjoining this are three wings of two storeys each, resting on handsome arches, which form a passage for craft between the big outer dock and the smaller inner basin. If the little lighthouse at Ellesmere Port is worth preserving, Telford's warehouses are a masterpiece in canal architecture and a heritage that must be saved at all costs. It is worth bringing your craft up from Chester to Ellesmere Port to have a look for yourself—the navigation has been improved since our cruise. One can spend a long time in quiet admiration of this product of genius and it is no wonder that the Lord Bishop of Chester who was with us, spontaneously appealed in his Diocesan leaflet for the restoration of 'these fine buildings and waterways to full use'. Adding that the 'brick and stone buildings have a Venetian touch about them, and the craftsmanship is splendid', the Lord Bishop suggested that the warehouses would make ideal youth club premises.

However, Telford's warehouses and the connection with

the Ship Canal have been threatened with demolition since 1967. The Manchester Ship Canal Company, which hold the lease of the area, wants to redevelop it to provide new berthing and other facilities for the Ship Canal. Ellesmere Port Council, local interests and canal enthusiasts have indicated that they would like to preserve the group and convert it into a marina and canal museum. To seal off the exit of the Shropshire Union into the Ship Canal would be disastrous, making a dead end of the Wirral Line and a mockery of the Government's declared intentions to retain the Shropshire Union main line and all its branches as amenity waterways. The area is too small to provide substantial facilities for the Ship Canal, yet Ellesmere Port is a natural focal point for the creation of new leisure amenities. Despite the recent fire Telford's warehouses should certainly be declared an historic monument, thus preventing their destruction, and then they should be adapted to provide both a youth club and canal museum. Below them one can easily visualise a great marina with boatyards, a restaurant and other amenities.

The nine-mile cruise from Ellesmere Port to Tower Wharf in Chester has no locks and after two miles of industry it is unspoiled countryside with herds of dairy cattle grazing in valley pastures. There are a number of interesting little villages along the winding course and a visit can be made to Chester Zoo at Upton from Caughall Bridge, easily identified by its number, 134, and its iron arch and parapet. As you get nearer to Chester the Welsh hills loom on your right and for such a large cathedral city, the waterways entrance is surprisingly open with only a short stretch of canal with houses backing on to it. Tower Wharf, just beyond the short branch leading through three locks to the River Dee, is a good overnight mooring. The Dee is tidal to Chester but those with some experience can cruise safely for ten miles along this pretty river to Almeree Ferry.

We cannot praise Chester too highly as a port of call. A guide book is a great help in exploring the city and no one should miss the panoramic walk round the city walls. The wide curving approach to Northgate Locks, three of the staircase type carved out of solid rock and carrying you up 33 ft, is very shallow and you should stay in mid-channel. The canal goes through a beautiful deep rock chasm for a quarter of a mile along the outside of the city walls and there are memorable views of King Charles's Tower and Chester Cathedral. The exit from Chester is industrialised for a couple of miles but from Chrisleton Bridge it is all beautiful countryside. After passing over the River Gowy there is a favourite mooring spot at Bates Mill Bridge, from which you can visit the ruins of thirteenth-century Beeston Castle with its famous 370 ft deep well in which Richard II is reputed to have concealed a vast treasure, the old mill and the Old Shady Oak Inn. There are picturesque hills all round as you cruise along to Wharton Lock and the two Beeston Locks. The first is known as Beeston Iron Lock and is unique, built entirely of bolted iron plates instead of stone because this was the only way to cope with the running sand at the site.

In the next five miles to Barbridge Junction and the southern end of the ten-mile-long Middlewich Arm there are five hire cruiser yards including that of Ladyline Cruisers at the junction, complete with chandlery, groceries and souvenirs, all available from sunrise to sunset. Above the junction stands the Jolly Tar which we found rather grand for a canal-side pub. It is only a wide sweeping mile to the mammoth Hurleston reservoir and junction. Immediately beside the reservoir on the right is the flight of four Hurleston Locks which will carry you over 34 ft up into what is widely regarded as the most beautiful canal in this country. The first lock is a tight squeeze and you should ensure when you hire the craft for your holidays that you can get into this canal. Of course, hire craft are available on the canal itself.

The Llangollen Canal, originally known as the Elles-mere Canal, runs for forty-six miles from Hurleston Junction to Llantisilio in Wales with twenty-one locks, the breathtaking Pontcysyllte and Chirk aqueducts, three tunnels and well over 100 bridges, and these include some of the most picturesque lifting bridges on the waterways network. It also has an inimitable inland harbour at Ellesmere and, in fact, it owes its origin to a group of industrialists and business men from the Ellesmere area who promoted a parliamentary Bill which authorised the construction of a system of canals radiating from Elles-mere and linking the Rivers Severn, Dee and Mersey. They engaged Telford in 1793 to build the system and the first section to be completed was the Wirral Line, the only section with broad locks. There were modifica-tions to the original plans but what is now known as the Llangollen Canal was opened all the way to Llantisilio by 1808.

Once through the Hurleston Locks the canal, with its low banks, looks out on prosperous farming country with brick farmhouses and outbuildings. The canal is lined with flowers and there are many birds, including king-fishers, and so beautiful you may be tempted not to go far from the water, even to visit the occasional nearby village. After two miles you will reach the two Swanley Locks, closely followed by the Baddiley three and the wooded park of Wrenbury Hall, now a training college. Wren-bury with its mill and charming lifting bridge is reminis-cent of Holland, although the Cotton Arms here is entirely British. We found amateur artists at work; indeed, one had hired a cruiser just to paint along the Llangollen Canal. From the next lock at Marbury it is just under half a mile to the village. This village is worth a visit to see the black and white, or magpie, style of architecture which is striking, and Marbury Mere is not only pretty but has a plentiful supply of coarse fish. The countryside is now flatter as you lock up the oddly named Quoisley, Willeymoor and Povey's Locks and approach the Grindley Brook Flight. The first three are orthodox locks but the top three are staircase locks with only four gates between them. Care must be taken at the latter for the bridge is out of line with the lock chambers. You will find a convenient canal-side pub here, a post office and general stores.

The canal is full of turns and twists after Grindley Brook but soon after Platts Lane Bridge, No. 43, it becomes wider and straighter and the scenery rapidly changes. The Prees Branch of the canal is on the left and although it is officially closed, craft drawing under 2 ft can cruise for about a mile and a half to Waterloo Bridge. This is peat country and Whixall Moss is still worked. The waterway now goes briefly into and out of Wales as it winds through wooded countryside and into what the locals call the 'Lake District'. Cole Mere and Blake Mere are beautiful and unspoiled lakes beside the canal. Near Cole Mere we saw the only 'no mooring' signs on the entire length of the Llangollen Canal and indeed mooring is possible virtually anywhere. Through the short, straight 87-yard-long Ellesmere Tunnel you reach a junction with the quarter-mile Ellesmere Arm. The route to Llantisilio is round to the left but if you venture under the pretty rustic wooden bridge into the arm you will find moorings in the neatest little inland harbour in all Britain. This gives easy access to the amenities of the town. The local castle has long since disappeared but the heights on which it stood have been converted into a bowling green and there are fine views over lovely countryside. The Ellesmere area is claimed to be the most prolific milk-producing area in the world.

As you return to the junction you will see a fully equipped British Waterways maintenance yard, well worth inspecting. There are unfortunately heaps of junk about but it was while we were nosing through these that we discovered and bought some rusty old canal signs which, refurbished and repainted, we took home to decorate a part of the exterior of the house, and also a heavy balance beam cap which, now repainted, we have placed at the curve in our drive.

The canal is broad and deep for a short stretch beyond Ellesmere and then narrows and winds through fields of grain and pastures with grazing cattle. Once past Bridge 65 you will begin to get magnificent views of the Welsh hills on the left. Passing under Bridge 69 there is a useful mooring near the entrance to the abandoned Montgomeryshire Canal which once led to Welshpool and Newton. The first bridge beyond the junction is not No. 70 as might be expected but is No. 1; the bridges from here to Llantisilio are numbered 1 to 49A. At Bridge 5 there are shops at the village of Maesterfyn. If you feel energetic it is 2½ miles to Whittington with its nineteenth-century castle ruins.

The countryside is more hilly and broken now and at Newmarton are the last two locks on the canal with thirty-four miles of lock-free cruising beyond. There is a canal-side bakery at Bridge 13 which is useful for delicious cakes and bread, and local butter and eggs can be bought. Beyond the Lion Inn at Bridge 17 the canal sweeps into the beautiful Ceiriog Valley for a good mile before reaching Chirk aqueduct over the River Ceiriog. This 701-ft-long aqueduct is 9 ft wide and formed of cast-iron plates flanged and bolted together. It was completed on masonry arched piers in 1801 by Telford at a cost of over £20,000 and is some 70 ft high. The railway bridge alongside it, from which you can get good photographs of your craft crossing the aqueduct, is much higher but was not built until forty years later. This is the first of the major aqueducts on the canal and is closely followed by Chirk Tunnel, 459 yards long, which is dry and has a well-fendered towpath. You can moor in the basin before the tunnel and follow a path on the right up an incline into Chirk. This is an appealing little town with good shops, a hotel, and an amusing antique shop. Chirk Castle, with its handsome wrought-iron gates, has a collection of paintings, armour and antiques and lies about a mile from the town. The 191-yard-long Whitehouses Tunnel is little more than a mile from Chirk and you emerge into the beautiful Dee Valley. The canal passes through wooded hillsides for another mile before sweeping round to the right to the highlight of the canal, the Pontcysyllte aqueduct. The views on the long approach to this astonishing memorial to Telford's genius are really glorious. The 1,007-ft-long aqueduct soars 120 ft over the surging River Dee below. Although it was completed in 1805 the eighteen massive masonry arches carrying the 7 ft 2 ins-wide trough of bolted cast-iron flanged plates are in superb condition. Along the right hand side of the trough runs a 4 ft 8 ins towpath at the same level as the base of the trough. The aqueduct is scheduled as an ancient monument and the towpath railings when they were renewed in 1964 were made to Telford's original design. There is no need to have any qualms about taking your craft across under power unless there is a strong wind blowing. In these circumstances it can be somewhat alarming as we discovered, for on the occasion of our crossing strong winds were blowing and the *Golden Eye* was being pushed against the edge on the left with a sheer drop into the valley below. It is possible to walk your boat across from the recessed towpath should your crew wish to do this, but whichever way you cross I am perfectly certain you will never have a more thrilling experience on the waterways. This structure, which cost only £47,000 when it was built 165 years ago, would cost millions today and is, without doubt, the finest example of canal engineering in this country.

You will find good moorings just across the aqueduct at the Anglo Welsh Canal Cruisers' base at Trevor. The remaining six miles of canal to Llangollen and Llantisilio follows the contours of the hills along the course of the Dee but for the most part is shallow and narrow. Craft with over 2 ft draught should not attempt passage, which will take a good four hours one way. You can take a bus from Trevor to Llangollen and then travel a couple of miles by horse-drawn lifeboat to the end of the canal and Horseshoe Falls. Llangollen is packed with visitors during the summer months. However, the town is worth exploring for here the River Dee tumbles over rocks and below the fourteenth-century bridge is a lovely salmon leap. There is a modern pottery, offering a wide range of hand-made earthenware; nearby are the ruins of Valle Crucis Abbey with its famous mutilated cross, the Pillar of Eliseg, and wishing well, and the eighteenth-century Plas Newydd which the local council keeps open to the public.

On turning round you have the whole of the beautiful Llangollen Canal to cruise once again and even rain on the journey will not diminish the wild beauty of this waterway. As you join the main line of the Shropshire Union again you will notice the relative tameness of the agricultural countryside to Nantwich. You can moor at the basin for a visit to the old salt town. The old English

word for salt-rock was 'wych', and thus the names Nantwich, Middlewich, Northwich, etc. Nantwich Junction
Bridge marks the end of the broad Chester Canal completed in 1779, and the remaining twenty-nine locks on
the thirty-nine mile run to Autherley Junction are narrow.
After the bridge the canal enters a long and high embankment, the first of many earthworks built by Telford
on the route south to Autherley, each providing excellent
views of the peaceful countryside. The canal goes up and
up through Hack Green Locks and then through the long
and delightful flight of fifteen Audlem locks stretching
over two miles and taking your craft a further 93 ft higher.
You can moor, water and shop at Lock 13, the third of
the flight, for the old coaching town of Audlem has good
shopping facilities.

A peaceful wooded cutting starts immediately above
the locks and then comes the Adderley Flight of five locks
taking you up another 31 ft as you cruise from Cheshire
into Shropshire. Only another couple of miles now to the
graceful Betton Coppice Bridge which takes the towpath to the opposite side of the canal in a handsome sweep.
Shortly afterwards there is a canal basin on your left and
the headquarters of Ladyline Cruisers and Holidays
Afloat. From moorings here you can visit Market Drayton
with its many charming old buildings, inns and churches.
Wednesday is still market day and a visit to the open-air
swimming pool, followed by a call at the Corbet Arms, will
refresh your crew after working so many locks.

You now cross the 'Forty Steps' aqueduct over the Tern
to enter a wonderful cutting hewn through sandstone
with trees forming an arch over the canal. This approach
to the Tyrley Flight of five locks is unforgettable. The
rise of 33 ft is immediately followed by another tree-lined
rock cutting over 1½ miles long before you come into open
countryside again. Once you are through Tyrley Locks

you are on a seventeen-mile pound which is 333 ft above sea level, and from the many cuttings, embankments, aqueducts and even a short tunnel you will appreciate even more the true genius of Telford, who had none of today's mechanical aids to help him create this waterways route; he had only hardworking navigators or 'navvies' with simple tools.

The canal now wends its way into Staffordshire with no noticeable change in scenery. The high Shebdon embankment is followed by a lovely wooded cutting with an enormously high canal bridge which is unlike any other in the world. About half-way up you can see a buttress upon which stands a telegraph pole and wires, directly underneath the road bridge itself. Another two miles will bring you to Norbury Junction, one of our favourite overnight moorings. The Junction Inn has been spruced up but the company one meets here is invariably good fun. Horse-drawn canal day boats operate from the wharf at the pub.

The valley of the Meese with its open fields and pastures nestling between the hills is never more beautiful than in the early morning. The ancient village of Gnosall is quite charming, not least for its church of St Lawrence and its various inns. There are good shopping facilities near the bridge. Cowley Tunnel, wide and carved out of rock, bores through a wooded cutting for 87 yards, and for the next few miles the canal passes along on more embankments and aqueducts and through still more wooded cuttings to Dirty Lane Bridge and then Tavern Bridge with the Hartley Arms and Wheaton Aston Locks close by. The canal then goes up again for 7 ft to the last pound on the main line, some seven miles from Autherley Lock and Junction, with almost continuous cuttings, heavily wooded or narrowly cut from rock. The bridges here have odd names like 'Skew' and 'Turnover' and for nearly half a mile before Autherley Junction you will see an enormous collection of moored pleasure craft, almost up to the old Stop Lock with its very small rise of 6 ins. This lock dates back to the days when rival canal companies jealously sought to maintain control over their own waters. What was once the toll office is now manned by British Waterways to give advice to holidaymakers and to sell souvenirs.

After locking out, turn sharply to the left for the twenty-mile run back to the Trent & Mersey Canal at Great Haywood Junction. The Staffordshire & Worcestershire Canal north of Autherley Junction is in complete contrast to the twenty-six miles south of the Junction and nothing like as beautiful. Only eleven of the forty-three locks between the Trent & Mersey and the Severn are on the canal north of Autherley but it does possess some interesting features. As you leave Autherley on the outskirts of Wolverhampton you are on the summit pound and after an unexpectedly wide stretch there is a cutting so narrow and overhung with long grass and shrubbery that your craft will rub against the banks from time to time. But soon there is open country with farmhouses and stretches of parkland.

One fascinating feature of the 'Staffs & Worcs', as we call it, is that the majority of the bridges are not only numbered but are also named, and some amusing names there are. Passing through wooded country, at Gailey Lock you begin your descent to the Trent & Mersey. There are now six locks quite close together, the last being Penkridge, which, because of the low bridge above the lock, appears at first sight to be a dead end. From the Boat Inn by the bridge the canal follows the course of the river Penk and there are four more locks in the next three miles, a humdrum stretch with only Teddesley Park providing pleasant views up to Stafford. There are good moorings at Radford Bridge, No. 98, by the headquarters of Radford Marine Ltd, and the nearby Trumpet Inn. From here you can visit Stafford by bus and this is also a convenient place to embark or disembark guest crew.

Just beyond Stafford the River Sow joins the River Penk and the two streams pass under the canal at Tixall. Beyond the aqueduct is Tixall Lock and then the lovely Tixall Broad, a small canal lake about a mile long with pleasant views to Tixall Park, where Mary Queen of Scots was once held prisoner. Fishing in this area is said to be very good indeed, particularly in the Penk. Once out of the Broad you are at Great Haywood Junction and the beautiful wide-span bridge that carries the Trent & Mersey towpath over the Staffs & Worcs canal.

The thirteen-mile cruise to Fradley Junction and The Swan was even prettier than the earlier cruise in the opposite direction. From Fradley there are four locks to Bridge 46 and one of our favourite waterways villages, Alrewas, once famous for its basket making. There is an old mill here, the friendly George and Dragon Inn and some delightful thatched cottages. We also found that the butcher makes delicious home-made sausages.

After Alrewas Lock the canal joins the Trent river for a short stretch. You will pass a heronry here. Once through Wychnor Lock the canal narrows, and becomes shallow and weedy. After Branston Lock the wooded Sinai Ridge is on the left as you enter Burton-on-Trent, famous for its beer. There are moorings at Bridge 13 from which you can catch a bus for the town for shopping or possibly for a visit to one of the many breweries. It is said that as early as the thirteenth century the monks used water from the local wells for brewing ale but certainly Burton has been world-famous for its beer since the eighteenth century. The suburbs of Burton to the last of the narrow locks at Dallow Lane are hardly impressive but you soon reach open countryside again. There are good British

Waterways moorings above Bridge 23 at Willington and you will find a friendly welcome at the Green Dragon nearby. The local railway station which serves both Repton and Willington is a gem right out of Victorian days.

Stenson, the first of the wide locks, is noticeably difficult to operate after the narrow locks. Beyond the abandoned Derby Canal, Swarkestone Bridge carries the road for a mile over the river and the expanse of meadows which have been subject to flooding from the earliest times. A pretty wooded cutting leads to Weston Lock with its watering point and nearby shopping facilities. It is now a mixture of pastures and power plants as you cruise on to Aston and Shardlow Locks. You can moor beside the Malt Shovel, an old-time canal pub with a snack bar, or you can visit the Lady in Grey for hot meals.

To lock out of Derwent Mouth Lock is a blissful experience for your boat will surge ahead in the wide deep waters at the junction of the rivers Trent and Derwent, but it is important to keep straight ahead and avoid the dangerous weirs. Sawley Flood Lock will be open at both ends and after going through you will be in one of the biggest and most modern boating centres in Britain, Sawley Bridge Marina. There are usually hundreds of craft moored in the Sawley Cut and you will find every conceivable facility here from new and used craft to fuel and chandlery, and a fleet of hire cruisers.

This is actually part of the River Trent and all too quickly you will pass through Sawley Locks and into Trent Junction, a kind of Scotch Corner of the waterways system. On your left you will see almost tucked away Trent Lock leading into the $11\frac{3}{4}$-mile Erewash section of the Grand Union Canal, still navigable as far as Ilkeston. Straight ahead is the rather narrow Cranfleet Cut and the water highway of the River Trent to the north. To the right of the yacht club on the island is a broad channel flowing under a railway bridge, and then over Thrumpton Weir. This branches sharply off to the right into the River Soar Navigation. The junction is well sign-posted and once you pass the yacht club ono the left turn into the River Soar, keeping close to the right-hand corner and well clear of the weir stream.

Having already cruised the narrow and shallow twenty-mile summit pound between Foxton and Norton Junction this end of the Leicester line will come as a surprise to you, for the Soar is wide and deep and very unlike a canal. A lovely sweep of river will carry your craft to pretty Red-hill Lock, with its little shop. Wooded hills and slender church spires demand your attention as you cruise on. There are pleasant moorings on the right about half a mile beyond Kegworth Top Lock, beside the Whitehouse Inn and the Soar Boating Club. Despite the nearness of road and railway along the canal, the only traffic to be heard are aircraft flying high over the wooded hills and woodlands. All along the canal on this stretch there are sleepy villages like Zouch and Normanton-on-Soar which will probably appeal to those who have to live in a town. There is a wharf and boatyard and shopping facilities in Loughborough, the town of the bells. Bells from the foundry here ring out round the world, and from here came Great Paul of St Paul's Cathedral, the biggest bell in England. You should visit the 151-ft-tall Grand Caril-lon in Queen's Park, the first to be built in England in 1923. The chamber houses forty-seven bells, the heaviest being over 4 tons and the lightest just over 20 lb.

The canal rejoins the Soar again after Pilling's Lock, in lovely Quorn hunting country. The village of Barrow-on-Soar is hard by Barrow Deep Lock with an amusement park on the right. As you approach Mountsorrel, famous for its granite, there are huge boatyards and hire cruiser bases on the right. Beside the lock stands the Waterside Inn which is to be highly recommended. The Soar continues to flow in and out of the canal like a writhing snake. Charnwood Forest is not far off and there are many delightful walks to nearby villages like Rothley, Cossington, and Newton Lindford with its thatched and timbered dwellings and cedar-shaded inn. Nearby is beautiful Bradgate Park, one of the homes of the ill-fated Lady Jane Grey, with a thousand acres of natural forest which have become almost a shrine to the nine-day queen.

To the right from Bridge 19 lies the Roman settlement of Wanlip whose secluded fourteenth-century church contains admirable brasses, including one dated 1393 of Sir Thomas Walsh and his wife, with the earliest prose inscription in English on any brass in the country.

It is now but three miles and three locks to Leicester and the last, Belgrave Lock, has a lovely weir with hundreds of swans. The best moorings for shopping and sightseeing are by the North Bridge Inn, Frog Island. The navigation out of Leicester is rather weedy and sordid but you soon reach pastures and fields of waving grain. From Bridge 87, which leads to Wigston Magna, once called Wigston Two Steeples, the countryside is glorious and the waterway one of utter peace.

The locks now take on most amusing names, such as 'Bumble Bee' and 'Turnover' lock. After nine more locks, all with an average rise of about 6 ft in the next four miles to Saddington Tunnel, the total is forty from the Trent. After the first four, Bridge 80 leads to Newton Harcourt and in the shady churchyard stands a miniature church with spire, porch, windows and battlements, perfect in every detail and of undoubted craftsmanship, set up in memory of a boy of eight. Saddington Tunnel is only 880 yards long, wide and in good condition, with no sign of the headless ghost said still to haunt it.

There are three more miles of winding and wild canal between Saddington Tunnel and Foxton with no locks and only one swing bridge. I had asked special permission to take the *Golden Eye* along this stretch in the dark. We turned on the spotlight and rigged our portable navigation lights and got through without mishap. It was a wonderful but eerie experience and one we have seldom repeated, but it made a perfect ending to looping the loop of the Midlands waterways when we put in to Market Harborough the next morning.

CHAPTER 13

INTO SHAKESPEARE'S COUNTRY

THE RECENT restoration of the southern section of the Stratford-on-Avon Canal from its junction with the Grand Union Canal at Kingswood in Warwickshire makes it possible once again to visit Shakespeare's Stratford-on-Avon by water. The £300,000 Stratford Canal which runs for twenty-five miles from King's Norton on the Worcester & Birmingham Canal via Lapworth was begun in November 1793, but owing to financial problems and canal politics, was not completed until June 1816. It was difficult to construct for it involved building fifty-six locks, a 352-yard-long tunnel at Brandwood, near King's Norton, one brick aqueduct and three iron ones. It was not a money spinner as unfortunately it was completed less than thirty years before the railway mania year of 1845. Intended as an alternative route between Birmingham and the Severn by way of the River Avon, it never captured substantial through traffic and was used primarily to carry coal to Stratford.

The southern section between Lapworth and Stratford ceased to be navigable about the end of the Second World War and in 1958 Warwickshire County Council announced that it was applying for a warrant of abandonment. This led to many public protests and sparked off a British Transport Commission Act of 1960 authorising a lease of the waterway to the National Trust with a government subsidy of £27,500, and the southern section was restored and reopened in 1964.

Our fortuitous discovery of the *Golden Eye* under the name of the *Flying Mexican* at Warwick meant that we had only a few pretty rural miles of the Grand Union, the Cape Flight of two, the Hatton Flight of twenty-one wide locks and the 443-yard Shrewley Tunnel to navigate before joining the short arm leading to the Stratford Canal.

Passing through Lock 20 at the end of the arm you enter a large basin. On the left are locks leading into both the northern and southern sections. Your course is 180 degrees to port into Lock 21 under an unusual type of bridge—a split bridge with a narrow gap in the centre. This, and other bridges, were built this way to allow tow lines to pass through when horses crossed the bridges in the days of horse-drawn craft.

Beside the lock is the National Trust canal office where for a toll of £1 2s 6d you can cruise for a week on the southern section. For a 10s deposit you can obtain a key which opens the padlock on the locks into the River Avon at Stratford and you will certainly want the 3s guide to the canal. It is wise to paste your licence in a window of your craft and to read the sheet of navigation notes which insist that all lock gates and paddles are closed after passage.

The Stratford-on-Avon Canal is a gem in the waterways system. You will find it somewhat narrow, but lined with wild flowers, shrubs, trees and fields of grain. The first ten locks to Lowsonford and the Fleur de Lys pub are within easy walking distance of each other and a very pleasant walk for one or two of the crew, moving ahead and preparing the locks. Beyond Lock 29 you will come to the outskirts of Lowsonford village, passing a demolished railway bridge which once carried the first railway to Henley-in-Arden, which is as beautiful as its name and contains a number of architectural gems. There are grassy moorings beside the towpath just before Lock 31 and nearly opposite the waterside gardens of the Fleur de Lys. These are convenient for visiting the pub and for going to the village of Lowsonford which has at least one shop which is open on a Sunday.

The pub is the home of the famous Fleur de Lys pies. The story is that the original chicken and mushroom pies were made here from mushrooms grown in the cellar. Today the pies are made in a factory but can be bought at the pub, either hot or cold, along with steak and kidney pies and a wide selection of sandwiches. It will take some searching to find the watering point at Lock 31, but it is in a shed abutting the lock cottage. Beyond Lock 31, the banks are green fields and meadows, grazed by sheep or cattle. Below Lock 36 the towpath mysteriously changes sides away from the small stream which parallels this winding contour canal from just beyond Lapworth Junction. Why this was done is a puzzle, for in so doing the canal builders created the biggest single cause of flooding on the southern section of this canal. Had they put the towing path embankment on the opposite side, between the canal and the stream, this would have prevented any flooding.

At Lock 37 you will notice an unusual type of lock cottage, owned by Mr and Mrs Wagstaffe. This 'barrel' type cottage is in effect the replica of a 14 ft wide canal tunnel above the surface, and was erected by the canal builders about 1812. The occupants have modernised the cottage in a most charming way and have turned it into a cosy residence. We were told that the tunnel-like brick-work can still be seen in their airing cupboard. They will be pleased to show you over their home on request but they do ask you to make a donation to the Stratford-on-Avon Society for the restoration of the Avon between Stratford and Evesham. Restoration of this navigation is already under way and will complete the waterways ring, as the waterways map will show you, and provide easy direct access between the River Severn and the Midlands canals. You will hear some interesting stories about Lock Cottage, about the days when tow-horses were stabled at the cottage for 6d a night and a bag of beans, or about the lock-keeper's wife who brewed beer for the boatmen.

There is good mooring between Locks 37 and 38 and it is wiser to moor here than at Bridge 47 where there is no ready access. Henley-in-Arden is little more than a mile along the road on your right. The Crab Mill Inn, 400 yards from the bridge, and the Manor House tea garden nearby are convenient for meals. Some two-thirds of the way along the pound between Locks 38 and 39, just after Bridge 53, you reach a long concrete quay by the attractive pink Navigation Inn. At the time of writing, Harborough Marine Ltd are building a new hire cruiser base here with full facilities.

From the moorings here the road under the nearby aqueduct leads to the oddly-named village of Wootton Wawen, one of the most charming little villages in Warwickshire, with a timbered inn, delightful old cottages, a fine hall in lovely grounds and the oldest church in the county.

Once over the aqueduct the scenery changes as the canal no longer follows the tributary stream of the River Alne which now joins the canal. The canal builders had to cut through higher ground to reach the side of the Avon valley. There are a number of cuttings with bushes hanging over the canal and from time to time an embankment giving pretty views across the countryside. One such cutting carries the Bearley or Edstone aqueduct over a road and railway. This early nineteenth-century aqueduct with a sunken towpath is exceedingly narrow and must be navigated at a very low speed. You are now in the lovely

Forest of Arden, not as thick as it was in Shakespeare's day for the trees were used to feed the iron works of the Midlands before the Industrial Revolution developed. The area is still more heavily wooded, however, than many other so-called wooded parts of Britain.

Bridge 59 is a new concrete bridge, so obviously stark after the graceful brick arches and split bridges you have passed. If you wish to visit Wilmcote you can moor at the watering point beyond the bridge. Pass through a gate and turn right on the road for Shakespeare's mother's house. Mary Arden's house is open daily from 9 a.m. to 6 p.m. and on Sundays from 2 p.m. to 6 p.m. A collection of antique agricultural tools is on exhibition. To the left of the bridge, at the road junction, you will find shopping facilities and also the Mason's Arms which sells paintings.

Moving along towards Bridge 60 you will get your first glimpse of the Cotswolds, about a dozen miles away on the other side of the Avon valley. Having now passed over a watershed you will now reach a flight of eleven locks, numbers 40 to 50, in three groups of three, five and three. There are wonderful views going down this flight of locks, Warwickshire being the most typically English of all English shires, and all the locks are easy to operate. There is a mile-long pound between locks 50 and 51 and after the latter you will be in the outskirts of Stratford. Some 300 yards beyond twin railway bridges there is a wooden wharf on the right, the base of the recently established Western Cruisers Ltd. There are two useful watering points with hoses on the wharf and a souvenir shop with canal books and various items connected with the canals. The entry to Stratford via the canal is shabby, but points of interest include the strange right-angled or cranked balance beam on the lower gate of Lock 53, constructed so that leverage can be obtained despite the close proximity of the bridge.

You may possibly find that wading is necessary at Lock 55 because water often flows over the top of the upper gate and floods the sides of the lock. All you have to do is to ensure that your craft is well away from the top gates when in the lock so that it is not caught in the 'falls' when the lock empties. You will also have to guide your boat down as you empty the lock slowly, so that the hull is not caught on the lock-side.

A sharp bend brings you to the lowest bridge on the canal and care should be taken to see that the super-structure will clear the underside of the bridge. If it will not, walk beyond the bridge past the basin to Lock 56 on the River Avon. Use your special key on the padlock, open a paddle and let some water run out into the river. This will lower the level of the pound and let your boat pass beneath the bridge. Keep left as you go under as there are submerged remains of a towpath on the right.

The Bancroft Gardens basin, once an ornamental pond with a fountain and masses of water lilies, has been cleared to make moorings near the Royal Shakespeare Memorial Theatre. This is convenient for shopping up Bridge Street or Sheep Street, both of which lead to more shops in the High Street. There are beautiful alternative moorings on the river, one north of Lock 56 and one to the right opposite the theatre along a line of poplars. There is easy access to the town across the old tramway bridge. River mooring can be uncomfortable and should be avoided if the river is in flood.

Stratford-on-Avon is such a popular holiday centre with so many guides and books describing it in great detail that no full description is needed here. The official guide costs a shilling and the inside cover has a useful town map. The theatre is open from April to December and it would be a pity to miss going at least once. Shakespeare's birthplace is in Henley Street, and many other places are well worth a visit. There is old Holy Trinity church where he is buried, medieval Clopton Bridge over the Avon, Shakespeare's statue at the canal basin, the classic town hall, Harvard House and the neighbouring Garrick Inn, the Shrieve's House and Emms Court, the Guild Chapel, Guildhall, the Grammar School and almshouses, and many old timbered houses and inns. Anne Hathaway's thatched cottage at Shottery is a mile from the town and there are buses running there frequently. Stratford is like the hub of a wheel with roads stretching in all directions, offering sights everyone should see at least once in a lifetime. The surrounding country-side is dotted with farms, market gardens, woodlands, parks and orchards, stretching into the Cotswolds, the Vale of Evesham and the Edgehills, and delightful villages like Henley-in-Arden, Shipston-on-Stour, Chipping Campden and many others are within reasonable distance.

There are many interesting items to note on the return journey such as the fact that the balance beams carry an iron plaque with the words 'Built from English oak by Wyckham Blackwell Ltd., Hampton-in-Arden 1961-5', or that the reconstructed lock sides often show the oak leaf emblem of the National Trust. The tops of the bollards at some locks have inscriptions on them and there are beautifully restored lock cottages at Lock 25. The tow-paths are sound and easy and give an opportunity for some lock-wheeling. There are a great number of different grasses, reeds, cat-tails, ferns and wild flowers, and in the hedgerows and along the banks scores of many species of birds, and even dragonflies. Fishing along the southern section is private, however, and no guns are allowed along the canal according to the notices. At several locks there are useful white square signs with black symbols showing, for example, a telephone, a farmhouse loaf, or a mug of beer.

We had another talk with Mr Bannister, the National Trust representative, when collecting the deposit on our key for Lock 56. He has been on the waterways all his life and lived in the cottage now occupied by Mr and Mrs Wagstaffe for twenty-two years as the lock-keeper. We found the southern section of the canal very pretty and a relaxing interlude. As regards scenery, the thirteen-mile southern section, in our opinion, comes very close to the longer Llangollen Canal and the southern section of the Oxford Canal.

The northern section of the canal, a little over twelve miles long and under the control of the British Water-ways Board, was something of a surprise. We had been told that it was scarcely worth navigating. The Lap-worth Flight of nineteen locks is admittedly hard going, but as they have to be emptied after locking through, they will all be with you and the bottom gate can be gently pushed open with your bows. There is mooring on the curving concrete wall below Lock 14 and the Boot Inn is a few steps along the road to the left, giving easy access to the little village of Lapworth with its varied shops. Within a few miles of Lapworth are some of the finest country houses in England, Chadwick Manor, Knowle, Broom and Bushwood Halls and Wroxall Abbey.

Working your way some 120 ft up the Lapworth Flight will be all the more rewarding if you stop at Bridge 31 to visit fifteenth-century Packwood House whose gardens contain a magnificent yew hedge clipped to represent the Sermon on the Mount. Nearby is moated Packwood Hall.

Beyond the Lapworth Flight the canal turns into a shady tree-lined cut with lifting bridges to Hockley Heath. There are moorings at Swallow Cruisers beside the Wharf Inn, which shows a 'R U 18' licence plate beside the bar.

There is now more open countryside with distant views and then miles of shady cruising past the Bluebell, a cider house, and Earlswood Marina. You can moor here if you wish to visit the Roman remains and moated manors in the countryside round Waring's Green and Earlswood. The canal side then becomes rather built up before the 352 yard long Brandwood Tunnel, then a swing bridge and an imposing open guillotine stop lock. This is two massive gates operated by huge pulleys once used to preserve water rights, and leads to a short cut and the junction with the Worcester & Birmingham Canal at King's Norton.

This latter canal, built between 1791 and 1815 after constant battling with rival canal companies, is a wide waterway running for thirty miles from Worcester Bar junction, Birmingham (within half a mile of the city centre) to the River Severn at Worcester, with five tunnels totalling some 4,260 yards in length and fifty-eight narrow 7 ft-wide locks with a total fall of nearly 450 ft. You join it some $5\frac{1}{2}$ miles from Worcester Bar.

While famous for the longest flight of locks in the country, the Tardebigge Flight, it is particularly remembered by us because of an incident above the tunnel at Wast Hill. My wife spotted a plaid carrier bag in the water and hoisted it aboard. When the bag suddenly emitted an extraordinary noise she dropped it back into the canal and shouted 'Cat...cat...cat', urging me to reverse and retrieve the bag. As it was pulled aboard we could all hear mewing. Inside, wrapped in a scarf, was a tiny marmalade kitten, yelling for the very last of its nine lives. The sodden little creature was shorter than my hand and looked more like a rat than a cat as we rushed it down below where my wife dried it and gave it a little whisky in warm milk and then held it to dry off completely in the gas oven. He was immediately named 'Worcester' and allocated a cardboard box and a soft towel in the shower. I may add that no one used the shower while he was there, but his escapes were so numerous we had to put a lead on him. He has since grown into a handsome ginger cat with a tail like a fox's brush and a temper to match.

Once through Wast Hill Tunnel you are in Worcestershire and the countryside is one of rolling hills and woodland. Ahead are the Lickey Hills and in the far distance the Malverns and the Cotswolds. All along the canal are black and white country houses and charming villages. This part of the country is crossed by old Roman roads. Beyond Hopwood and the Bittel Arm lies Bittel reservoir, a bird watcher's paradise.

The waterway goes through wonderful scenery to the 613-yard-long Shortwood Tunnel and a mile beyond lies the first glimpse of big orchards, the Tardebigge Boat Company hire base and the Tardebigge Tunnel. This tunnel has been hewn largely from stone and both the width and height vary considerably. Outside the tunnel and past a British Waterways yard is the top of the famous Tardebigge Flight. In $2\frac{1}{4}$ winding miles there are thirty easily-worked locks with a total fall of 217 ft, but the views from the flight are magnificent throughout the $2\frac{1}{2}$ hours it will take to go through.

Here George Bate made friends with us and we found in him a fountain of local knowledge. He lockwheeled with me down a dozen locks and I learned that he had started work on the Worcester & Birmingham Canal at fourteen, eventually becoming a lock-gate maker. He retired in 1968 at the age of sixty-seven, with a British Empire Medal, but had returned to oversee the Tardebigge Flight for the 1969 season. His father had been a maintenance man on the canal all his working life. His grandfather had been a trader on the canal and had been the innkeeper at the Queen's Head between Locks 29 and 28 and also the local blacksmith. His great-grandfather was the blacksmith who founded the smithy behind the Queen's Head when the canal was being built. In this smithy the first horses and donkeys which towed the boats along the canal had been shod.

The Tardebigge Flight is followed almost immediately by the Stoke Flight of six locks with a total fall of 42 ft. Along this flight are signs of old canal arms which once carried boats to the salt workings at Stoke Prior. Brine was first brought up from great depths here by the inventor, John Corbett, who devised the most perfect system of salt manufacture in the world. Near the bottom lock is an unusual shop with canal souvenirs for sale and rare 'pie crust' plates recovered from working narrow boats, and the clever woodcraft of R. G. Sherwin. This shop also has authentically designed working boatmen's corduroy and moleskin front-flapped trousers.

Through the Astwood Flight of six locks dropping 42 ft you will find that the canal is higher than the surrounding land, with long views of rolling wooded hills. Next comes Hanbury Wharf and Marina, all that remains of the disused Droitwich Arm, built by James Brindley along the Roman road of Salt Way to Droitwich. This town, one of the oldest in England, is famous both for its salt and as a spa. The springs are so impregnated with brine that the water is reputed to be over eleven times the strength of sea water and with a greater density than that of the Dead Sea.

After the weir at Hadzor you will reach Dunhampstead Tunnel, the last and lowest of the five on the canal, and only 275 yards long, and as you emerge the Malvern Hills loom ahead. Then follows the Offerton and Tolladine Flight of eight locks, falling a further 56 ft into open countryside with the spires of Worcester Cathedral in sight some four miles away. From here you can visit Hindlip Hall and Park, which is less than a mile from the canal.

The approach to Diglis Yacht Basin is built up and the water becomes literally black. Entry into the River Severn is through two barge locks operated by a lock-keeper.

You will find excellent moorings at Worcester, below the railway bridge to the right. The town is hardly impressive, but the cathedral, which took 500 years to complete, and the Royal Porcelain works are worth visiting.

From Worcester it is only a four-hour run down the Severn to Tewkesbury and the beautiful River Avon. You will certainly want to make the few stops possible on the fast-flowing stream. As you leave Worcester you will pass once more under the main bridge and will notice high brick walls on the left with mooring rings in them. These were put there long ago but there is now little water beneath them and the town has done no dredging. Leaving the cathedral and the entrance to the Worcester & Birmingham Canal on the left, you come to a river junction. Keep to the left here as the right-hand stream leads to a dangerous weir. Diglis Locks nearby are electrically operated, one being over 93 ft long and 17 ft 9 ins wide and the other 142 ft long and 30 ft wide, both controlled by 'traffic lights'. The banks of the Severn are some 15 ft high with huge boulders to prevent erosion piled along the right-hand bank, and trees on the left.

There are few landmarks but you will soon see the narrow mouth of the River Teme, which rises in Wales. The countryside is now heavily wooded and the Malvern Hills dominate the landscape. Despite the high banks, there are many lovely views. Moorings for the charming village of Kempsey are on an old barge. You can explore the Malvern Hills and visit the town of Malvern from appropriately named 'Cliffey Wood' on the right.

The Severn along the next few reaches is rather like a miniature Rhine. There are manors and churches perched high above the river, as are the Rhineland castles, on the approach to Upton-on-Severn. This town, once a flourishing port for two shires, is pure delight, but not at weekends. There are moorings on the stone steps at the foot of the bridge on the right. Most of the pubs in this fishing town are above average, and offer superb meals, particularly at the Old Swan, and excellent rough cider or 'scrumpy' at the Plough. Giving the little town a kind of French air is a national monument, the remains of a church on whose thirteenth-century tower a copper cupola, which is now blue, was erected in 1780.

Beyond Upton there are more wooded banks and after rounding Sandy Point and abreast of Uckinghall Meadow the spires of Tewkesbury Abbey can be seen. There are many pretty villages in this part of the country but mooring on the Severn is not easy. The chart of the river must be consulted, coupled with probing with the boathook, to find suitable moorings along the wild banks. Twenty minutes after the M50 bridge, and it is wise to note that the Severn speed limits are 6 m.p.h. upstream and 8 m.p.h. downstream, you will pass under Wythe Bridge and it is then only five minutes to the mouth of the Avon on the left. This is a hazardous spot, with shoals extending well out into the main river and you must pass the junction before turning wide to enter the Avon from downstream of its mouth. Keep to the right once you enter the Avon as far as the lock gates and the unusual new lock cottage, on stilts. Lock charges vary according to the size of your craft and length of stay, but with our boat of over 40 ft long, through all eight Avon locks over a seven-day period, it cost us £2. The official handbook on navigation of the Lower Avon is on sale at the lock house. There are also various souvenirs for sale here. To the right are public moorings by Healing's Mill, or you can moor just upstream of the 800-year-old King John's Bridge on the left as you leave the lock.

Tewkesbury is a pleasant blending of old with new, and the town is laid out in three main streets in the form of the letter Y, the stem leading to the splendid Norman abbey church at the southern end of the town. The handsome water mill close by the abbey is twelfth-century. Shopping is a pleasure here and the High Street has ancient shop fronts and signs. Fowler and Sons supply sherry from casks by the gallon. The white timbered The Ancient Grudge restaurant and delightful alleys are reminiscent of medieval times. The inns of the town are good value too, including the Bell, associated with the book *John Halifax, Gentleman,* the Hop Pole Hotel, mentioned in *Pickwick Papers,* and Ye Olde Black Bear. reputedly 'Gloster's Oldest Inn'.

CHAPTER 14

BACK THROUGH BIRMINGHAM

THE AVON is undoubtedly one of England's most beautiful and peaceful rivers. You owe your holiday on it to a number of people, not least the Lower Avon Navigation Trust, a charitable organisation formed in 1950 which restored the navigation between Tewkesbury and Evesham after twelve years of arduous labour. Today, although a few locks leak, the navigation is maintained in good condition by voluntary private subscriptions without any help from the government, and it is the first successful restoration of its kind in the world. Craft up to 70 ft long, 13 ft 6 ins in beam and 4 ft draught can now safely cruise on the twenty-seven miles from the River Severn to Bridge Inn above Evesham Lock.

For some strange reason the speed limit on the Lower Avon Navigation is 10 m.p.h., which we consider is too fast and should be brought into line with the River Severn limits. After passing under the biggest but angled arch of King John's Bridge, you enter a broad and deep reach with a great many sailing craft about. You must give way to these boats, even if they cut right across your bows. Some 2½ miles out of Tewkesbury you will come to Twyning Fleet on the left with moorings by the Fleet Inn. Tewkesbury has virtually no outskirts along the river and you are at once in a rural setting with cattle grazing in the fields, pretty woodland and lovely hills ahead.

Bredon, little more than a mile from Twyning Fleet, has a lovely fourteenth-century Tithe Barn and a little church

with an almost needle spire. You will find the lock-keeper
at Strensham Lock most helpful. He is treasurer of the
Staffordshire & Worcestershire Canal Society and can tell
you much about the waterways in the area. He owns and
runs a little and useful shop there. From this lock the
river winds its way through beautiful countryside to the
charming sixteenth-century red sandstone Eckington
Bridge, the most perfect of all the old bridges surviving in
the county. As you cruise along the Avon you will see not
only meadows and hills, fields with sheep and cattle and
many orchards, but countless willow trees lining the banks.
The unspoilt beauty is broken only by a few villages and
houses, some almost as large as 'stately homes'. The settings
of the locks cannot be bettered on any waterway. It is only
three-quarters of a mile from Eckington Bridge to Swan's
Neck bend where the river narrows and twists with a bend
of 180°, and it is wise to reduce speed here. There is a
swing bridge over Nafford Lock which should be closed
again after going through. If you follow the path leading
off from the left of the lock to the road, you will come to
the old-world village of Birlingham with its orchards and
cottages. Here is the Swan Inn, and a shop. St James's
Church can be found through a gateway, once the twelfth-
century chancel arch of the church.

You are now coming into the supreme beauty of the
River Avon. Swans will come close to your boat for food
and you may see graceful terns and marauding hawks, as
we did. Near Pershore you will pass under the centre of
two bridges almost side by side, one relatively modern,
and the other a thing of beauty built for wayfarers of the
fourteenth century. The lock here is an unusual one,
having shallow diamond-shaped sides and a deep centre
portion which is parallel-sided. Put your boat up against
the planks instead of on the sloping beams on the right. It
is only two minutes from moorings at the foot of the rec-

reation grounds to the small market town of Pershore, said to have derived its name from the pear trees that once grew on the 'shores' of the Avon here. Some parts of the lovely abbey with its delightful lantern tower date from 1090, but work was not completed until the fourteenth century. It is the only church I know of which has a lock key or windlass on its interior walls, with a plaque reading: 'To the Glory of God as a symbol of Thanksgiving for the completion of the work of restoration this lock key was placed here by the Lower Avon Navigation Trust—1962'.

Pershore and Wyre locks are only just over a mile apart and sailing dinghies often use this short reach. At the lock there is an old grist mill converted into a social club. There are moorings here for water. Beyond Wyre Lock the river twists and turns through orchards and beautiful country-side with superb views of Bredon Hill. You may notice that there is no towpath along the Lower Avon. This is due to the fact that horse-drawn traffic was unknown on this river. Early craft using the navigation were sailing barges carry-ing grain and flour and coal, and when necessary, these 35 ft barges were bow-hauled by men.

Standing high on the left bank beyond Wyre Lock is the little village of Wyre Piddle with gardens coming right down to the waterfront. The Anchor Inn serves really good food and you can have your meal brought to you on board if you wish. There is little sign of habitation on the three-mile winding reach to the 1887 Jubilee Bridge, carry-ing the road between the villages of Fladbury and Crop-thorne. There is a very narrow navigation with a blind corner leading to Fladbury Lock. If I had to choose one lock as the loveliest in England I would have to choose Fladbury, with its impressive weir and two picturesque old mills.

As you reach the undulating Evesham golf course, you will find big loops in the river with delightful water meadows below the Woodnorton hills. Chadbury Mill and Lock, the last lock before Evesham, follow and soon you will see Abbey Manor through the trees. An obelisk in the grounds marks the site of the Battle of Evesham in 1265 in which Simon de Montfort, Earl of Leicester and reputed to be the founder of English parliamentary government, was slain. Closer to the river is the Leicester tower, built in 1840.

A huge horseshoe bend makes the prosperous market-garden town of Evesham into a peninsula. At the warning sign for Hampton Ferry blow three blasts on your horn to have the ferry rope lowered, and when passing over it put the engine in neutral as a safeguard against propeller fouling. Evesham Borough moorings are on the right, near a watering point in the little park. The handsome bridge ahead is Workman Bridge, about a hundred years old. Navigation is possible as far upstream as the Boat Inn, beyond Evesham Lock, but the Lower Avon Navigation Trust's control ends at Evesham Lock, and until the entire river from Stratford is made navigable again the shoals above this lock are likely to remain and cruising is inadvisable.

Opposite the moorings are lovely gardens sloping to the river and behind them Evesham's Bell Tower, dating from 1539, with its famous peal of twelve bells. There was once a massive abbey church here, founded on the basis of a vision of the Virgin by a swineherd, but little remains of it now, but the parish church of All Saints and the Pilgrims' church of St Lawrence with their noble spires still stand proudly. The abbey gateway is a memorable corner and the Almonery Museum in the fourteenth-century Almonery of the former Benedictine monastery, has exhibits on view which tell the story of Evesham from prehistoric times.

Heavy rains in the Midlands for several days before our

arrival at Evesham caused the river to flood and shortened our stay. As the water rose we hastily returned to Tewkesbury to make sure that we could get under King John's Bridge, the lowest on the navigation, before the floodwaters marooned us on the Lower Avon. In spite of the dark and glowering skies, mist hanging over the hills and for a time a torrential downpour, the return cruise of about twenty seven miles with six locks in under six hours was a happy one. It was very peaceful as no other craft were moving, the cattle were lying huddled in their pastures and the willows along the banks were literally weeping.

Locking out of Avon Lock for the River Severn we were tempted to run down once more to Gloucester and Sharpness, and on to the Bristol Avon. However, I have deliberately excluded detailing such a cruise from this book; although Gloucester, Bristol and Bath, the pleasant riverside and canal-side pubs, and the prospect of visiting the Wildfowl Trust at Slimbridge were all very inviting, this is a cruise filled with dangers for the inexperienced. The Severn is one of the oldest navigations in Europe and tidal effects increase as it nears Gloucester. However, the spectacular and famous Severn bore, that peculiar formation of a tidal wave rising at times to as much as 10 ft, which sweeps up the river at the head of each spring tide, will not affect your cruising above Tewkesbury.

Although you have already cruised from Worcester to Tewkesbury you will find that the wide river is more beautiful than ever when travelling upstream. The river runs fast too, so it will take you somewhat longer to cruise back to Worcester. Above Worcester you are quickly into wooded banks and open fields. Three miles from Worcester is Bevere Lock, operated by lock-keepers as are all locks on the Severn, and three hoots on the horn will get you through between 6 a.m. and 7.15 p.m. You now go past the silted entry to the derelict Droitwich Barge Canal. On this 'Wich Barges', sailing craft similar to those on the Severn, used to travel to Droitwich for cargoes of salt.

The river now goes through meadowlands to Grimley. As wooded hills rise on the right you will see tiny chalets in rows on the right bank with freshly painted fences and miniature gardens. The turrets of Holt Castle are visible on the left and Holt Lock follows with moorings for the Lenchford Hotel, an old and attractive building. We had here the most hilarious meal we have ever had on this kind of holiday. Silver salvers were topped by tins of baked beans and slices of toast, there were French mustard pots with leaping jacks-in-the-box, coffee cups the size of chamber pots and hinged spoons which had us all in hysterics. This kind of service would perhaps not always be welcomed but we were in the mood to appreciate the fun.

I have not mentioned all the inns and pubs on the banks of the Severn, of which there are many, as your chart will show, but the names are fascinating. Many have nautical ones, Ship, Sloop, Barge and Jolly Waterman, and others are named after animals, birds and fish, such as Lion, Hart, Bull, Dog and Duck, Bird-in-Hand, Salmon and even Plate of Elvers. As might be expected there is a Shakespeare. Virtually all were once navigation inns, catering for river men. Many carried on 'sidelines', trading in coal, fodder, bricks or general merchandise, and some were possibly engaged in smuggling.

Lincomb Lock is a mile below Stourport where the banks are lined with timber yards, factories and oil depots. On the left is the cliff knows as Redstone Rock with a great labyrinth of chambers. The British Waterways moorings are disgraceful and it is advisable to go on past the big barge locks of the Staffordshire & Worcester Canal on the right to the humpbacked bridge entry to the narrow locks, installed in 1781 to save water, a few dozen yards further on. The lock-keeper will help you through the two pairs of staircase locks to the four basins 42 ft above the Severn where there are good moorings and facilities.

The Staffordshire & Worcestershire Canal, which was opened in 1772, is linked to the Severn by these locks and basins, all interconnected and criss-crossed by pathways and bridges. The old Tontine Hotel, which stands here, was named after Lorenzo Tonti, the originator of a 'life assurance' scheme whereby a number of people contributed to a fund and the last survivor took the lot. The ancient warehouse with the white-painted clock tower is a masterpiece of its kind and fortunately has been declared an 'ancient monument', being used by the Stourport Yacht Club.

Stourport is an example of a canal town which still retains its old-time character with its waterway attractions which are happily under a Conservation Order. It owes its very existence to Brindley for he brought the canal here only after the nearby town of Bewdley had rejected the scheme. The views from Areley Kings church on a nearby hill are memorable and the churchyard shows many amusing epitaphs.

The narrow York Street Lock, with its nearby 'Boat Shop', has excellent souvenirs of the canal and delightful watercolours of waterside scenes. Once past the 60 ft weir and Upper Minton Bridge (No. 8) you will be in open countryside. Most bridges appear to be sited on blind corners but are distinctly numbered and named on pleasant iron plaques. The canal runs high above meadowland with hills rising gently beyond, through many one-sided red sandstone cuttings with bracken-covered banks and profuse growth of trees, vying for the sun. You cruise past Olding Woods to Falling Sands Lock with a cast iron split bridge, similar to those on the Stratford-on-Avon canal. From here you can see the factory chimneys of carpet-making Kidder-minster. Mooring is a problem here for there are several miles of industrialised canalside before you reach Wol-verley Court Lock and open countryside once again. There are lovely flowers here and flowering weeds amidst cat-tails; the pound is one of the most delightful on any canal, with low-lying meadows on one side and wooded sandstone cliffs on the other. Near Wolverley Lock is the Lock Inn with one of the finest collections of horse trap-pings ever seen outside a museum. If you walk along the road on the other side of the canal you will come to the top of the hill and will find the unique 'Wolverley Pound', an open-topped cavern of sandstone with an iron gate once used to impound straying animals until they were claimed. Down the one-way road, past the red brick eight-eenth-century Italianate church, is the enchanting 'lost village' of Wolverley. It nestles beside a little stream, with ancient stone cottages and the former Sebright Grammar School, which was built in 1620 by Sir William Sebright and has unexpectedly noble proportions. It is no longer a school but is used to some extent by the local council. Were it not for the Kidderminster factories this canal would challenge the Oxford and Llangollen for being the most beautiful. Beyond Wolverley Forge Bridge it narrows and passes through a rock-hewn bed and creeper-covered sand-stone cliffs. At Debdale Lock with its rock cliff and cave you will find a circular weir, one of many built when the canal was constructed to save space, and possibly the first you have ever seen.

After the sixty-five-yard-long Cookley Tunnel the canal is bordered by ferns and wild balsam and many kinds of trees flourish along the banks. Past aptly named 'Hanging Rock' you enter Staffordshire. The narrow Whittington Horse Bridge is the place to moor if you wish to visit the famous oak-timbered Whittington Inn, dating back to 1300 and reputed to be haunted by Lady Jane Grey.

Beyond the Horse Bridge you will see more cave dwellings amidst the trees. Until the turn of the century they were inhabited by boating families and this particular area became known as 'Gibraltar'. From Kinver Lock you can visit the town of that name and also nearby Kinver Edge, a wild area of woodland gorse, once the home of prehistoric men. The National Trust now preserves the ancient cave dwellings. A narrow cut soon brings you to small Dunsley Tunnel and Stewponey Lock, with a pub, a modern steak bar, a shop and garage. There are buses from here to Stourbridge where the famous crystal glassware is made. Then comes the entrance to the Stourbridge Canal, which links with the Birmingham Canal Navigations. It is only just over five miles long with twenty narrow locks through pleasant agricultural country and is a boon to those who wish to 'pub-crawl' for it has at least two pubs for every mile of waterway.

You now go on past an area known as Devil's Den and through six more locks, bordered by pubs ancient and modern, under Giggety Bridge to moorings for beautiful Wimbourn. From Bumble Hole Lock modern housing estates begin to encroach but there are pleasant views of the Orton hills. The unique Bratch Locks need particular care. They are not staircase locks but three individual ones separated by very short pounds fed from side ponds. Locking instructions must be followed to the letter or you may ground your boat on a flooded lockside. There is normally a lockkeeper on duty to help you. The flight is most attractive with its white bridges and white octagonal toll house.

After seven more locks at the rate of one a mile you are on the summit level, 294 ft above the Severn at Stourport, having navigated 33 locks and one of the loveliest stretches of canal anywhere. It is less than two miles to Aldersley Junction and the Birmingham Canal Navigations.

Today all but sixty-eight miles of the vast complex of canals on three levels round Birmingham, known as the Birmingham Canal Navigations, are navigable, a total of 112 miles having been adopted as official 'cruiseways'. Cruising these waterways, for the most part running through heavily industrialised areas, may seem dull, sordid and uninteresting but unless you go through at least some of them you will have missed the very heart and soul of our inland waterways. The Inland Waterways Association held a special rally at Farmer's Bridge on the B.C.N. in July 1969 in a publicity bid to save the remaining sixty-eight miles of these fascinating canals. Birmingham is the centre of the country's canal system and the focal point of the St Andrew's Cross which forms the rough layout of the network and connects the main rivers of the country. If you count the currently unnavigable canals, this large city is said to have more miles of canals than Venice. The 7 ft lock (many are a little wider) is standard throughout the system which is fed by drainage pumped from the many disused mine shafts and other pumping wells in the vicinity. The Wolverhampton level is the highest of the three levels on the system, being 473 ft above sea level, the Birmingham level is 453 ft and the Walsall level is 408 ft above sea level.

From the Staffordshire & Worcestershire Canal the 'Wolverhampton 21' flight carries you up to the Wolverhampton level, and into the city of Wolverhampton. The countryside is quickly taken over by industry and there is virtually nothing to stop for through this flight of locks. Factories standing cheek by jowl along the canal side are not such eyesores as the countless arms and basins leading from the canal, now largely dumps or graveyards for rotting narrow boats. As you go along you can watch hot steel rods like long flares coming from the blast furnaces, or penetrate deep into the Black Country by taking the Wednesbury Oak loop for the two mile run into Bradley. The main line continues through the wide Coseley Tunnel, 360 yards long and with railed towpaths on both sides. At Factory Junction you can turn right through Tipton and follow the Wolverhampton Level to Smethwick 6 miles ahead via Oldbury, which is Brindley's original line, or, as we did, lock through the three Tipton Factory Locks on to Telford's Birmingham Level.

We had no choice, for the M5 motorway was under construction when we were cruising here and huge signs warned us to use the Birmingham Level. We had planned to explore Dudley Tunnel on the nearby Dudley Canal, an unusual 3,172-yard tunnel built in the 1790s with a complete system of basins, branches to old workings and limestone caverns.

By the locks you will find the first of the former gauging stations where commercial craft were measured for displacement in order to make life easier for the toll clerks on the B.C.N. Below the locks is the first of a number of twin-arched bridges. Always take the left-hand arches into Birmingham at each of these bridges as only the left hand channels have been dredged. Also pass to the left of the 'toll islands' you will meet.

The canal now runs straight as a Roman road through Dudley Port past the junction for the Netherton Tunnel branch to the Dudley Canal. Netherton Tunnel was completed in 1858, is some 2,027 yards long and was the last canal tunnel built and is the biggest in circumference. Two boats can pass inside, it has twin towpaths and is actually lit, first by gas and later by electricity.

Now on a high embankment the canal soars past junction after junction to Spon Lane locks, the oldest working canal locks in the country, and the new M5 motorway

with only a 7 ft 3 ins gap left for navigation. It was somewhat harrowing passing by the tall steel girders of the
motorway with the clanging of work going on high overhead. Brindley's old line also shortly passed overhead on
the Stewart Aqueduct.

The Main Line now lies in a valley some 40 ft deep,
Telford's famous Galton Cutting, the sides being most
attractive with gorse and wild flowers. Next comes the magnificent arch of Telford's Galton Bridge, one handsome
span of cast iron across the 150 ft gap. From all the loops
you have passed since Deepfield's Junction you will
appreciate the scope of Telford's canal-straightening project
here.

At Farmer's Bridge there is a round island with signs
pointing to Coventry, Worcester and Wolverhampton. By
following the sign to Worcester, a few hundred yards will
bring you to Worcester Bar and Gas Street Basin with
excellent overnight moorings, only five minutes from the
centre of Birmingham. There are alternative overnight
moorings along the route to Coventry, just above Farmer's
Bridge Locks. We moored here where the city of Birmingham and British Waterways have restored the canal to its
former glory. A lovely marina has been built by the shining
white lock cottages and the British Waterways Board has
opened an information centre and a canal shop. An old
30 cwt crane stands beside the marina, and a new pub, the
Longboat, was being constructed when we were there. The
lane from the marina to the British Waterways Board
centre has been appropriately named 'James Brindley
Walk' to mark the exemplary cooperation between the
city and waterways authorities.

We found Farmer's Bridge most attractive. The flight
of thirteen locks, with L-shaped pounds and freshly painted
black and white balance beams, falls sharply to disappear
after half a dozen locks under a bridge. After leaving

the flight there is a short factory-lined pound with the Birmingham & Fazeley Canal continuing to the left at Aston Junction through the 11 Aston Locks. Keep right here into the Digbeth Branch, almost a mile long, and after two bridges you will reach the six Ashted Locks, which are in rather sordid surroundings. You have to make a sharp left turn under Bridge 96 into the narrow Warwick Bar and it is easy to miss. The Birmingham Canal Navigations will appeal to the enthusiast much more than to the novice who must remember that weekend passage can be restricted and that pleasant overnight moorings are very limited indeed.

Although now out of the B.C.N. through Camp Hill Locks the Grand Union flows past factory after factory with only a few glades of overhanging trees for some six miles to Bridge 79. Here you now reach open countryside again. You will find pleasant moorings just beyond Bridge 78 or Catherine de Barnes Bridge. The attractive village of the same name lies sprawled on either side of the canal. The Grand Union now wends its way through prosperous farming country to the first of the wide locks on the long route to London. Knowle Locks, a pretty flight of five, falling 42 ft from the summit level of 379 ft, provide splendid views of Warwickshire. The delightful village of Knowle is less than half a mile away and not far from Knowle is the Forest of Arden and the Tudor Grimshaw Hall.

Beyond the locks the canal runs high above the meadows and fields. Then comes the Black Buoy Cruising Club on the right with the Black Boy Inn on the left by Bridge 69. The front door of this tiny plain pub is on the canal side and, according to the present publican, has been for over 200 years, making it older than the canal itself which was completed in 1799.

Here we met Mr Neville Bent, Commodore of the Black Buoy Cruising Club, and owner of the *Iron Duke* narrow cruiser moored in front of the pub. It boasts two original paintings of the Duke of Wellington and is a unique craft, the 35 ft hull coming from a British Waterways steam pump boat, formerly used to clean out locks. Mr Bent built the superstructure and fitted her out himself in well-planned comfort to sleep six. The unique feature of the *Iron Duke*, apart from her specially commissioned portraits, is that she has twin screws, something we had never come across before in a narrow canal cruiser. One is powered by a small Enfield diesel and the other by an electric motor and batteries.

Three bridges beyond the Black Boy is Rising Bridge, No. 66, and from here you are within easy reach of Baddesley Clinton, one of the best examples of Tudor architecture anywhere in Warwickshire. The village is charming and a fine centre for pleasant country walks. One more bridge and you are back at Kingswood Junction and the short cut to the Stratford-on-Avon Canal. There remains only the dripping Shrewley Tunnel, the Hatton Flight and Cape Locks with its boaters' pub and you are at Warwick, having covered, if you have done the entire trip, $244\frac{1}{2}$ miles and 300 locks, or $544\frac{1}{2}$ lock miles. Our actual cruising time was 103 hours and 28 minutes which means an average speed of just a fraction over five lock miles per hour.

With time in hand you can tour beautiful Warwick, with its magnificent castle, or continue along the canal for a couple of miles and take in gracious Leamington Spa. Your cruise has taken you through the very heart of England—Shakespeare's country. You have been exposed to history and heritage, to the works of many craftsmen both on and off the canals and rivers in the four counties of Warwickshire, Worcestershire, Staffordshire and Gloucestershire. It is, along with the adventure of the canals of the Black Country, a voyage of enchantment.

CHAPTER 15

ADVENTURES TO COME

THE INLAND waterways already described will keep any boating convert happily in holidays for a decade or more. Apart from the River Thames, which could not possibly be excluded, all these ribbons of water are still remarkably unpublicised and still largely empty of pleasure craft, even in the height of summer. The amateur can cruise any of them with complete confidence and, escaping from noisy crowds, find a forgotten heritage in perfect peace. They offer such endless variety and extensive choice that boredom is impossible, however discriminating or eccentric the tastes of the skipper or crew may be.

There are more inland waterways, of course, many hundreds of miles of them. They are not less interesting, exciting or beautiful but if I am to follow my own advice to the novice of not attempting to travel too far too soon I must leave you with the expectation and anticipation of more thrilling boating adventures to come.

The short River Wey and Lee & Stort navigations have not been described for they are more suited to weekend outings or brief excursions from cruises on major waterways. Nor have I dealt with the Kennet & Avon Canal and the two short river navigations which once formed a broad water route across the south of England to link the Thames and the Severn. There are a few isolated navigable sections but the vast majority of this waterway is derelict and through navigation is impossible. The Kennet & Avon Canal Association, formed in 1951, was transformed in 1962 into the Kennet & Avon Canal Trust and restoration work has been undertaken and is continuing in many places. The pace is slow, the problems formidable and the finance hard to come by but one day with luck we may yet cruise from Reading to Bristol.

I must confess to some slight prejudice in giving the Broads so little space. The Broads, however, are the most popular and most publicised of all our inland waterways and today boats per mile on these waters are more dense than vehicles per mile on our roads, with one reliable source estimating over eighty as compared with seventy-four. The navigational areas are being extended but after holidaying on the cuts where there are only about four boats per mile, the Broads have less appeal to one seeking essentially to escape from the hustle and bustle, the noise and stress of everyday life.

I am in no way suggesting that you ignore the Broads, particularly if you want to be in on what is called 'the scene'. But unless you want lots of company and prefer socialising to privacy I would recommend that you book your hire craft for either early or late in the season. If the popular resort type of holiday appeals to you, you will greatly enjoy the Broads and its many amenities. You will find many reports on the Broads when holiday supplements are published in newspapers, magazines and other mass media. Any of the three Broads hire craft associations will provide copious literature about these pleasant waterways.

You will have noticed that while the waterways of the South, East, West and the Midlands have been explored in this book, the waterways system of the North has not. There are many good reasons for this. The Trent, Humber and Yorkshire Ouse tideways are no places for beginners to learn the rudiments of navigation and boat handling.

In any case, special permission is necessary to take hire craft on these tideways.

The Trent, of course, is the waterways artery to the North, linking up not only with the Humber, Yorkshire Ouse, Ancholme, Don and Hull rivers but with a vast network of navigations that join Rotherham, Doncaster and Sheffield, Wakefield, Huddersfield and Sowerby Bridge, Goole, Leeds, Burnley, Wigan, Leigh, Manchester, Runcorn and Liverpool by water and sprawl across the north of England. On the way to the North the Trent picks up the ancient Fossdyke and Witham Navigations and the semi-derelict Chesterfield Canal. Beyond these junctions bows can be pointed west to Hull and Grimsby, north to Goole, Selby, York and Ripon, and west into a canal network that encompasses the Aire & Calder, Calder & Hebble, Huddersfield, Stainforth & Keadby, Selby, New Junction, Sheffield and South Yorkshire, all of which still throb to commercial traffic, some surprisingly heavy. Some experience is desirable in order to obtain maximum enjoyment from these waterways. The remote and isolated Lancaster Canal must be included in the canals of the North on geographical grounds and, of course, that pride of the North, the cross-country Leeds & Liverpool Canal, which is the very heart of the system.

Although the Lancaster and the Leeds & Liverpool Canals are eminently suitable for beginners and are among the wildest and most beautiful in the country, they cannot be divorced from an appreciation of the waterways of the North which deserve a book of their own to do them justice. I and most of my boating friends tend to reserve the Leeds & Liverpool for that last great fling, holding holidays upon it in abeyance so as to have one last prize to enjoy.

This explains why I am reserving the waterways of the North for a sequel to this book which has been written essentially for those who have never enjoyed a holiday on

our inland waterways. The novices going for their first
venture on skis wisely head for the nursery slopes rather
than risk their limbs on terrain that gladdens the hearts of
the experts. There is challenge and scope and excitement
enough for the beginner and convert alike on the inland
waterways described in previous chapters. Taking on more
than you can handle, exposing your crew of family or
friends to unnecessary risks, defeats the whole purpose of
carefree, peaceful holidays on the water. If you have no
confidence in your ability to cope and worse still if your
crew suffers from anxiety because you are clearly out of
your depth, the boating holiday will be spoiled for everyone.

From experience I can assure you that you and your
crew will get so much more out of holidays on the waterways of the North if you reserve them for later adventures.
I still get a thrill every time I recall locking out of Keadby
and taking the tide to Trent Falls, arriving just after low
water to catch the tide there all the way to Naburn Locks
just below York, particularly as I had worked out the
precise timings for myself. I remember with some chagrin
grounding momentarily in the rushing Trent off Torksey
and the entrance to the Fossdyke Navigation in the glowering dusk. The sudden meeting of a long train of 'Tom
Puddings', those coal-laden compartment boats linked in a
convoy of nineteen and towed by a tug, as we swung into
the Aire & Calder from the Selby Canal is stamped indel-
ibly in the minds of our crew and none of them will forget
the exciting navigation of the Linton 'clay huts' on the
Ouse above York. Many memories come back sharply:
roaring down the New Junction with half a dozen massive
barges and locking through the Sheffield & South Yorkshire with craft that made our cruiser look like a lifeboat in
comparison; shooting the fast flowing Ouse current under
the battered wooden bridge at Selby; the sight of mount-

ains of detergent foam on the dangerous Don; manoeuvering with ocean-going shipping at Goole and slithering smoothly across the tide past the tall open lock gates at West Stockwith. When eventually you go on the waterways of the North you will find a completely different kind of boating holiday, and get supreme satisfaction from mastering the tides, the shifting sands, the obstructions to navigation and even from little things like countering the high wake of passing barges without allowing your bows to move off course.

I would emphasise that your craft is the most important element in your boating holiday and time spent in ensuring that the craft you hire suits your particular needs is never wasted, indeed pays you handsomely in the enjoyment of your holiday. We have tried broad and narrow-beamed cruisers from only a few of the many hire firms now operating and with regret have not had the time diligently to inspect every boatyard and the craft they offer for hire, although we have covered quite a few. We have for the most part travelled with a sizeable crew on combinations of waterways and therefore craft that have suited us perfectly may not be your particular cup of tea. No one can supply you with a list of 'best boats' or classify hire firms in order of importance, convenience or value for money, although I stand by my comments on those already mentioned. If you neglect the basic 'homework' described in earlier chapters you will only have yourself to blame for unnecessary disappointments on your boating holiday. You may feel that you wish to have the minimum of planning, but to make sure of the greatest possible enjoyment of your holiday on the waterways do give yourself plenty of time to choose your hire craft carefully.

POSTSCRIPT, 1986

ARE ENGLAND's inland waterways still a fascinating heritage bringing peace and pleasure to all those forsaking humdrum routine for freedom and adventure? Fifteen years have elapsed since the first publication of *Slow Boat Through England*, during which the country has been inflicted with recession and violence and sorely tried by savage cuts in public expenditure and steep rises in inflation. Membership of the European Economic Community has brought gradual closer orientation towards, if not integration with, the Continent. And all through the period concern for the environment and pressure for conservation has mushroomed and spread as never before.

Can you, therefore, seriously expect to find the inland waterways—a long-neglected and ageing system crumbling under the ravages of time—anything as described a decade and a half ago? The answer to both questions is a surprising and resounding 'yes'—and a story with many elements to enhance your appreciation and enjoyment of a waterways holiday in the 80s and 90s.

The 1968 Transport Act dividing the 1,950 miles of nationalized inland waterways into commercial, cruising and remainder waterways, has significantly helped to stop the rot, foster new hope and spur authorities and enthusiasts alike into a massive campaign for waterways improvement.

Of course, the further decay and deterioration of the fabric of canals going back some two centuries was not and could not be miraculously stemmed by a 'waterways charter'. It continues, often drastically and dramatically, to this very day. At this writing the famous century-old Anderton Lift, which carries boats between the Trent and Mersey Canal and the Weaver Navigation, is, despite costly repairs in 1981, once again closed to traffic. Its restoration may well depend upon whether it has a useful role to play in the possible development of a major tourist attraction in the area. In the past year canal beds have failed, embankments have been breached, and erosion has continued to take its toll on waterways as different as the commercial Aire and Calder Navigation and the popular Llangollen Canal cruiseway. There have been unparalleled disasters, too. As recently as 1983 no fewer than seven strategic tunnels were closed simultaneously for repairs. The 1¾-mile Blisworth Tunnel on the Grand Union, main link between the canals of the north and south, was closed for four years until repairs, using modern technology and equipment, were completed ahead of schedule in 1984 at a cost of £4.5 million, over 10% of the total annual budget of the British Waterways Board's engineering department.

Nevertheless, when viewed in retrospect against conditions fifteen years ago, both our nationalized and other inland waterways are in much better condition. Miles upon miles of banks have been protected and restored, the channels have been extensively improved and dredged and related lock gates and other waterway structures renewed. The general level of care has markedly improved.

Remarkably, no waterways have been lost to navigation. Indeed, over a hundred miles have been added to the more than 3,000-mile long combined accessible network of rivers and canals controlled by the British Waterways Board and over a dozen other navigation authorities. All provide more scope for all waterway users but boaters will find particularly valuable the restoration of the Ashton and Lower Peak Forest canals which revived the exciting 'Cheshire

Ring', and the re-opening of the River Avon from Evesham to Stratford, forging another scenic ring route.

This is not the full story; much more has and is being done. There is no doubt that the Fraenkel Report was a major turning point. This two-year engineering study of the operating and maintenance costs of the nationalized inland waterways commissioned by the Department of the Environment exposed a massive backlog of maintenance and reported in 1975 the need for a £168 million programme over 15 years. The government was slow to react—additional grants did not begin until 1979—and it was not until 1982 that the Board, faced with a formidable programme of work on major structures including reservoirs, bridges and tunnels, began to receive anything like realistic grants. Provided grant levels are maintained the Board's new Corporate Plan for the ten years 1985/86 to 1994/95 estimates that most of the arrears of maintenance will have been overcome in that time.

Despite a complete change in attitude towards the inland waterways vigilance must be maintained. The 82 miles of remainder waterways—the lengths of the Ashton, the Erewash, the lower Peak Forest, the Monmouthshire and Brecon canals and the Caldon and Leek branches and Slough Arm—although restored in the early 70s, were not actually upgraded to cruising waterways, thus securing their future, until 1983.

These and literally hundreds of ongoing large and small restoration projects are not the exclusive arena of the navigation authorities, although their cooperation is obviously essential. Ever since its formation in 1946, the now 20,500-strong Inland Waterways Association has pioneered and led an aggressive and enthusiastic campaign for waterways survival, abetted by a host of local canal societies and trusts and other charitable bodies. Since setting up a Restoration and Development Fund in 1969 the IWA alone has raised over £200,000 for grants and loans to worthy projects. Its Waterways Recovery Group coordinates the great voluntary movement of do-it-yourself canal navvies who have and are contributing so much to restoration, often working under conditions they would not for a moment tolerate from an employer.

Navigation authorities, and not least the British Waterways Board, have come to appreciate and work closely with voluntary groups. They are also now getting cooperation and financial support for the improvement of inland waterways and their surroundings from local authorities and other statutory organisations, and these informal partnerships are invaluable. The BWB's new Corporate Plan adopts a highly commercial approach to attract more private sector investment as well, both for amenity and freight transport where applicable.

It is apparent that more private funds are coming to the waterways as their future becomes more secure. Fortunately, waterside development is not allowed to reflect the ugly face of capitalism but is subject to environmental planning to protect and improve the quality of waterway surroundings. The BWB's excellent 'Waterways Environment Handbook', for example, is used for its own guidance and that of riparian local authorities, most of whom in practice send any waterside planning applications to the BWB for advice. The results can be admirable, like the picturesque transformation of Camden Lock and the development of towpaths along the Regent's Canal in the heart of London, the refurbished towpath along the Aire and Calder in central Leeds, the development of a canal centre at Devizes Wharf on the Kennet & Avon, the revived terminus of the Calder and Hebble with its 'Moorings' pub in a converted canalside warehouse, to say nothing of the unique Museum of Inland Navigation established in the historic buildings round the basins of Ellesmere Port.

At any one time restoration work of one kind or another can be going on simultaneously on over four score inland waterways, many hopelessly derelict as far as navigation is concerned or of more historical than current interest to all but local enthusiasts. Improvements to all of these will certainly add to their amenity value but as a matter of practical fact—apart from the Kennet & Avon, hopefully navigable between the Thames and Bristol Channel in another decade, the two trans-Pennine waterways of the Rochdale and Huddersfield Narrow canals and the Montgomery Canal in Wales—restoration to through powered navigation is hardly likely. Major rehabilitation schemes are currently underway on all four exceptionally beautiful waterways. The full restoration of the Huddersfield Narrow is strongly championed, but anyone who has penetrated and explored the 5,698 yard-long Standedge Tunnel, the longest and highest (645 ft) in Britain, since its closure in 1948 cannot help but wonder if this unique underground multi-purpose labyrinth can ever be restored to safe navigation. The problems were thought serious enough to warrant launching a £100,000 engineering study late in 1985 to determine the feasibility and cost of doing so.

In recent years a new dimension has been added to waterway improvement, an extensive programme of waterways projects under the Manpower Services Commission's 'Community Programme'. At the end of the BWB financial year in March 1985 there were over 50 such projects in progress, sponsored by local authorities, Community Task Force, private companies and voluntary agencies. These gave employment to over 1,300 adults and young people. Projects involving an additional 450 places were also being considered.

The work done varies widely, including restoration of locks and canalside buildings, improvements to towing paths, the provision of various facilities for boaters, anglers, walkers and other users, and ecological studies. The object of the latter is to produce an inventory of the flora and fauna associated with the canals and the adjoining land so that the maintenance and restoration of the waterways can be carried out with proper regard for the wildlife and the countryside.

Projects like these and those undertaken by volunteer groups and canal societies will add much to your pleasure. Mileposts have been replaced and interpretive signs installed, picnic sites have been constructed, rubbish has been cleared from canals, moorings have been constructed, brickwork repairs made, hedges laid, trees felled and a bruised environment healed in countless ways. At the same time, irrespective of ownership or classification, the cruising range of many waterways, such as the River Derwent and the Chesterfield, Pocklington and Ripon canals, is being extended. On others like the Basingstoke, Droitwich, Sleaford, Stroudwater, Somerset Coal and Wey & Arun canals, isolated lengths are being reinstated. And fresh proposals continue to emerge for extending the navigable length of the River Severn, restoring the disused northern reaches of the Lancaster Canal, re-opening the Wendover Arm of the Grand Union Canal and reviving the Bridgewater and Taunton.

Waterside projects are often as remarkable as waterways restoration. The inclined plane which carried the ingenious boat lift beside the Foxton Flight of locks on the Leicester Arm of the Grand Union is being cleared and excellent progress is being made in converting the old boiler house into a museum and visitor centre. Tasks like transporting 41 hollow concrete beams up the 300-yard long incline and lifting them into position for the concrete roof were cheerfully undertaken by volunteers of the Foxton Inclined Plane Trust.

While exploring the waterways you will inevitably discover a fascinating collection of 'listed' buildings of special architectural or historic interest and they are being added to at a rate often approaching 150 a year. Along BWB waterways in England and Wales alone you will find no less than 586 buildings or structures listed under the Town and Country Planning Acts. These include tunnels, portals and airshafts to tunnels, locks, bridges, aqueducts, back pumping stations, workshop buildings, cottages, overflow structures, side ponds and other features of industrial archaeology. A further 64, including the Anderton Lift and the recently replaced old iron Stanley Ferry Aqueduct, are scheduled as Ancient Monuments. Some of these items preserved for posterity are, of course, no longer suited to actual use, but many continue to operate and others are converted to modern use. For those wanting to be on the waterways without negotiating any locks or bridges it is now possible to hire a canalside cottage converted to a holiday home by the BWB at Nantwich in 1984 and more such conversions are planned.

Movement on the waterways, however, is easier today than it was 15 years ago. Literally millions of tonnes of dredgings are being removed from the waterways each year, miles upon miles of piling are being constructed and banks protected in other ways, many locks are being improved or repaired, defective culverts renewed and even swing bridges are being electrified. Apart from these and other channel improvements new weir signs and direction signs are being installed as part of an extensive scheme to improve navigational aids and safety standards. But sufficient funding has not yet been made available to prevent some cruising waterways from becoming very shallow.

Working locks means hard work for some and lots of fun for others. Some can still prove tiring but generally locks present no formidable problems. There are no locks at all on the Broads and the Ashby, Bridgewater and Lancaster canals and all locks on the River Thames are worked for you. Tidal locks and others on commercial waterways naturally have lock-keepers. You will also find lock-keepers assigned to busy flights of locks and other areas where water supplies require special safeguarding. Lock-keepers are on duty at specific stated times. On some waterways advance notice of lock passage may be required and on others late and Sunday passage may be banned or restricted but there are good reasons for this. In any case moving at night is generally pointless and can be foolhardy.

There is no official 'cruising' season but March to October are recognized as the most favourable months for comfortable waterway adventure. Emergency breaches, collapses or other mishaps can bring sudden closures of parts of any waterway at any time but stoppages for scheduled repairs are notified well in advance and every effort is made to confine them to the October-March period. With so many arrears of maintenance to catch up on more work than ever is taking place and it may not always be possible to carry it out to everyone's convenience. Since 1975 the BWB has operated a Canalphone Service to advise on stoppages and other waterways developments with two telephone numbers, one dealing with waters in the southern areas and the River Soar section of the Grand Union Canal and the other with waterways in the northern areas and Scotland. Since its introduction it has continually been well patronised, handling no fewer than 206,899 calls to Christmas 1985. The 'south' number is 01–723 8487 and the 'north' 01–723 8486.

Another recent innovation on the nationalized waterways has been the appearance of Patrol Officers, introduced in 1976 to help curb vandalism and enforce a code of conduct for the safe enjoyment of the waterways by all users. By boat, car and on foot patrol staff not only check boat licences and deal with speeding and navigation offences, but also warn about the dangers associated with swimming in the canals and discourage those tempted to ride motor-cycles on towing paths, dump rubbish into the waterways, fire weapons or otherwise misbehave.

The latest development is the appointment of special Project Officers in England and Rangers in Scotland to help promote the wider use and improvement of particular waterways. Of course, all water authorities cater to the obsession of angling. In the 60s and 70s boaters and anglers were often at daggers-drawn but wiser counsels have prevailed and seething hostility has all but faded away. There has been a steady improvement in canals and rivers as fisheries over the past 15 years with regular restocking by the various water authorities and angling clubs. Considerable progress has been made with cooperative efforts for fish rescue operations and pollution control. Fishing rights may lie with the owner of the bank or with the water authority, and in either case may be let to an angling club. There is a 'Closed Season' in England between mid-March and mid-June and other restrictions are generally posted. But licences are usually cheap and easy to obtain.

There are more activities of all kinds on the waterways network than at any time in their long history. Of course, the Inland Waterways Association is noted for its successful national and branch rallies almost since its inception, and canal societies have joined in with their own rallies of boats which are also open to all comers. In 1983 the IWA introduced a National Waterways Fortnight greatly extending the range and scope of waterway events to boost its campaigning image and results. In 1984 the Association's national rally at Hawkesbury Junction on the Coventry Canal attracted no fewer than 720 boats, the largest number ever gathered for such an event, and a crowd of over 30,000 people. By 1985 the Fortnight had become National Waterways Summer involving over 200 happenings of all kinds, including a National Rally at Milton

Keynes and 45 other rallies, run by 107 different bodies over a period of six months.

There is no doubt that this massive operation provided much work for a relative few but tremendous fun for many, although no one knows the total number of people attending the events, some staged in rather remote places. Certainly many learned about waterways, their attractions, values and needs for the first time, and television, radio and press carried the campaign further still. The profits in pounds and pence cannot be measured either but the impact of this magnificent campaign for waterways survival must be unparalleled. It also fostered a closeness of cooperation between IWA branches, canal societies, boat clubs and commercial firms which would have been considered wishful thinking only a few years ago.

Last year, too, brought another unprecedented dose of stimulant to waterways enthusiasts. The BWB agreed to sponsor three major IWA events in 1985—the Ellesmere Port International Waterways Festival, the Pewsey National Trailboat Rally and the National Rally at Milton Keynes—to the tune of £30,000. In effect this transferred the costs of the three events from the IWA to the Board's Leisure Promotions rather than engineering budget and means an extra £30,000 to devote to restoration.

In 1971 I wrote that, apart from the Broads and the River Thames, which have their own distinctive appeals, our inland waterways were 'unspoiled and uncrowded even if pleasure craft were suddenly to double or treble overnight'. In the decade after those words were published we did, in fact, have a rapidly accelerating boom in boating as well as in other amenity use of the waterways. By 1980 the BWB had announced that more boats were using the waterways than at any time since the canals were built.

Back in 1970 there were just 9,850 powered pleasure craft and 663 powered hire craft licensed or registered on the nationalized waterways. By 1980 the numbers had swelled to 18,836 and 1,983 respectively. But this was the peak for, with the recession biting, the numbers have dwindled since to 18,512 and 1,535 in 1984, the latest year for which figures have been published. The trend has been the same on other waterways (the Broads, Thames, Wellend, Nene, Medway and Bridgewater etc.): ten years of rapid expansion followed by decline and consolidation. Compared with the 50,000 powered craft on all waterways in 1970 there are now some 75,000 licensed or registered. The number of powered hire craft just exceeded 4,000 in 1970 but today just approaches 5,750. Of course, the total number of all types of powered and unpowered craft of all sizes on broads, rivers, canals, reservoirs and lakes is estimated at over 750,000 but all are not simultaneously afloat.

Does this mean overcrowding and congestion? The answer is 'rarely', and there definitely are many waterways today where relative isolation can be found if desired, and even in peak season. There is more than enough water space; although waterside facilities on the Broads can be hard-pressed at times, there is certainly waiting at Thames locks at peak periods and it is true that the Llangollen Canal and the southern Oxford Canal have reached new heights of popularity. In recent years as many as 200 craft a week have been moving through these two favourites.

An NOP Market Research survey for the BWB indicated that in 1984 over 170,000 people aged 15 or over had used hire boats on the nationalized waterways, 640,000 had used other powered craft, 360,000 had been unpowered boating, 770,000 had been angling and over five million had used them for informal recreation. Experience leads to the conclusion that these figures can virtually be doubled to encompass all waterways.

Do explore the lesser known waterways which have countryside just as beautiful, architecture and heritage every bit as fascinating and pubs just as friendly. Try the Macclesfield, or indeed any and all sections of the Cheshire Ring. The lockless Lancaster Canal has a special appeal to anglers and real ale fans. The River Nene is like a journey back in time and the Leeds and Liverpool is, perhaps, the most peaceful, cleanest and uncrowded of them all.

It is considerably easier to hire a boat today than it was 15 years ago for there are not only more boatyards ranged over the waterways but readier access to them. There are now a number of hire agencies representing a large number of boat holiday firms countrywide (and abroad), the two giants being Blakes Holidays Ltd, Wroxham, Norwich NR12 8DH (06053 3221) and Hoseasons Boating Holidays, Sunway House, Lowestoft, Suffolk NR32 3LT (0502 62211). Both offer sailing yachts, houseboats and holiday homes on the Broads as well as broad-beamed cruisers and narrow boats on rivers and canals.

Then there is the Blue Riband Club, Weltonfield Farm, Welton, Daventry, Nothants NN11 5LG (0327 842282); Boat Enquiries Ltd, the doyen of them all, which operates a bonding scheme safeguarding your money if the hire firm goes out of business, at 41–43 Botley Road, Oxford OX2 OPT (0865 727288) and Eurocruisers, Freepost, Haslesmere, Surrey GU27 2BR (0428 54001), which has its own hire boat network in Britain and acts as agent for boating holidays in France and Ireland.

Today, too, there are 24-hour Dial-a-brochure services (Blakes on 0533 701701 and Hoseasons on 0502 62101) or you can phone or write to other agencies or individual hire firms. The Inland Waterways Association (114 Regent's Park Road, London NW1 8UQ) publishes annually at £1.85 an 'Inland Waterways Guide' which describes each waterway and up-to-date details of boat hirers and services available on them. The British Waterways Board, Leisure & Tourism Division, Melbury House, Melbury Terrace, Lon-

6711), also publishes an annual 'Waterway Users' Companion' in the form of a pack of five leaflets covering hire boat operators, water points, sanitary stations, angling and water authorities, for 75p including postage. You will find them invaluable both before and after booking.

Waterway holiday brochures are now as glossy, sophisticated, information-packed, well-presented and lavishly illustrated as those promoting the most expensive holidays to the most exotic areas of the world. The boats they offer for hire are little different from those first described in *Slow Boat Through England*. Narrow boats and cruisers generally have a long useful 'working' life and many refurbished oldtimers still sail along smartly with new craft of various types but of similar design and layout. Modifications for comfort and convenience have been introduced, of course, but no revolutionary changes have been made.

Quality and standards have improved, however. Fittings on the whole are better and more comprehensive. Little things like insulation and central heating systems add greatly to comfort, especially when holidaying out of season. More craft have television available although I have never seen the point in letting an idiot box divert me from nature. As anticipated, virtually all hire craft now have hygenic toilets for which a pump-out service is available for about £3 or so at strategically located sanitary points.

Latest innovation, from Blakes, is a Video Holiday Preview specially created for those who have never tried a boating holiday before. Comforts of the hire craft and glimpses of holidays on the Broads, English canals and Scottish waterways are compiled on a 30-minute film at the beginning of a high quality blank 3-hour video cassette costing just £9 including post and packaging. You keep the cassette and record on it as you wish.

Once you have selected your top choice of boat for the weeks you want on the waterway(s) of your preference, it is a simple matter to telephone the computerized booking services and reserve it on the spot. Agencies keep up-to-date details of last-minute vacancies all over the country. There is no reason at all why you should not opt for the personal attention of an individual firm, particularly if you want to look over the hire craft and get a sneak preview of at least some reaches of the waterway. My family enjoy pre-holiday outings like this.

Agencies like Blakes, however, have experienced Reservation Consultants at the end of six telephone lines every day of the week, in the busiest booking periods as late as 9 p.m., and this simple but expert service shows why eight out of ten bookings are made this way. The different telephone numbers relate to different waterways in Britain and abroad and to different sizes and types of craft.

Whether booking with family-run boatyards or agencies, do read the conditions of hire carefully for they may vary widely and check equally carefully what your hire fee includes and what extras must be paid for. It is as advisable to obtain insurance and cancellation protection for a boating holiday as it is for a package holiday to Spain, but note that while some boatyards incorporate some aspects of this in their hire fee, others treat it as an extra. All boatyards insist on a deposit of at least £30 to cover the first part of any damage to the craft but this is refundable shortly after the end of your holiday. Back in the old days I always found parking for cars belonging to hirers was free but today some boatyards are charging what I regard as outrageous sums for this open-air service.

Although hire charges today seem high in comparison with those 15 years ago they do carry a 15% VAT surcharge and are still very good value for money. Check back on the cost of package holidays in 1970 compared with the cost today, or on train or air fares. Do remember boat hire charges include home, transport and amusements.

Back in the late 60s it was possible to hire the type of six-berth narrow boat we used on our holidays for between £38 and £80 per week according to season. Average 1986 rates for comparable craft and seasons come to between £40 and £70 *per person per week*, roughly six times as much.

Average 1986 rates per person per week for two-berth craft range from £79 to £125; for four-berth from £44 to £75; for eight-berth from £35 to £60; for ten-berth from £28 to £50 and for twelve-berth from £26 to £45. Rates for river cruisers of similar capacity and standard are about the same. There is sometimes no charge for children under 12 but taking a dog or other pet along—rarely forbidden–can set you back about £12 a week. This is a fair charge, for I can clearly recall how the seemingly perpetually moulting 'Wiggers'—long since departed and undoubtedly enjoying some celestial barque—used to shed tawny hairs which spread to every nook and cranny of the craft including the engine room and bilge. When extra crew are permitted aboard certain boats there is a charge per person of between about £10 and £20 a week.

The boat hire industry today is as professionally organized as the rest of the travel trade. Hirers invariably have to make an initial payment when completing the booking form, covering a deposit on the hire fee ranging from about £35 to £85, a cancellation insurance premium from about £10 to £15 and an optional personal insurance premium of anything from £3 to £15—all per boat per week. The balance of the hire terms must usually be paid not later than 28 days before the hire starting date.

I note a new condition of hire these days to the effect that you are not permitted to bring any heater of any kind, lighting equipment, TV sets or 'any other electrical equipment or anything which may cause danger to the boat, the equipment or its occupants', a sensible precaution. And as always you are not allowed to cruise after dark, tow or race any other boat or enter tidal waters without express permission.

Most hire craft these days have diesel engines which are very economic on fuel. You usually pay a fuel deposit of between £30 and £50 when you set out with a full tank and the value of unused fuel at the end of your holiday is refunded. And you may well use little more than 10 gallons a week.

The canals are unsuitable for sailing but yachts can be hired on the Broads, the Thames and some other rivers and in the Lake District. Some hire firms have camping boats, usually ex-working narrow or wide boats, with camping under canvas in the original hold. Some have a professional crew, others may be self-navigated, and they provide inexpensive holidays for groups of young people. The up-market end is the hotel boat, few and far between 15 years ago, but today offered by at least ten firms. Generally these are narrow canal boats converted into floating hotels and usually travelling in pairs. Clients have nothing to do but enjoy themselves as they are carried and cosseted through some of the most beautiful canal scenery in the country. There are single and double-berth cabins with comfy bunks, hot and cold water and electric light. There is a large saloon and a lounging deck from which to watch the world go by. Passengers may help at locks or explore during planned stops. Hotel boats moor for the night either in remote places or within easy access of a pub or restaurant. They carry about 8–12 passengers usually on weekly or fortnightly schedules. Wider hotel boats with similar facilities operate on rivers like the Thames and Trent. Costs vary according to season and bookings may be made direct or with Boat Enquiries.

Since *Slow Boat Through England* and *Slow Boat Through Pennine Waters* were first published—the first waterways books to go into paperback editions—there has been an almost non-stop flurry of waterways maps, guides, leaflets, books and compendiums rushing into print so that today you have a wealth of waterways reference material of all kinds, as well as a number of waterways magazines to keep you up-to-date. The British Waterways Board has a number of information offices and shops stocking literature, most hire firms have a selection of guides, booklets and general reading and for a stamped self-addressed envelope the IWA will send you its comprehensive list currently offering over 150 items covering all aspects of the inland waterways.

So the canals and rivers and broads that make up the holiday cruising network of England are much as they were a decade and a half ago but in somewhat better fettle and actually being extended. Appreciation of the heritage they uniquely encompass is more widespread and they are being enjoyed by more and many kinds of users under sensible regulations to protect their integrity for posterity. They are being genuinely cared for with brigades of keen enthusiasts not only digging in for restoration but challenging nationally and locally the slightest threat to their well-being and preservation.

You will miss little my crews enjoyed, with the exception of chatting with old-timers like the mole-catching Albert Armsby, the gravel-snatching Ike Argent, the lock-gate making George Bate and garrulous boatmen like old Jack James. Perhaps wild areas may be a little tamer now and some eyesores may have been removed. Some pubs may have more nautical names and decor and some derelict warehouses may have altered, converted now to restaurants, museums or shops. Most changes have been for the better.

There is more on the inland waterways today than ever before for all who want to escape and unwind. The delight, interest and pleasure they bring lies in the eyes and minds of the beholder.